The Poetics of Unremembered Acts

The Poetics of Unremembered Acts

Reading, Lyric, Pedagogy

Brian McGrath

Northwestern University Press
Evanston, Illinois

Northwestern University Press
www.nupress.northwestern.edu

Printed in the United States of America

10 9 8 7 6 5 4 3 2 1

Library of Congress Cataloging-in-Publication Data

McGrath, Brian M., 1973–
The poetics of unremembered acts : reading, lyics, pedagogy / Brian McGrath.
p. cm.
Includes bibliographical references and index.
ISBN 978-0-8101-2849-1 (pbk. : aka. paper)
1. English poetry—18th century—History and criticism. 2. English poetry—19th century—History and criticism 3. English poetry—18th century—Study and teaching. 4. English poetry—19th century—Study and teaching. 5. Romanticism—Great Britain—History and criticism. 6. Reading. I. Title.
PR590. M26 2012
821.709145—dc23
2012022487

♾ The paper used in this publication meets the minimum requirements of the American National Standard for Information Sciences—Permanence of Paper for Printed Library Materials, ANSI Z39.48-1992.

For Mom, John, and Dad

CONTENTS

ACKNOWLEDGMENTS

I am fortunate to have many people to acknowledge and thank for helping me to complete this book. Not all forms of teaching are accidental, even if the full significance of that teaching remains always on the horizon. This book would not have been possible without my many teachers in the Department of Comparative Literature at Emory University. Cathy Caruth directed the dissertation from which this book emerged. She has been for me a guiding example, and I am grateful for her teaching, astute listening, and remarkable generosity. I am grateful to Geoffrey Bennington for his playful irreverence and for helping me to conceptualize the contingent intersections between philosophy and literature, and to Deborah Elise White for helping me to think the unfinished project of romanticism more deeply. Other mentors and teachers at Emory University were integral to the project's initial formation: Maximilian Aue, Michael Elliott, Shoshana Felman, Dalia Judovitz, Walter Kaladjian, Elissa Marder, Claire Nouvet, Walt Reed, and Jill Robbins. Numerous friends in Atlanta read my early work and at key moments inspired me to continue writing: Rachel Bowser, Jennefer Callaghan, Tony Cuda, Angela Hunter, Michael Johnson, David Kelman, Sarah Peterson, Lisa Schneider, and Petra Schweitzer. Before Emory, I was lucky to study with Peter Fenves at Northwestern University and Tony Brinkley and Burton Hatlen at the University of Maine at Orono.

A year spent at Colgate University was crucial to my development as a scholar and I could not have written this book without Peter Balakian, Jennifer Brice, Susan Cerasano, Morgan Davies, Deborah Knuth Klenck, Margaret Maurer, and Jane Pinchin. I am grateful for their intellectual conversation, collective insight, and friendship. At Clemson University, I am grateful to my colleagues for building and sustaining such an intellectually rich and gratifying community of writers and teachers. Cameron Bushnell, Kim Manganelli, Dominic Mastroianni, Angela Naimou, Catherine Paul, Elizabeth Rivlin, and Rhondda Thomas read, commented on, and helped vastly improve an early version of the introduction. I thank my various department chairs, Lee Morrissey, R. Barton Palmer, and Sean Williams, and deans of the College of Architecture, Arts and Humanities, Chip Egan and Rick Goodstein, for the research support and release time necessary to finish this project. Many conversations with Lee Morrissey about models of reading have helped to shape the book and have made it better. Mike LeMahieu read and commented on the whole manuscript, and I am grateful to him for his excellent and thoughtful responses. I am grateful to many friends and colleagues working in romanticism and literary theory for their complex dialogues, crucial interventions, and deeply resonant writing: Cynthia Chase, Anne-Lise François, Sara Guyer, Eric Lindstrom, Jonathan Mulrooney, Marc Redfield, Emily Rohrbach, Emily Sun, and Orrin Wang. The book would be very different, and much poorer, without them. The anonymous readers for Northwestern University Press provided invaluable feedback. I would also like to thank my editor at Northwestern University Press, Henry L. Carrigan Jr., for much help and encouragement. Thanks also to Sara Dreyfuss, Heather Antti, and Lori Meek Schuldt for expert help in preparing the final manuscript.

I thank my family and especially my parents, Ronald McGrath, Pamela Sergey, and John Sergey, for their continued love and support. I dedicate this book to them. My sister, Sarah Scully, reminds me several times a year that I am lucky to get to spend my time thinking and talking with students. She is, as always, right. And finally, I would like to thank Erin Goss for all of the things I have not yet found words for. The traces of her timely interventions and critical responses are present on every page of this book and have made it immeasurably better. She helps me find joy in the small things and laugh when moments appear bigger than they actually are.

Portions of chapters 1 and 2 appeared previously in print as "Rousseau's Crusoe: Or, on Learning to Read as Not Myself," *Eighteenth-Century Fiction* 23, no. 1 (2010): 119–39. Chapter 4 was originally published as "Wordsworth, 'Simon Lee,' and the Craving for Incidents" in *Studies in Romanticism* 48, no. 4 (2009): 565–82. I am grateful to the journal editors and to the Trustees of Boston University for permission to reprint.

The Poetics of Unremembered Acts

Introduction:

Reading in the Dark

. . . little, nameless, unremembered acts
—William Wordsworth

In February 1808, William Wordsworth confesses in a letter to Sir George Beaumont, a wealthy British nobleman and art patron, that he "wish[es] either to be considered as a Teacher, or as nothing."[1] Given the opposition, to be considered a teacher is to be considered "something." And if Wordsworth were not going to be considered something, then he would rather be considered nothing. He would rather not be considered at all.[2] In the same letter, Wordsworth declares that all great poets are teachers, which may help explain why Wordsworth chose to write poetry and not become a teacher by profession. But what, given the starkness of the ultimatum, does the poet teach? What *can* poetry teach?

In *The Prelude,* Wordsworth attempts, among other things, to explain his decision to write poetry. Early books of the long, epic poem show how nature instructed the young Wordsworth. With the fifth, Wordsworth turns to the function books played in his youth (and so as well to the function they are to play in the model of education *The Prelude* itself outlines): "Hitherto / In progress through this verse my mind hath looked / Upon the speaking face of earth and heaven / As her prime teacher."[3] The goal of book 5 is to show that books, and, one assumes, *The Prelude* itself, are "things that teach as Nature teaches."[4] Wordsworth posits an analogy between books and nature and borrows from nature metaphors to describe books. Books are full of "heights" and "hollows" and rich with "indigenous produce." Reading books is like traveling through a natural landscape. In this way, Wordsworth argues that poems are capable of offering the same instruction as Wordsworth's "prime teacher." The passage from the speaking face of earth and heaven to books of poetry does not represent a departure from nature but a continuation of the particular kind of teaching nature offers.

To employ a slightly more technical vocabulary, the aim of book 5 is to unite the structural and ahistorical aspects of poetic language together with the "natural" and referential aspects of ordinary language. If

Wordsworth can organize language around a "speaking face" (in much the same manner that he organizes nature's teaching around one, "the speaking face of earth and heaven") then it might be possible to bring together the structure of language (arbitrary and differential) and its various referential effects. Reference might then, in turn, be understood as phenomenal (just as meaning is often figured as a question of "seeing" or "looking"). While Wordsworth describes and even celebrates accidents and chance encounters in *The Prelude,* the articulation of linguistic structure and phenomenal reference will be possible only if the poem can account for the possible interruptions language occasions within the text.[5] Wordsworth, in other words, can articulate the structure of language and its referential function only if his own language is not subject to accident. But Wordsworth's analogy presents a surprise that is difficult to inscribe within the narrative argument Wordsworth pursues in *The Prelude.* And my argument in *The Poetics of Unremembered Acts* is that such moments of surprise are precisely what poetry occasions, even when the reception of individual poems often denies them. Reading poetry exposes one to a language that does not know what it means.

Wordsworth's use of the word "as" in the line that explicitly links books and nature interferes with the figurative identification that makes easy passage between them possible. The aim of book 5 is to unite books and nature (structure and reference) and show that readers can pass from one to the other without incident or interruption. Wordsworth celebrates the power of figurative language in the analogy he draws—books are "things that teach as Nature teaches." But "as" also introduces a problematic ambiguity at the same moment that the language is to overcome difference through identity, asserting the importance of figure over grammar. As an adverb or a conjunction, "as" can mean either "to the same degree or extent that" or "at the same time." Here, "as" is to function in the first manner mentioned (like "like"): books are things that teach like nature teaches, that is, to the same degree or in the same manner. Thus far—"Hitherto / In progress through this verse"—Wordsworth has explained the manner in which nature teaches; now he is going to show that books teach as nature teaches. And yet, "as" might also be read as "while" or "at the same time." In this case, the line suggests that books are not only things that teach like nature teaches but also things that teach *while* nature teaches. The ambiguous grammar of Wordsworth's poem celebrates the poem's ability to teach but prevents the full identification of books and nature at the same time that it works to unite them through analogy. As a result of Wordsworth's grammar, readers cannot determine for certain whether books teach the same thing as nature teaches or if they teach at the same time that nature does. Books teach, but what do they teach? Wordsworth hopes with the early books of *The Prelude* to demonstrate the phenomenal power of nature's teaching. He has looked upon the face of nature as prime teacher. Whether what books teach (at the same time that nature teaches) is compatible with what nature teaches is a question that Wordsworth cannot answer definitively because it is not clear that he knowingly asks it.[6] In working to unite books and nature, Wordsworth works to bind together the critical insistence of poetry's independence from the material world with a corresponding insistence of historical reference. But Wordsworth's line poses a question that emerges from the attempt formally to bind them together. The two readings of Wordsworth's line are possible because the language of analogy that Wordsworth uses to harmonize competing linguistic models (the semiotic and the referential) stages the potential incompatibility of both models and, subsequently, the potential impossibility of perfect linguistic formalization.

Unlike the surprising interruption of the imagination that Wordsworth integrates into his argument in book 6, where the imagination comes "athwart" the speaker, here the grammar of Wordsworth's poem interrupts the union of poetry and nature but in a manner that is not fully accounted for within *The Prelude*. "As"—and Wordsworth's insistent use of "as"—manifests some recognition that the language of poetry might always produce an additional surprise, one that complicates the poem's argument even as Wordsworth narrates in *The Prelude* the potentially positive effects of surprise. The language of poetry is always capable of an additional surprise that cannot be included within the narrative argument of *The Prelude* if *The Prelude* is to succeed in resisting the mighty workmen who would bridge the chaos of futurity. Only with the recognition that the language of poetry must exceed even Wordsworth's celebration of surprise in *The Prelude* is the poem guaranteed a future. "As" guarantees this future even if (even while) it undoes the narrative argument of Wordsworth's poem: that poetry teaches as—in the same manner that—nature teaches.[7] With "as," Wordsworth guarantees that he is a teacher but at the price of the figurative identification (things that teach like nature teaches) he works otherwise to achieve. Poetry's method of teaching, it seems, is unavailable to the poet himself, since poetry no longer teaches just what nature teaches. Wordsworth's language stages the potential irreconcilability of the grammatical and rhetorical aspects of language and displays language's resistance to the kind of formalization Wordsworth elsewhere pursues. Far from merely celebrating the mystified unknowability of poetry's teaching, Wordsworth's poem registers the impact of a teaching that cannot be known in advance. This effort to bear witness to the future possibility of teaching is the challenge Wordsworth's words pose, a challenge that cannot be faced without passing over "as," as if "as" were not also capable of its own surprise. Poetry teaches the difficulty—if not impossibility—of learning to read it, which is not to suggest that it teaches one how to overcome this difficulty.

❖ As the Wind Blows

In recent decades, literary criticism, in the attempt to assert its relevance, has focused largely on historicist or cultural studies approaches to literary texts.[8] As long as the literary object offers readers the chance to think "critically" about history or culture, then an easy defense of literature follows, for literature provides a unique perspective on history and culture. While such an argument privileges history and culture over the experience of reading literature, it also assumes that one can move from the literary text to history and culture unproblematically, as if literary texts do not pose questions about themselves as "objects."

In the last several years, though, literary criticism has witnessed numerous attempts to rescue the literary from oblivion. In her report published in *PMLA,* "What Is New Formalism?" Marjorie Levinson identifies a set of shared commitments present in recent studies that focus on literary form. Like members of most critical "schools," New Formalists do not present a unified front, but Levinson demonstrates how they "seek to reinstate close reading both at the curricular center of our discipline and as the opening move, preliminary to any kind of critical consideration."[9] In response to the historical turn, New Formalism aims to reinvigorate specifically literary approaches to texts through a rededication to close or slow reading. In this way, New Formalism is also a response to what Franco Moretti has polemically called "distant reading," in which a premium is placed on an expansive quantity of reading over close examination of one or a limited number of texts.[10] Indeed, the linguistic and historical turns have been followed by an expanding list of reading methods: "paranoid," "reparative," "critical," "uncritical," "postcritical," "hyper," "machine," "surface," and so on.[11]

When New Criticism introduced close reading in the early to middle decades of the twentieth century, it helped determine the study of literature as a profession. In her defense of close reading from 2007, Jane Gallop argues that close reading is the "most valuable thing English ever had to offer": "Not because it is necessarily the best way to read literature but because it, learned through practice with literary texts, learned in literature classes, is a widely applicable skill."[12] Gallop acknowledges that there exist numerous reading methods, but for Gallop close reading offers the best defense of literary study. To defend the study of literature, one must defend the importance of close reading. In a related piece also published in *Profession,* "Shakespeare in Slow Motion," Marjorie Garber calls for "redirecting attention to the language of the plays, scene by scene, act by act, moment by moment, word by word."[13] For Garber, critical attention to context has come at a cost to all that distinguishes the literary object. Like Gallop and those Levinson identifies as New Formalists, Garber redirects attention to words, though she is careful to switch her metaphors, calling for "slow" as opposed to "close" reading.[14]

As will be clear from the specific readings that make up *The Poetics of Unremembered Acts,* I find much to value in the recent turn to formalism and the accompanying focus on close, slow, even rhetorical reading. However, when Levinson describes the critical practices that New Formalism reinvests in (New Criticism, Burkean performativity, Frankfurt school dialectics, and Crocean appreciation), oddly missing from the list is "deconstruction."[15] As a result, the latest turn to formalism raises for me several related questions. In defining her reading method, Garber substitutes a temporal metaphor (slow) for a spatial one (close) but both metaphors assume the phenomenal availability of the literary object.[16] To defend close or slow reading must one assume that literature is something one can "approach"? Does not formalism, despite its own metaphors, challenge the phenomenal availability of the literary object? Or, phrased differently, when and how does formalism, especially the radical formalism pursued through deconstructive reading practices, question the primacy of phenomenology and phenomenological models of language? These questions lead me to a second set. Must New Formalism return to phenomenology to enable practical, pedagogical success? In her defense of close reading, Gallop understands it as a skill learned through practice. And in "What Is New Formalism?," the last title Levinson refers to is Elizabeth Harris Sagaser's "Flirting with Eternity: Teaching Form and Meter in a Renaissance Poetry Course," which Levinson admires for its "hands-on approach to the problem of helping students" address questions about culture without "lapsing into an alienating technicalism."[17] Focusing on the literary object, close readers argue that literature teaches one how to read (slowly, with patience) in order to transfer these skills to other classes and pursuits. But it seems to me that this focus on the ability of literature to teach is often enough what literature itself questions. In this way, both historicist and formalist critics deny literature its pedagogical imperative to question its own pedagogical success.[18] I interpose "Lyric" between "Reading" and "Pedagogy" in the subtitle to *The Poetics of Unremembered Acts* because figures that dominate the lyric interrupt the easy movement from reading to pedagogy or from pedagogy to reading.[19]

Given the above, it may be no surprise that this book began many years ago with Paul de Man's enigmatic claim in *The Resistance to Theory* that "it is better to fail in teaching what should not be taught than to succeed in teaching what is not true."[20] Too often, what is not true is all the easier to teach precisely because it is not true. One need only confirm what another wishes, however unconsciously, to hear. So how does one fail in teaching what should not be taught? How can one be sure one has failed adequately? Famously, de Man was commissioned to write *The Resistance to Theory* for a Modern Language Association (MLA) volume entitled *Introduction to Scholarship in Modern Languages and Literature,* but the essay was rejected. "I found it difficult," writes de Man, "to live up, in minimal good faith, to the requirements of the program, and could only try to explain, as concisely as possible, why the main theoretical interest of literary theory consists in the impossibility of its definition. The Committee rightly judged that this was an inauspicious way to achieve the pedagogical objectives of the volume and commissioned another article."[21] If de Man's essay is sometimes understood as an attack on pedagogy, for de Man this attack is constitutive of literature and so, too, of literary teaching, a teaching that takes seriously the often-surprising encounter with the language of literary texts. When Barbara Johnson quotes these sentences in her essay "Deconstruction, Feminism, and Pedagogy," she summarizes the problem with characteristic wit: "It is not pedagogically auspicious, it seems, to be sent on a mission of scholarship and to come back with a tale of impossibility."[22] The intervening years have not proved kind to such tales. As the name for a particular form of attention, literary texts, like poems, expose readers to a certain not-knowing about how to proceed with reading; they expose readers to the impossibility of reading, an impossibility that is, of course, the very chance to begin. "Reading," writes Thomas Keenan, "is what happens when we cannot apply the rules."[23] In *The Poetics of Unremembered Acts* I contend that it is precisely in giving unprecedented insight into the impossibility of reading that literature opens teaching to what one does not yet know about the enterprise.

❖ Unremembered Acts

The Poetics of Unremembered Acts is divided into two parts. The first part features chapters on John Locke's *Some Thoughts Concerning Education* and Jean-Jacques Rousseau's *Émile, or On Education* and approaches questions about literature and teaching not through conventionally defined literary texts but through practical treatises on education. The second part brings together focused readings of Thomas Gray's "Elegy Written in a Country Churchyard," William Wordsworth's "Simon Lee," and John Keats's "Isabella, or the Pot of Basil." Each poem prominently features a figure of direct address to the reader and so allegorizes the attempt to move from rhetoric to cognition by demanding that the reader acknowledge his or her implication in the poem's construction. Each poem stages its own readability as a question even as it calls "directly" to its reader to respond appropriately.

The question for both Locke and Rousseau is: how does one teach children to read? Even as the calls for utilitarian practicality and accountability increase in volume in school reform today, the texts that have come to define the history of education bear witness to the difficulty of teaching reading. Potentially surprising is Locke's suggestion in *Some Thoughts* that learning to read not be available to cognition. To borrow from Wordsworth's "Tintern Abbey," learning to read must, for Locke, go "unremembered."[24] Locke states explicitly that the child must not know that he is learning to read if the child is to continue reading in the future and offers a die-rolling game useful for instruction in reading. The first text that the child will read will result from random rolls of dice with letters inscribed on their faces. The child is to understand that he is playing a game but not understand that he is learning to read. I take seriously Locke's suggestion that the event of learning to read is one that must be missed. In "Tintern Abbey," Wordsworth hopes—against the possibility that his hope is just "vain belief"—that "little, nameless, unremembered acts / Of kindness and love" have "no trivial influence / On that best portion of a good man's life."[25] In *The Poetics of Unremembered Acts,* the missed event of reading similarly conditions the possibility of an ethical encounter, but one in which the reading subject is dispossessed of his ability to know the ethical imperative he transmits.

In *Émile,* Jean-Jacques Rousseau singles out Locke's die-rolling game for ridicule. The first text that Rousseau's imaginary pupil, Émile, will read will be a note left for him describing an outing that he will miss because he will not yet know how to read. Émile will be inspired to decipher the note to participate in future outings. While Rousseau ridicules Locke, in his *Confessions* he admits to the very ignorance about reading that Locke suggests is constitutive of learning to read. Rousseau, in other words, announces straightforwardly: "I do not know how I learned to read."[26] For Rousseau, the child should not be tricked into learning to read (as with Locke's die-rolling game); Émile must know that he is learning to read, and he will choose to read because he will want to experience events in the future similar to the ones he has missed. In his *Confessions,* however, Rousseau repeats and in repeating foregrounds the philosophical questions raised by Locke's practical suggestion for improving reading instruction: one should not know that one is learning to read when one in fact learns to read. Rousseau's fascination with reading in *Confessions* emerges from the inaccessibility of its origin to memory. *Confessions* bears witness to the missed encounter that Locke identifies as crucial to reading instruction.[27] If memory is from the start another metaphor for reading (and vice versa), can one remember learning to read? Must one already know how to read to remember learning how to read? Why should the event of learning to read so often turn on a missed encounter? Why should the event of learning to read be conditioned, paradoxically, by the absence of a memory trace?[28] And how does learning to read question the availability of teaching (specifically the teaching of reading) to phenomenal perception and cognition?

In the introduction to her edited volume of *Yale French Studies,* "The Pedagogical Imperative: Teaching as a Literary Genre," Barbara Johnson focuses on Samuel Taylor Coleridge's *The Rime of the Ancient Mariner* and contrasts Coleridge's later inclusion of the poem's gloss, which attempts to anticipate and explain away all the questions a reader might have about the poem, and the mariner's compulsion to repeat his tale over and over again. "The gloss," writes Johnson, "stands for a pedagogy that would repress the very stuff that literature is made off. But on the other hand, a reading of the mariner himself would suggest that teaching is a compulsion: a compulsion to repeat what one has not yet understood."[29] Johnson turns to the punctuation of the poem and finds in the dash that divides the wedding guest's question from the mariner's resumption of the tale—

> "Why look'st thou so?"—"With my cross-bow
> I shot the albatross."

—the pedagogical moment represented "as inherently and constitutively missed—represented by the dash that marks the place where what is not known is evoked as the blank that makes the story go on forever."[30] One does not teach what one knows. All too often, in other words, one "teaches" what one does not know. The purpose of the gloss is to help readers to decode the poem's message, though the necessity of the gloss suggests that the poet is not in control of the message communicated.

Johnson identifies a tension within Coleridge's poem that is crucial to the debate between Locke and Rousseau over reading instruction. Locke, anticipating the mariner's confusion over what exactly happened at sea, suggests that to learn to read, one must miss the event and fail fully to understand its significance. While Rousseau ridicules Locke for tricking children into reading, his own experience of reading is similarly structured around an absence or gap in cognition. He does not remember learning. One will learn to read only to the extent that one misses the event of its teaching. Reading, like the unconscious itself, introduces a constitutive difference between what one knows and the meaning of what one knows. In this instance, reading, like teaching, describes a form of knowledge that does not know itself.[31] The mariner "teaches" precisely because knowledge of what he teaches is foreclosed to him. He teaches readers to read what he himself does not know.

❖ The Blank Goes on Forever

The first two chapters of *The Poetics of Unremembered Acts* show how attempts by Enlightenment pedagogues to articulate a successful strategy for reading instruction falter around the question of address, which anticipates the turn to lyric figures in the second part of the book. For Locke, the first text is not addressed to the reader precisely because it is produced by chance rolls of dice. The addressee is not determined in advance or even considered. For Rousseau, the first text is specifically addressed to the one learning to read. Why should a question of address come to play such a primary role in the theories of reading instruction that Locke and Rousseau offer? Why, in other words, should learning to read depend on the ability of the philosopher to control (either through its elimination or guarantee) the question of address?

Locke offers his die-rolling game as the best way to teach children how to read even though the chance that one can read in the absence of any identifiable intention or addressee is precisely what Locke works to limit in his *Essay Concerning Human Understanding*.[32] Strangely, the first text the child should be exposed to is the end result of a text-producing machine; what is "written" is unconnected to any human agent. The game foregrounds the degree to which language functions even in the absence of a human subject who aims to use it for some purpose; and so the game demonstrates the complicated independence of language from human will. Rousseau, however, foregrounds the importance of human intention as well as the importance of an identifiable addressee. Émile's education in reading notes is a belated attempt to catch up to and so master retrospectively the mechanical aspect of language essential to Locke's die-rolling game. With his die-rolling game, Locke suggests that learning to read requires exposure to a radically formal, mechanical, and nonhuman aspect of language that must simultaneously remain undisclosed to consciousness. In the passage from Locke's die-rolling game to Rousseau's notes one senses the importance of disguising this moment of dispossession within an encounter with language that privileges language's referential (and later, aesthetic) aspects. If for Locke the child learns to read because language utters in the absence of human intention, for Rousseau the child learns to read only because language carries forward and transmits often accurately human intentions. The passage from Locke to Rousseau, from Locke's die-rolling game to Rousseau's note, humanizes a language that for Locke remains (and must remain) stubbornly mechanical.[33]

How does the lyric—the poetic form most invested in the phenomenal presence of the human voice—play on and so allegorize the attempt to eliminate or guarantee address? How do poems preoccupied by figures of address take up again the question of reading, when learning to read for both Locke and Rousseau stumbles on the question of address? In "Uncritical Reading," Michael Warner describes the emergence of the phrase "critical reading" in the eighteenth century and argues that romantic conceptions of art "deepened the ideal of critical reading, as opposed to any other kind of reading, making it seem like the unfolding of the necessity of art itself."[34] Today, critical reading is dominant in literature departments and key to the institutional role of literary study. Warner argues that critical reading is so dominant that we have forgotten that it emerges in the eighteenth century to further particular ideological ends. A critical reader is capable of extracting himself or herself from the "immediate situation of address" to assert his or her own freedom and agency as an enlightened subject.[35] We label all other forms of reading "uncritical." In my focused readings of specific poems by Gray, Wordsworth, and Keats that feature prominently figures of direct address to readers, I show how poems stage the ability of the reader to transcend textual address as a question. When is address avoidable? When is it unavoidable? In the second part of *The Poetics of Unremembered Acts,* I do not oppose "critical" and "uncritical" reading but show how certain forms of "uncritical reading"—associated with the power of lyric address discovered, for instance, in what Keats calls a "yawning tomb"—emerge only from the corresponding attempt (and subsequent failure) to be critical enough in one's reading. From within critical reading emerges a new power of lyric address.

Poets frequently associated with romanticism explore through figures of address the difficulty of satisfactorily aligning the mechanical or radically formal aspect of language and its commitment to address—its commitment to carrying forward the lived intentions of those who write and speak. I argue that the power of address cannot very easily be eliminated because figures of address determine the act of reading itself. The movement from Locke's *Some Thoughts Concerning Education* to Rousseau's *Émile* turns on the philosopher's attempt to control the question of address. In contrast to Locke's die-rolling game, Rousseau's notes organize the child's reading around figures of facing, like prosopopoeia, as what is written (and so mute) is transformed into a voiced utterance, an utterance addressed to the one who finds himself reading. This transformation is one the poems restage.[36] In this way, poems ask (or force with maximum gentleness) readers to reflect on the divergence of reference and grammar (which is not conceivable without the suspension of referential meaning).[37]

Paul de Man calls prosopopoeia—a figure that describes the granting of faces and voices to the absent, dead, or inanimate—the master trope of poetic discourse in part because it frequently (and perhaps unavoidably) governs critical discussions of poetry, where "voice" is a commonly employed metaphor. In identifying as a listener the one who "overhears" the poem, John Stuart Mill famously transforms the mute, written word into living speech, granting a voice (and so therefore a face, the locus of speech) to the inanimate object (the poem, as inscription, "read"). One may be unable to answer why the poet of "Ode on a Grecian Urn" addresses an urn, but what is at first an extreme example of the lyric poet animating an inanimate object turns out to describe what many observers—what all, perhaps unavoidably—figure by reading. Keats's animation of the urn is fully realized when the urn speaks its famous closing lines. In reading, one often takes oneself as the text's addressee, therefore granting the text a voice. One animates the text one reads so that it will then "speak" a message one must hear and decode. In this way, prosopopoeia describes Rousseau's response to Locke's die-rolling game. The attempt to control the power of inscription requires an act of figuration.

The figure one commonly employs when one reads (when one finds oneself "addressed" by what one reads) is the same one that lyric poets frequently employ—the same figure that defines the lyric poem as lyric. It is precisely, in other words, in granting a face and a voice to the notes he reads (and so discovering himself the addressee) that Émile will learn to read. In this way, the lyric poem may potentially alienate readers not simply because it excludes the one who reads (as the poet turns his "back" on his reader) but also because it shows one something about the figures one employs as one reads, the figures, for instance, that rescue readers from the arbitrary and differential (the iterable, capable of being repeated) structure of language. Like lyric poets, readers grant the inanimate, the nonliving, the dead (the mute, written word) a voice, a speaking face, and a new life. One animates the inanimate, brings the dead back to life. What one thinks one knows from reading turns out to belong to the poets, to the figure lyric poets know best.[38] It may be that readers sometimes find lyric poems boring or uninteresting not because they are too distant but because they show readers something about reading that readers would rather ignore.

The poems that I discuss throughout *The Poetics of Unremembered Acts* allegorize the movement from language as mechanical and iterable (produced by random rolls of dice, for instance) to language capable of expressing the particular intentions of an author or speaker (intentions that must then be decoded). One passes from blank repetition to knowledge and understanding only via particular figures of facing. But these figures of address in poems, like the Ancient Mariner himself, continually repeat the same tale over and over again without full cognition of the significance of what they repeat. In my readings, I focus on figures of direct address (like Gray's "for thee" or Wordsworth's "gentle reader") that seem to call to the one reading for a response. With such figures of direct address, the poem's "voice," what William Waters calls "poetry's touch," is strongly felt.[39] At these moments, the transformation of mute text into living speech is accomplished via tropes and the text, now a speaking face, is animated. At the same moment, however, such figures allegorize this transformation precisely *because,* like the Ancient Mariner, they repeat the same call over and over again. What appears at first a human voice is always also a recording, a sign of language's own mechanical and iterable structure, something tropes of address both erase and foreground. Such tropes restage at one and the same moment both Locke's insistence on language's mechanical and inhuman structure and Rousseau's insistence on language's ability to overcome its own semiotic structure to become the living presence of an absent intention.

❖ (Passing On) Future Departures

In turning attention to tropes of address in Gray, Wordsworth, and Keats, I argue in the second part of *The Poetics of Unremembered Acts* that poems, and in particular poems associated with the romantic expressive lyric, pursue through these various figures of address a mode of transmission that is not understanding but the performance of passing on the failure to know (what Barbara Johnson, for instance, calls the pedagogical imperative). Formalism produces something for which form cannot account. Through their employment of figures of address, these poems stage the passage out of cognition, from language as cognition to language as performance. These figures repeat the scene of instruction in reading, a scene that must go unremembered—for Locke—for reading to commence.[40] I explore how poems bear witness to an encounter recorded paradoxically only in the event that understanding is missed. The poems do not, however, leave readers with the security of negative knowledge, as if reading poems could help improve one's knowledge of ignorance. Gray, Wordsworth, and Keats intensify a question about the possible intersections of reading, poetry, and pedagogy that they inherit (however unconsciously) from the practical Enlightenment texts of Locke and Rousseau. As I explore in part 1, the movement from Locke to Rousseau allegorizes the broad attempt to determine reading as primarily a process of decoding and understanding. The poems discussed in part 2, however, explore the manner in which this attempt to determine reading as primarily a question of cognition results, paradoxically, in the passage out of cognition; the poems offer a pedagogy that passes on what is not understood with the force of an event unavailable to phenomenal perception.[41]

Wordsworth's attempt in *The Prelude* to explain how poems teach (they teach *like* nature teaches) introduces a form of teaching (performed at the same time *as* nature teaches) unavailable to the argument of the poem. While Locke and Rousseau attempt to articulate how children should learn to read, poems do not figure prominently in their discourse. The poems I discuss in the second part of *The Poetics of Unremembered Acts* begin to offer an explanation as to why. Preoccupied as they are by figures of address, these poems pick up on what the authors of practical advice on education disclose unconsciously. In foregrounding tropes of address, these poems show that we have not yet learned to read slowly or closely enough. But our failure is not a failure of patience or focus. Instead, it conditions the very possibility of learning to read in the first place. In this way, lyric poetry (overdetermined by figures of address) has a unique role to play in education, even if its role is to remind one that one always reads in very dark light.[42]

In the late twentieth and early twenty-first centuries, numerous books have been published that attempt to account for poetry's lack of cultural significance.[43] It may, however, not be a coincidence that the story of poetry's steep decline in cultural significance often begins with the narrow definition of poetry as lyric that emerges with romanticism, when various mimetic poetic subgenres were collapsed into the expressive romantic lyric.[44] What is remarkable, however, is that poetry's decline in cultural significance should correspond historically with the lyric's rise. For the lyric would seem to satisfy certain cultural demands for self-presence and immediacy, demands that have only increased with various technological advances. And yet the lyric, and poetry more generally, has become less and not more important.

I understand poetry's declining cultural significance as a symptom of a cultural fascination with immediacy and self-presence that the romantic lyric in fact exposes and thereby throws into question.[45] Throughout this book, I trace the lyric's resistance to unmediated contact and argue that the idea of the expressive romantic lyric emerges in opposition to the rhetorical situation explored *by* the lyric even as the lyric becomes synonymous with poetry in general. Poetry's decline, in fact, has much to tell us about our own cultural fascination with aesthetic immediacy and readerly praxis. The more strenuously reading is defined as the process of decoding a message, the more easily reading is confused with listening, as if writing were always and only an extension of the writer's presence in space and time, as if the break in presence that constitutes writing were not structurally necessary. Within the history of reading instruction, solidification of the definition of reading as a process of decoding is accompanied by the prevalent increase in lyric tropes of address explored in romanticism.[46] A popular and all-too-common strategy for resisting the way the lyric reflects on and throws into question the conventional understanding of "reading" is to find poetry (and romanticism) irrelevant.[47]

It may be impossible, in this age of excellence dominated by notions of professionalism and practicality, to attend adequately to poetry's insistent self-questioning, always too easily confused with its insistent impracticality. For the poets I discuss here in *The Poetics of Unremembered Acts,* reading comes to describe an ethical project carried on in the absence of understanding and knowledge. For instance, in the conclusion to "Isabella," Keats describes the story of Isabella's suffering and eventual death being passed from mouth to mouth through all the country. I argue that this mode of transmission bypasses understanding (the ear as metonym for the mind) but enables a new relationship to the power of address. When poetry and teaching meet, they meet by accident with a force that is registered by the absence of cognition. In response to such practical pedagogical texts as Locke's *Some Thoughts Concerning Education* and Rousseau's *Émile,* which turn on missed encounters necessary to reading instruction, the lyric poems I discuss discover in these missed encounters an ethical call to bear witness in the absence of full understanding. As a result, lyric poems offer, however accidentally, a theory of reading less practical than ethical, a theory of reading that educational institutions—given the current push to align absolutely education and immediate, phenomenal, and measurable results—strive to eliminate. If there is no longer a chance for missed encounters, then there is no longer—suggest Gray, Wordsworth, and Keats—a chance to bear witness with inhuman patience and a mind not entirely one's own to teaching's surprise.

Part I

Reading—Pedagogy

1

"Cozen'd" into Knowledge: Locke

The machine performs all alone, without even the intention of the user.
—Blaise Pascal

Cheat him into it if you can.
—John Locke

Sometimes it is better not to know what you are doing. For John Locke, teaching children to read involves a game in which letters are inscribed on the sides of dice, creating words spelled by chance when rolled together. Locke's reasons for including the die-rolling game are entirely practical. Because children might resist learning to read, they should think they are merely playing a game and so play themselves into a reading lesson that they might at other moments resist. But when Locke's practical treatise on education is compared to the more philosophical work of *An Essay Concerning Human Understanding*, the fact that the first text children will read is produced mechanically and by chance contradicts Locke's suggestion that words are only words if they represent some prior intention in the mind of the speaker or author. In *An Essay,* he goes so far as to suggest that sounds that do not represent ideas already in the mind of the speaker are "noise" and not words. The words spelled by the die rolls have no relationship to ideas the die roller intentionally communicates. They are "noise." Why does instruction in reading require that which Locke elsewhere rejects, words that are hardly words?

The tension between Locke's philosophical project in *An Essay* and his practical one in *Some Thoughts Concerning Education* raises questions about the structure of language and the supposed priority of intentions in considerations of textual meaning. Many literary critical debates in the second half of the twentieth century centered on just these questions: Can or should language be considered independently of authorial intention and context? And how significant is the intended addressee in making determinations of meaning or valuing particular readings or interpretations over others? Jacques Derrida explains in "Signature Event Context" that for writing to function as writing it must continue to function not only in the absence of the addressor (why else write?) but also in the absence of the addressee: "My 'written communication' must, if you will, remain legible despite the absolute disappearance of every determined addressee in general for it to function as writing, that is, for it to be legible."[1] As writing, what is written must continue to be legible even in the absence of any determined addressee, which also means that the addressee of any written communication cannot be determined in advance. A written communication must remain legible to anyone who happens upon it; no addressee can fully lay claim to what is written (as writing). Derrida identifies this structure of writing, but this same structure also conditions the possibility of language more generally. To be minimally understandable (readable or legible), language too must continue to signify in the absence of addressor and addressee. Locke, perhaps unintentionally, raises a similar point about the structure of writing through the die-rolling game as he relies on the chance that words might be spelled even in the absence of a subject who means to write. What looks like a simple enough game exposes an aspect of writing (and so too of language) that more often and elsewhere in Locke is viewed as a problem to be overcome.

While in *Some Thoughts Concerning Education* Locke advises parents not to let children become poets, Locke's die-rolling game borrows from the lyric what he cannot, in *An Essay,* abide: the chance that one might use language and not intend to transmit a particular message to another. In *An Essay,* Locke privileges the referential function of language over what Roman Jakobson calls the poetic function, which stresses the material form of the message over the meaning conveyed.[2] The poet takes an interest in language independent of the will to use it to communicate a particular message to another. This rhetorical situation is exploited by lyric poets. The lyric poet, often through apostrophe, turns his or her back on the reader to address himself or herself, an absent other, or an inanimate object. And so readers find themselves "overhearing" an utterance not intended for them. In this way, the poet's indifference to the reader (however staged) counters Locke's understanding of the purpose for language as articulated in *An Essay:* to transmit a message to another. The lyric plays on address and foregrounds questions of address through its dominant tropes. Like a lyric poem, the first text the child will read, for Locke, does not communicate a particular message to a determined addressee. At the origin of modern reading pedagogy, in other words, rests an utterance, like the lyric, that takes no interest in its addressee, an utterance that is not, at least not in any simple sense, addressed to the one who reads. Historically, lyric poems are not often the result of die-rolling games, but the rhetorical situation staged in and by the lyric echoes (and is echoed by) Locke's game. One learns to read, Locke suggests (perhaps without fully acknowledging the implications) from an utterance that ignores one. One must read the lyric first to learn to read at all.

The priority of the lyric, however, is doubly denied in the history of reading pedagogy. After describing the game, Locke suggests that children should not understand that they are learning to read when they are playing the game. Children must be "cozen'd" into knowledge of reading. When Rousseau responds to Locke's *Some Thoughts Concerning Education* in *Émile,* he singles out the die-rolling game for ridicule. The first texts a child will read, for Rousseau, will not be spelled by chance but will instead take the form of notes directly addressed to the child. The repeated missing of events—dinner, walks, an outing on the water, a public festival—will inspire Émile to decipher notes describing such events in preparation for a future in which events will not be missed. In this way, *Émile* acknowledges that Locke's die-rolling game complicates an understanding of language structured around authorial intentions and questions of address. In *Émile,* Rousseau works to close the possibility that Locke opens—that to learn to read, the child must read an utterance that goes unaddressed and does not aim to communicate a message. In this chapter, I trace the passage from Locke's to Rousseau's theory of reading pedagogy, a movement that begins with Locke's enigmatic suggestion that the first text children read will be composed of words that have no relationship to the conscious intentions of the die-roller prior to the compositional act, a text that is not addressed to the one who reads.[3] Why should a linguistic structure that will come to define the lyric poem condition the possibility of reading? Why must this structure be denied? What does the lyric disclose about reading that modern pedagogy must—inherited as it is from Locke and Rousseau—keep a secret?

❖ Voluntary Impositions

In *An Essay,* Locke famously acknowledges the arbitrary and conventional relationship that exists between a word and the idea it is meant to communicate. Words, writes Locke, become the signs of ideas "not by any natural connexion . . . but by a voluntary Imposition."[4] It cannot be assumed, asserts Locke, that the specific sound patterns and individual letters that make up the word "scarlet," for instance, have any natural connection to the idea of the color scarlet that is signified by the word. If such were the case, he surmises, there would exist only one language. When Ferdinand de Saussure, several centuries later, links the arbitrary nature of the sign to language's differential structure, he extends Locke's insight: "it is evident, even *a priori*, that a segment of language can never in the final analysis be based on anything except its noncoincidence with the rest. Arbitrary and differential are two correlative qualities."[5] Because language is a system of arbitrary signifiers, any given signifier gains its significance not from the signified but from its relationship to other signifiers. For this reason Saussure famously describes language as a system of differences without positive terms. As Jacques Derrida has shown, if language is structured differentially, then there is always (and necessarily) a chance for play, a chance that one's words communicate otherwise than one intended.[6]

One has the sense that Locke was uncomfortable with his own insight into language. Indeed, much of book 3 of *An Essay,* on words and language, reads as Locke's attempt to overcome the potential complications for any philosophical understanding of language that result from the observation that words have a conventional (as opposed to a natural) relation to what they signify. He confesses that when he began *An Essay* he "had not the least Thought, that any Consideration of Words was at all necessary to it" (*Essay,* 488), and yet his consideration of words came to occupy a central place in the work.[7] Locke asserts that the only proper function of a word is to communicate the idea it represents in the mind; he labors to ground the arbitrary relation between words and ideas on the communicative intentions of the language user. While the relation between word and idea is not natural but imposed, the word, argues Locke, does not have an arbitrary relationship to a speaker's or author's intention to use it for some purpose: "When a Man speaks to another, it is, that he may be understood; and the end of Speech is, that those Sounds, as Marks, may make known his Ideas to the Hearer" (*Essay,* 405).[8] Locke relies on intention to rescue him from the dilemma that emerges from his own understanding of language's structure.[9] If language does not excite in the hearer the same idea as in the mind of the speaker, "Men fill one another's Heads with noise and sounds; but convey not thereby their Thoughts, and lay not before one another their Ideas, which is the end of Discourse and Language" (*Essay,* 478). By indicating a difference between words and noise, Locke addresses the possibility that what is heard might not correspond with the internal thoughts of the speaker. If words do not correspond "exactly" with the idea in the mind of the speaker, then what others hear are not words but noise. But how can one tell the difference in advance?

To help distinguish words from noise, Locke opposes the language of human beings from the "articulate sounds" of parrots. The ability to frame articulate sounds, words, "is not enough to produce Language; for

Parrots, and several other Birds, will be taught to make articulate Sounds distinct enough, which yet, by no means, are capable of Language" (*Essay*, 402). While parrots may make articulate sounds distinct enough to be mistaken for words, the ability to produce articulate sounds is not enough to consider these sounds words. The parrot utters noise because it has no intention to use language to communicate an idea. For an articulate sound to be considered a word, the speaker "should be able to use these Sounds, as signs of internal conceptions; and to make them stand as marks for the Ideas within his own Mind" (*Essay*, 402). The goal of language use is making these ideas known to another. Parrots should not be considered capable of language because, Locke implies, they cannot be considered to have ideas and internal conceptions that they wish to convey.[10]

Locke spends a great deal of time and energy in *An Essay* working to ensure that language is grounded in the intentions of the speaker to communicate an idea received through the proper sensory inlet, but all of this time and energy serves almost as a defense against the force of Locke's insight from the beginning of book 3: noise (like articulate sounds spoken by a parrot) might always possibly be mistaken for words.[11] What one hears as words may turn out upon further consideration to be noise, and what one hears as noise may turn out to be words.[12] If such is the case, then the difference between articulate sounds (noise, words spoken without intention) and language (words spoken with intention and with the proper internal conceptions of sense-data) is difficult to determine absolutely.[13] That parrots are capable of articulate sounds in the absence of ideas (of the intention, that is, to produce meaningful sounds) is a problem for Locke because it foregrounds the material aspects of words—sound patterns, or, with written texts, the shape of individual letters—that are always open to duplication in the absence of ideas and intentions. If parrots are capable of producing articulate sounds that might be mistaken for language by those who listen, then language cannot be grounded once and for all in the intentions of an individual speaker.[14] Locke does not engage with this insight directly in *An Essay*. However, he will come to address this question in *Some Thoughts Concerning Education*.

❖ Intentionless Meanings

The child reads what no one intends to write. The game that Locke describes in *Some Thoughts Concerning Education* is possible only after the tutor inscribes letters on a series of dice and relies on the introduction of an element of chance, which Locke claims is necessary for reading instruction. The dice are rolled and the child records the meaningful words he or she discovers: "I know a Person of great Quality . . . who by pasting on the six Vowels . . . on the six sides of a Die, and the remaining eighteen Consonants on the sides of three other Dice; has made this a Play for his Children, that he shall win, who at one cast throws most Words on these four Dice."[15] After rolling the dice, the child arranges and rearranges the dice, producing letter combinations and counting the number of meaningful words he or she finds. Locke describes the game as "so easy and useful that it will be hard to find any better, and there will be scarce need of any other" for reading instruction (*Education,* 257). The child is to find within meaningless and arbitrary collections of letters as many words as possible. To learn to read, the child will first read not what anyone intended to write but what is written nonetheless, a "chance-writing" that has no prior relation to the intention of the "author" to communicate a particular message. The dice will spell words that appear meaningful but have no relationship to the die roller's will. What is written is set down at a distance from, and therefore is cut from, the intention to communicate. To learn to read (though unaware of the full significance of what they have learned), children must also learn that words do not have a natural connection to thoughts and appear meaningful even in the absence of an author's intention to communicate.

Locke offers the die-rolling game for practical reasons. He would prefer that the child not associate learning with work and, as Rousseau will later do in *Émile,* imagines a child who desires to learn. "I have always had a Fancy," Locke writes, "that Learning might be made a Play and Recreation to Children; and that they might be brought to desire to be taught, if it were propos'd to them as a thing of Honour, Credit, Delight and Recreation, or as a Reward for doing something else; and if they were never chid or corrected for the neglect of it" (*Education,* 255). Children, argues Locke, are much more likely to continue to learn if they associate learning with delight and recreation, if learning is not forced upon them, and if they are not punished physically or corrected verbally for not learning properly. Locke recommends these die-rolling games because he fears that if children think about learning to read as work, then they will soon lose interest in reading. If children are "tied down to their Books" (*Education,* 256), if they are forced to read, then they will develop an aversion to reading: "their being forced and tied down to their books, in an Age at enmity with all such restraint, has, I doubt not, been the reason, why a great many have hated Books and Learning, all their Lives after: 'Tis like a Surfeit, that leaves an Aversion behind not to be removed" (*Education,* 256). The die-rolling game prevents the association of reading with work in part because the "message" communicated by the dice—the words the dice spell—cannot be ascribed to the conscious intentions of the tutor or the die roller. The child is to associate the game not with other pedagogical tasks in which the message the adult communicates has priority but rather with free play, with an aesthetic mode divorced from predetermined goals. With respect to Locke's die-rolling game, which words appear to have been spelled by the dice is less important to the child's development as a reader than the fact that any are spelled at all. While Locke is not responsible for inventing the game, his interest in the game poses complicated questions to his philosophy of language as developed in *An Essay.*[16] If, as Locke's interest in the game suggests one might, one stresses the ability of language to signify in the absence of an idea present within the mind of the author, then this ability of language complicates the conventional (and assumed) priority of the signified to any understanding of the development of language. In asserting the importance of games such as these to reading instruction, Locke foregrounds the structuring independence of any given word from the goal of communication. What is written by the chance rolls of dice is readable only if writing is no longer (or at least not entirely) "inside" thought. Such a notion of writing proves troublesome for Locke's more general philosophical pronouncements on language from *An Essay* because what is written is not dependent on the die roller's prior intention to transmit a message.[17] In his practical treatise on education, Locke implies that the independence of linguistic signs from the objects to which they are meant to refer, and, additionally, from any intention to use them, is necessary for instruction in reading. Far from preventing practical pedagogy, such writing—the writing produced by throws of dice—is constitutive of learning to read.[18] Although Locke in *An Essay* blames the great controversies of human society on the tendency of words to communicate otherwise than intended, in *Some Thoughts Concerning Education* it is the chance that words might be read in the absence of determinable intentions that makes learning to read possible.[19] Learning to read comes to depend on the possibility of reading what was never intended consciously by the author to be communicated.[20]

❖ "Without Knowing"

Learning to read requires a trick. With the use of die-rolling games, "Children may be cozen'd into a Knowledge of the Letters, be taught to read, without perceiving it to be any thing but a Sport, and play themselves into that which others are whipp'd for" (*Education,* 256). Locke recommends deceiving students because he wants to ensure the game's success. If children come to recognize that the game is not only for sport—if, in other words, they associate the game with learning to read—then they might lose interest in playing it and so also lose interest in reading.[21] As a result of playing the game, the child will "learn to read, without knowing how he did so" (*Education,* 257).

Why is such deception necessary? Why should children never know that they are learning to read? Locke's focus on the importance of a child's not knowing how he or she learned to read is, I argue, a sign of Locke's resistance to what the game discloses about language. Language functions independently of the author's intentions to communicate. To learn to read, and to continue to read in the future, what the game discloses about language must be kept from the child for it threatens the very idea of reading (as decoding) that Locke advocates for in *An Essay.* Perhaps more dangerous than the chance that children come to think of learning to read as a task (more dangerous than the chance that children come to understand that the game is not just for play) is the chance that children come to understand that the words written by the dice have no relationship to the thoughts of the die roller. The adult's deception of the child and the child's subsequent ignorance of "reading"—ignorance of having learned to read a text written by chance and in the absence of authorial intention—both testify to the potentially disruptive observation that language signifies in the absence of intention. No one signs his or her name to the first text the child reads. This the child cannot know.

In a 1960 text offering advice in reading instruction, *Reading Games: Strengthening Reading Skills with Instructional Games,* Guy Wagner and Max Hosier express a similar worry. They offer an impressive array of games similar to the die-rolling games described by Locke and popular in past centuries. In the foreword to the book, however, they present one particular caution: "*Word games* have a tendency to isolate words from the context and therefore should be used only after the pupils have met these words in meaningful situations."[22] Wagner and Hosier do not elaborate on the negative repercussions that will result from children coming to read words in isolation. Meaningful situations, they warn, must determine the reader's encounter with language. One suspects that the danger Wagner and Hosier allude to is not unlike the danger Locke identifies: because these games emphasize words as words and do not immediately subject words to the ideas they represent, the child who plays too many word games is always, possibly, in danger of focusing on words as a poet does. Such a focus potentially strands the reading child in an understanding of language's material properties, as if language had no referential function to speak of.

Locke resists the insight into language that his invocation of the game demonstrates when he stresses how important it is that children not know that they are learning to read. The idea of reading that emerges in Locke's practical treatise on education designates as necessary to reading instruction the chance that language signifies even in the absence of an intention to use language. Reading is made possible by those aspects of language that are not reducible (or limited) to language's referential function. Necessary to the success of the game, though, is the child's ignorance of what he or she is doing when he or she "reads" the dice. Only to the extent to which children are ignorant of learning to read is it possible for Locke, in *An Essay,* to assert the primacy of intention and address. In this way, Locke builds into his own educational theory the necessity of forgetting (or of never consciously knowing) that one has learned to "read"—a necessary erasure from history of the chance that language is readable even in the absence of an author's intentions to address another. What guarantees a future for reading is that children forget that they learned to read what Locke would never have had them read at all.

❖ Lyric Reading

When Jean-Jacques Rousseau wrote *Émile* in 1762, he engaged many of Locke's theories of education and singled out the die-rolling game for ridicule. Objecting to such contrivances, Rousseau focuses his pedagogical experiments on increasing the child's interest in reading. For Rousseau, children will learn to read only after they understand the utility of literacy: "A great business is made of seeking the best methods of teaching reading. Desks and cards are invented; a child's room is made into a printing shop. Locke wants him to learn to read with dice. Now is that not a clever invention? What a pity! A means surer than all these, and the one always forgotten, is the desire to learn."[23] Rousseau will increase Émile's desire to learn by using his desire for sweets and outings. Émile will learn to read when he understands that literacy will help him to satisfy his desire. Wagner and Hosier follow Rousseau in suggesting that "meaningful situations" are necessary for reading instruction.

For Rousseau, children will take an interest in learning to read only after it has been made clear to them why they should want to know how to read in the first place, only, that is, after they know what reading is good for. "The art of speaking to and hearing from absent people, the art of communicating our feelings, our wills, our desires to them at a distance without a mediator," writes Rousseau, "is an art whose utility can be rendered palpable to all ages."[24] In contrast to Locke's die-rolling game, Rousseau stages a scene as if from a play. Émile will receive numerous notes from friends and relatives asking him to join them for a walk or watch some public spectacle. Because no one is present to read the notes for him, Émile will miss the events that have been planned for the day: "Thus the occasion, the moment, is missed [Ainsi l'occasion, le moment se passé]."[25] Only later will Émile find someone to read the note to and with him; and he will come to understand that had he been able to read the note, he would have been able to participate in the outing. He continues to receive more notes. After repeatedly missing events announced by the notes, Émile will decipher part of a note himself: "It has to do with going tomorrow to eat custard . . . he does not know where or with whom . . . how many efforts he makes to read the rest."[26] Émile will learn to read these notes because he will wish to be included in the social outings that they announce. Because he will fail to read the notes, he will take an interest in learning to read so that he will be able to read future notes left for him. For Rousseau, children should not play themselves into reading. They should learn to read whole messages that have been addressed to them with a particular message that they will take an interest in deciphering. In this way, Rousseau sutures what had begun to come apart in Locke's *Some Thoughts Concerning Education*—reading, according to Rousseau, should always be directed toward deciphering and understanding particular messages.

Locke's game exposes, however unintentionally, an aspect of language that Émile's education in reading is to overcome. The game points to a structuring mechanical or nonhuman aspect of language that allows for language to function even in the absence of the human subject, a machinelike quality without which language would cease to function; the game exposes the way that language functions independently of referential determination, as also "a system that is both entirely arbitrary and entirely repeatable."[27] Once discovered, Locke ensures that this structure of language is hidden behind the tutor's trick. The child is not to understand that he is reading when he is playing the game. Rousseau, by contrast, would rather the game not be played at all. For Rousseau, what one does with language and not what language "does" in one's absence is of primary importance.

Underway in the passage from Locke to Rousseau is an attempt to limit and so eliminate language's ability to signify aberrantly or atypically (its ability, in other words, to signify in the absence of intention). In attempting to limit this chance, Rousseau, however, cannot help but draw attention to Locke's game and so to the very possibility he works against. In *Émile*, Rousseau develops a series of measures meant to ensure that Émile always recovers the intentional messages conveyed by writing. These measures will be explored in the next chapter. Rousseau privileges the ability of language to convey particular messages and the ability of the reader to recover those messages, a reading that privileges language's referential function over its mechanical and iterable structure, what Jakobson calls "poeticity." Reading (as defined by Rousseau) is an attempt to put an end to the very chance that makes reading possible (for Locke).

If Locke's game, like the rhetorical tropes that determine the lyric, raises address as a question, then Rousseau's reading pedagogy develops a lyric reading that pretends to overcome the question of address. What has come to define the lyric is the poet's reticence to communicate a message to another. The reader overhears the lyric poet's utterance, one that is not addressed to him or her. Mutlu Konuk Blasing describes the lyric in terms now familiar to readers of Locke's game: "Lyric poetry is not mimesis. Above everything else, it . . . keeps in view the linguistic code and the otherness of the material medium of language to all that humans do with it—refer, represent, express, narrate, imitate, communicate, think, reason, theorize, philosophize. It offers an experience of another kind of order, a system that operates independently of the production of the meaningful discourse it enables."[28] In this way, the rhetorical situation that defines the lyric shares a structure with Locke's die-rolling game, though few observers would confuse them. Stéphane Mallarmé comes to seem the unnatural result of Locke's pedagogical method.[29] Despite the fact that after romanticism the lyric is frequently celebrated for its ability to carry and convey the poet's voice and full presence, the lyric also names a difference within language, the ability of language to do something other than communicate. If the die-rolling game touches upon considerations of the lyric, as I have suggested, because the text produced by rolls of dice is not addressed to the reader and does not communicate a particular message, then Rousseau labors to deny the lyric any role in education. Locke's game makes difficult granting a human face to the text one reads, as it is produced by chance. However, Émile is to learn that a text worth reading is specifically addressed to him; it aims to convey a predetermined meaning. In this way, though, lyric reading is central to reading instruction for Rousseau. While lyric reading aligns the text with the representation of a human voice,

Locke's die-rolling game offers an extreme form of the lyric (a form of the lyric familiar to readers of John Cage's chance operations). This lyric writing stages a question of address that lyric reading aims to overcome through the figures of address that have come to dominate the lyric as a genre. As Paul de Man suggests in "Anthropomorphism and Trope in the Lyric," "the lyric is not a genre, but one name among several to designate the defensive motion of understanding."[30] In other words, lyric reading, which aims to recover (or discover) a voice within the text, defends one against the ways the lyric questions address (through its investment in the rhetoric of address). Rousseau substitutes lyric reading for the encounter with the lyric utterance offered by Locke. And so reading comes to be defined by the figure that dominates the lyric: prosopopoeia. Reading is possible only after one grants to letters a face and a voice. For Rousseau, the note must be understood to transmit a message to Émile, who will take an interest in reading only after he takes himself as the addressee.

As will be explored more fully in later chapters on Thomas Gray, William Wordsworth, and John Keats, the dominance of the lyric—and the ways in which one grants to the lyric a face and voice—is meant to overcome the questions of address that preoccupy Locke and Rousseau. In other words, the dominance of the lyric in romanticism inherits a question that troubles eighteenth-century reading pedagogy. One grants to language a face and a voice so as to overcome the chance that language is not addressed to one, the chance that it does not always correspond to the human voice.

❖ Addressing Words

For Locke, in *Some Thoughts Concerning Education,* children will learn to read without knowing how they did so. The event of their learning to read must be missed if there is to be a future for the sort of reading Locke celebrates in *An Essay* and elsewhere in *Some Thoughts Concerning Education.* Similarly, Rousseau's method for reading instruction as offered in *Émile* is meant to guarantee that the reader understand himself or herself as addressed by the "voice" in the text; the reader works to recover the original intention "voiced" by what was written. One must grant to the text, through the figures that dominate the lyric, a face and a voice.[31] To contend with the fact that language does not address one as entirely human, one must (like a poet) grant to the text a human face and a human voice. In this way, Locke's suggestion that children not know that they are learning to read when they are reading words spelled by chance also acknowledges the ways that the lyric disrupts the notion of reading defended elsewhere in Locke and Rousseau. The importance of intention and address returns in *Émile,* but it returns as a strategy for readers to defend themselves against the lyric utterance.

In a well-known passage from the close of book 2 of his *Confessions,* Rousseau recalls an utterance not unlike one produced via Locke's die-rolling game, a chance utterance that becomes the very condition of possibility of his *Confessions.* When employed as a servant in an aristocratic household, Rousseau confesses, he stole a pink-and-silver ribbon. After his theft was discovered, he accused Marion, a servant girl Rousseau desired who also worked in the household. Rousseau remembers being so troubled by the memory of falsely accusing an innocent girl that he could not sleep. She approaches, and reproaches, him in his dreams. But never before, he writes, has he confided his crime: "The most that I have been able to do has been to confess my responsibility for an atrocious deed, without ever saying of what exactly it consisted. This burden, then, has lain unalleviated on my conscience until this very day; and I can safely say that the desire to be in some measure relieved of it has greatly contributed to the decision I have taken to write my confessions."[32] He confesses what he has never before fully confessed. Without this accusation leveled against an innocent girl, and without the desire to confess, he might never have written and there might never have been a *Confessions.* In his reading of this moment included in *Allegories of Reading,* Paul de Man focuses on Rousseau's description of the event of naming "Marion." "I have never been less motivated by malice than at this cruel moment," Rousseau writes, "and when I accused this unfortunate girl, it is bizarre, but it is true, that it was my fondness for her that was the cause of it. She was on my mind, and I had simply used as an excuse the first object that presented itself to me."[33] De Man focuses on the vocabulary of contingency that emerges out of the more familiar vocabulary of explanation. Rousseau admits to thinking of Marion, who was present in his mind. And yet, he does not explain that it was because he was thinking of her that he named her. Instead, he excused himself on the first object that offered itself. "Marion" is spoken as if without intention or forethought. "Marion," as a signifier, is simply the "first thing" that offers itself: "Je m'excusai sur le premier objet qui s'offrit."[34] The speech act that makes the *Confessions*—to some extent—possible is spoken without agency: "By saying that the excuse is not only a fiction but also a machine one adds to the connotation of referential detachment, of gratuitous improvisation, that of the implacable repetition of a preordained pattern."[35] Rousseau does not "mean" to accuse Marion. He randomly (mechanically, without aim or intention) utters "Marion." The name—or more accurately, perhaps, the random series of letters—produced by Rousseau at this all-important moment shares the structure of words produced by Locke's die-rolling game. Both arrive arbitrarily and contingently, untied to any intended content and unaddressed. Much of Rousseau's confession may be understood as an attempt to catch up to what he uttered as if mechanically, or what was uttered in his name but without him, without his being fully present to himself. Locke's story of the origin of reading (which emerges in his advice for reading instruction) and Rousseau's story of the origin of his *Confessions,* and so much else of his writing, an origin, almost, of writing itself, turn on an encounter with the otherness of language—as nonreferential, nonrepresentational, and nonexpressive.

After Immanuel Kant, many scholars have justified poetry by celebrating its autonomy, its purposiveness without purpose.[36] But the story of poetry's autonomy becomes all the more complicated when it runs up against Locke's die-rolling game, which introduces, or at least plays on, an autonomy of words. The die-rolling game estranges the mission usually identified with romanticism, in which the immediate, expressive (and therefore human) utterance is judged philosophically significant. In response to the questions raised however subtly by Locke and Rousseau, I argue, emerge poets invested in language's otherness, its ability to function independently of human will and interest—its lyric potential to arrive unaddressed and as if by accident. This investment exists alongside (and so allegorizes) the more familiar investment in language's ability to place the poet, the human author, center stage, an investment one usually identifies with romanticism and its expressive lyrics. What Locke identifies as a necessary aberration, an accident, one that should remain in some sense inaccessible to the child, returns in Novalis's "Monologue," in which he writes, "Language is such a marvelous and fruitful secret—because when someone speaks merely for the sake of speaking, he utters the most splendid, most original truths. But if he wants to speak about something definite, capricious language makes him say the most ridiculous and confused stuff."[37] Novalis overturns the goals of communication that govern Enlightenment pedagogy. Instead of privileging the speaking subject who aims to use language to communicate a particular message to another, Novalis privileges the one who speaks without interest or intention. This reversal of Locke's position in *An Essay* and Rousseau's in *Émile* is most fully embraced by Novalis when he asserts that "perhaps the ultimate book is like an ABC book,"[38] the reading primers that "reading machines," like Locke's die-rolling game, were meant to extend.[39] In light of Locke's die-rolling game, as well as his own and Rousseau's resistance to it, the assertion of the voice of the poet, manifested in and through words, risks seeming yet another strategy for protecting readers from what I am calling the lyric potential of language, the potential of language to function even in the absence of a specified addressee. How does the lyric's unique willingness to raise questions of address tell anew the story of reading instruction?

The rise of the lyric in the nineteenth century repeats the gesture that Rousseau performs when he counters Locke's die-rolling game and asserts the importance of address. But in repeating Rousseau's gesture, romantic poets preoccupied by the lyric inevitably also allegorize Rousseau's gesture and so allegorize the passage from chance to reference. In this way, lyric poems tell the story of an encounter with the belatedness of reference. The addresses to the reader that I focus on in the second part of this book restage the attempted denial of the lyric in turning toward a language of address, a conception of language that privileges the intentions of the speaker to communicate a message to another, a conception of language built around the very figures of address (like apostrophe and prosopopoeia) that lyric poets know well.

2

On Learning to Read as Not Myself: Rousseau

I do not know how I learned to read.
—Jean-Jacques Rousseau

If the goal of reading pedagogy is to ensure that readers are properly trained to decipher the message transmitted, then Rousseau's *Émile* demonstrates, perhaps unintentionally, the cost of training readers to disregard language's lyric potential—its potential to exceed the intentions of the user and to refer aberrantly or address readers indiscriminately. Rousseau counters Locke's suggestion that a text produced by chance rolls of dice—and so one with no determinable addressee—will teach the child to read. Notes specifically addressed to him will constitute Émile's first reading material. The notes, however, are not capable of succeeding on their own, and so Rousseau turns to Daniel Defoe's *The Life and Strange Surprizing Adventures of Robinson Crusoe* (1719) to supplement Émile's instruction in reading. Attempting to prevent the child from reading to the "wrong" or "improper" end, from deciphering the message incorrectly, Rousseau somewhat enigmatically suggests that Émile will learn finally how to read properly only once he learns to read as Robinson Crusoe. To learn to read, Émile must learn to read as a literary figure. But in the very pages of *Émile* in which Rousseau articulates the importance of Robinson Crusoe to Émile's education, the language of Rousseau's text poses interpretive difficulties that are not easily resolved. The text of *Émile* itself questions the reader's ability to perform the action Rousseau so carefully describes as reading. The lyric potential of language cannot be eliminated without undoing the very structure of the text itself, something that *Émile* showcases even despite its own best efforts to limit the possibility of future misreading.

Although Rousseau himself considered *Émile* his best book and although Kant compared the event of its publication with the event of the French Revolution, suggesting that its publication was of political and not simply pedagogical import, *Émile* remains an obscure text. Unlike some of Rousseau's better-known texts, such as *Julie* or *The Social Contract*, *Émile* has not found a place in university curricula. This may be due not only to its length but also to the fact that *Émile* crosses traditional generic boundaries. A somewhat rambling and even unfocused text, *Émile* is both a novel and a philosophical treatise on education. It offers both the fictional story of the education of a young man, concluding with his marriage and his fathering of a child, and a literal model for the progress of human society. As a result, readers of *Émile* have tended to privilege one of these options over the other. The philosophical reading of *Émile* privileges Rousseau's pedagogical advice, while the literary reading privileges the narrative aspects of the text: either *Émile* is a treatise on education that relies on fiction to clearly assert its position or it is a novel with Émile as its title character that happens to offer practical advice on education. To read *Émile* as *both* a novel and a practical treatise on education would be to reconcile the literary and philosophical aspects of Rousseau's thought. As the "or" (*ou*) that divides the title suggests, *Émile, ou de l'éducation* struggles to unite these discourses. The difficulty (if not impossibility) of reconciling literature and philosophy opens onto larger difficulties, for what is at stake in *Émile* is one's ability to be free and independent as well as committed to a shared world.[1] Émile's ability to reconcile his freedom and self-sufficiency with his commitment to human society depends on his ability to learn to read the only book he should ever need to read, Daniel Defoe's *Robinson Crusoe.*

Émile begins as a philosophical treatise but slowly drifts toward the literary. Such a generic transition runs counter to the title, from which one might expect *Émile* to move from being classified as a novel (*Émile*) to a philosophical treatise on education (*de l'éducation*). Although Rousseau produces Émile as a fictional character, a figment of his imagination, the opening of *Émile* consists of practical advice for the raising of real children. By the end of *Émile,* however, Rousseau begins to tell Émile's *story* and no longer uses Émile merely as a pedagogical aid for the illustration of his philosophy of education. The literary *Émile* takes over from the philosophical *de l'éducation.*

The move in *Émile* from philosophy to literature is analogous to the corresponding development of the pedagogical practices Rousseau uses Émile to demonstrate. In the early books of *Émile,* Émile is to have a relationship to the world that is entirely grounded in his direct empirical experience of it. Émile is to be educated through his experience of things. Only later in his development will he be offered the opportunity to engage with signs. For Rousseau, signs are a problem because they allow one to mistake them for things. In the second half of *Émile,* however,

Rousseau recognizes and accepts the necessary importance of signs as he acknowledges the necessity of reading. Just as the text of *Émile* moves from the philosophical work of practical education to the literary work of the novel, so too does Émile's education move from the experience of things to the experience of signs.

Émile's education has the shape of a chiasmus. Initially, signs are capable of leading Émile astray from his proper, natural education, and Rousseau relies on direct experience of the natural world to keep him on track, but by the opening of book 4 it is the world that threatens to lead him astray, and Rousseau must turn to signs to keep Émile's education on track. While Émile's exposure to signs is to be kept to a minimum, history books come to play a necessary role in Émile's education. If in the first half of *Émile* present things are privileged over signs, in the second half of *Émile* signs of absent things are privileged over the present social world. This switch from things to signs is possible, however, only after Émile has safely learned to tell the difference between signs and things, rhetoric and experience, literature and philosophy—that is, only after Émile has learned to read.

The reconciliation of these oppositions has practical consequences for Émile, whose education is designed to reconcile his experience of nature, based on a natural relationship to things, and of society, based on a conventional relationship to signs. Émile will be able to articulate the natural and social only after he has aligned a philosophical and literary relation to signs—that is, a referential and semiotic approach to language, which is possible only through a particular model of reading that Rousseau describes in book 3. Émile's reading of history, the establishment of a proper relationship both to things and to signs, depends on a scene of reading found almost exactly midway through the text of *Émile,* where Rousseau describes how Émile should read *Robinson Crusoe.* This one book will teach Émile to read all others; it prepares him for the future reading of history books that, in turn, makes possible his return to the social world. And yet, this scene of reading complicates Rousseau's larger philosophical enterprise as presented in *Émile* because Émile will only come to learn to read to the extent to which he learns to think of himself as Robinson Crusoe. The understanding of reading that emerges most forcefully from *Émile* aims to guarantee that texts transmit their proper (and most useful) meaning. Rousseau wants to guard his reader from reading texts to the wrong end. But this desire to guarantee reading—to guarantee that what is read is always read properly—instead produces a text, *Émile* itself, that is split and divided from itself. The attempt to guarantee that Émile always reads properly produces a text, *Émile,* that struggles to know its own meaning. The grammar of *Émile* introduces a split within *Émile* that Émile (and pedagogical practices Rousseau outlines) cannot anticipate or overcome.

❖ The Reconciliation of Opposites

The goal of *Émile* is to produce an exceptional man who is in harmony with his own natural tendencies and yet also capable of participating in human society without being adversely affected by its conventions and institutions. Rousseau describes the natural man: "L'homme naturel est tout pour lui: il est l'unité numérique, l'entier absolu, qui n'a de rapport qu'à lui-même ou à son semblable" ("Natural man is entirely for himself. He is numerical unity, the absolute whole which is relative only to itself or its kind") (*Oc,* 249; *OE,* 39).[2] Natural man is self-coincident and exists entirely for himself. He has no need for others and, indeed, no need for knowledge of them. In contrast: "L'homme civil n'est qu'une unité fractionnaire qui tient au dénominateur, et dont la valeur est dans son rapport avec l'entier, qui est le corps social" ("Civil man is only a fractional unity dependent on the denominator; his value is determined by his relation to the whole, which is the social body") (*Oc,* 249; *OE,* 39–40). The civil man depends on the social body for his existence. Because he needs others and cannot exist without them, he is cut off from himself, split by his relationship to and dependence on the community. Natural man, who is independent and free, however, is absolutely so. As a result, he is alone. Rousseau asks: what will a man raised uniquely for himself become for others? Natural man may be independent, but he is entirely independent; there is no society for the natural man. The price of citizenship is one's independence or uniqueness. The loss of independence and self-determination, though, is the very possibility of society itself. Unlike the *Social Contract,* for example, in which Rousseau hopes to transform the civil order, in *Émile* he hopes to transform the individual through new pedagogical practices. These are two different methods for arriving at the same end: a more perfect human society. Either the civil order must be revised or people must be more perfectly educated. If society cannot be changed or transformed radically enough from the outside, it must be changed from within. Man must be newly fashioned, and in the process society itself will be reformed.[3]

Neither the natural man nor the civil man is adequate to the task as Rousseau imagines it. Rousseau's goal is to fashion an individual in harmony with himself *and* with others, to reconcile natural freedom with the constraints of society but not at the expense of society itself. Rousseau argues that the natural tendencies of man must be protected from the corrosive influence of human society, which perverts the natural world, but he does not wish to sacrifice society itself along the way. Simply to preserve the sentiments of nature is to privilege the natural over the civil man to the detriment of society. In contrast, Émile is to be educated in order to enter human society freely and independently. His education is not set in opposition to society, even if he is to be kept apart from society for a time.

The end goal of Rousseau's pedagogy, in other words, is to preserve and protect Émile for a time from the untoward influence of society; however, his aim is not to keep Émile from ever entering society. If Rousseau's goal were to set natural pedagogy in opposition to society, then the success of Émile's education would free him from the influence of society but simultaneously doom him to solitude. Instead of revolutionizing society, the pedagogical practices that Rousseau describes in the beginning of *Émile* would replace sociability with solipsism. The end goal of Rousseau's philosophy of education, however, is a more perfect society, and thus Émile must find a way to return and bring with him the lessons he has learned during his natural education.

Rousseau's choice of *Robinson Crusoe* as his crucial pedagogical example is particularly telling on this point. If Rousseau celebrated a mere return to nature, then the choice of *Robinson Crusoe* would be an odd one, for this book tells the story of a man who is shipwrecked alone on an island for many years but returns to society to tell the tale of what he learned on the island. The success of Émile's education rests on his being removed from society for a time, but the ultimate success of *Émile* rests on Émile's reintroduction to society. Émile must come into society as a man who has learned from nature. Nature will provide him a relationship to things, but to bring that relation into society he must become a reader of signs. If the encounter with signs were delayed indefinitely, then Émile would never be able to participate in the conventions of human society. This is not to ignore, however, the fact that, for Rousseau, signs present real dangers to the child's education.

❖ The Sign Absorbs Attention

In the opening half of *Émile,* Rousseau declares his distaste for signs. Signs, he argues, have no educational value. Signs are meaningless without prior experience and knowledge of the things that signs represent. Rousseau writes, "En quelque étude que ce puisse être, sans l'idée des choses réprésentées les signes réprésentans ne sont rien" ("In any study whatsoever, unless one has the ideas of the things represented, the representative signs are nothing") (*Oc,* 347; *OE,* 109). Without an idea of the thing represented by a particular sign, and without an appropriate experience of the thing, the sign is nothing. It has no meaning. Given this logic, and the prejudice against signs that underlies it, it is understandable that Rousseau privileges experience over rhetoric, things over signs, doing over talking. Tutors err when they try to instruct using signs and not things, when they attempt to instruct using reason instead of allowing the child to experience what is necessary to experience to understand the tutor's lesson. As an example, the tutor may wish to communicate why it is important for the child always to take his bearings before setting out on a journey, because the experience of being lost is unpleasant. But this lesson will mean nothing to the child without his first experiencing what it is like to be lost. "Lost" will have no meaning for the child without the experience of the idea of "lostness." An education based upon the use of signs will fail to produce the kind of adult that Rousseau aspires to produce in Émile.

Elsewhere, Rousseau suggests that signs not only are meaningless without the prior experience of the idea or thing that they represent but also present a real danger to the child's education: "En général, ne substituez jamais le signe à la chose que quand il vous est impossible de la montrer. Car le signe absorbe l'attention de l'enfant, et lui fait oublier la chose représentée" ("In general, never substitute the sign for the thing unless it is impossible for you to show the thing. For the sign absorbs the child's attention and makes him forget the thing represented") (*Oc,* 434; *OE,* 159). The price paid for an introduction to signs is the now forgettable world of things. Signs are not innocent, for Rousseau imbues them with real power; they actively participate in the derailing of Émile's education as they substitute themselves for the things represented. Signs will not only lead the child to misunderstand the world but also distract his attention from the world and the things that make it up. Signs kidnap the child's attention and hold it hostage. The world is replaced by a fiction. Émile's introduction to signs risks his attention, which in turn endangers the natural education designed to make him a model citizen. To safeguard his proper attention, Émile's education must be determined by his experience of things, and therefore he should be kept safe from signs for as long as possible.

The danger that Rousseau identifies with signs helps explain his claim, in *Émile,* that he hates books: "Je hais les livres" (*Oc,* 454). Rousseau's hatred of reading, though it may seem a strong dismissal of an activity he describes as essential to his own development in *Confessions,* offers an important insight into the problems that reading can sometimes occasion. For Rousseau, a child will take an interest in learning to read properly only after it has been made clear to him why he should want to know how to read—only, that is, once he knows what reading is good for. As discussed in the first chapter, Rousseau stages a scene for Émile, who will receive numerous notes from friends and relatives asking him to join them for a walk or to watch some public spectacle. He will take an interest in learning to read so that he will be able to read future notes left for him and thereby participate in similar events. In this way, Rousseau unites for Émile the act of reading with his reception of particular messages conveyed in and through the text he reads. Even from his early education in coming to read these notes describing missed social opportunities, the child who learns to read learns to subordinate sign to thing, signifier to signified.

Rousseau elaborates on the potential danger that reading poses to children's moral education when he describes the dangers implicit in a child's reading of La Fontaine's fables. Rousseau notes that children who are allowed to read fables before they are capable of adequately determining the moral of the story are in danger of being led astray by fables. He offers as an example La Fontaine's fable of the fox and the crow, in which a fox encounters a crow carrying cheese in its beak. In an attempt to win the cheese, the fox flatters the crow's singing voice, hoping that the crow will sing and so drop the cheese from its beak. The child is to identify with the crow and so learn the moral of the fable: "do not give in to false flattery." And yet, remarks Rousseau, if the child is allowed to read this fable too early in his career as a reader, it is possible for him to—and indeed highly probable that he will—take the opposite lesson as the moral. The child might identify with the fox and learn from the fable how better to acquire cheese. "Le fromage gâte tout" ("the cheese spoils everything"), writes Rousseau (*Oc*, 356; *OE*, 115). Children "are taught less not to let it fall from their beaks than to make it fall from the beak of another" (*OE*, 115). "Suivez les enfans apprenant leurs fables," continues Rousseau, "et vous verrez que quand ils sont en état d'en faire l'application ils en font preque toujours une contraire à l'intention de l'auteur" ("Follow children learning their fables and you will see that when they are in a position to apply them, they almost always do so in a way opposite to the author's intention") (*Oc*, 356; *OE*, 115). One must protect future readers from the possibility of such a monstrous misreading. If Émile were to read his early notes in the same way, he would, of course, miss (again) the desired outing.

Because children may always read to the wrong end, Émile will hardly know what a book is before he is twelve. He will know how to read—

this is important—writes Rousseau, but reading, which is the "plague of childhood" (*OE,* 116; *Oc,* 357), will be kept from him until he understands the proper role of communicating with others "at a distance." Once he understands that fables, like the notes left for him, communicate a message that he must decipher, he will understand the importance of reading to the right end. He will no longer, as he might have done when he was younger, read in a way opposite to the author's intention; instead, he will recognize in the text the message he is meant to decipher. As the notes left for Émile illustrate, to read against the author's intentions—or to refuse to prioritize the author's intentions—will result in harm done to oneself. Just as he would continue to miss out on the events the notes announced were he not to know how to read properly, he will miss the lessons offered to him in fables and so put at risk his ability to live a moral life.

Later in *Émile,* Rousseau takes up again his discussion of fables, suggesting that a return to the lessons offered by fables after a fuller experience of the world will improve the pupil's reading. Émile should only be allowed to read the fable of the fox and the crow, for instance, after he has experienced human trickery, which will guarantee that he reads the fable to its proper end by allowing him to receive the messages addressed to him: "The child who has never been deceived by praise understands nothing of the fable I examined earlier. But the giddy young man who has just been the dupe of a flatterer conceives marvelously that the crow was only a fool" (*OE,* 247–48; *Oc,* 540–41). Émile should not be allowed to read fables until he is in a position to understand the moral questions involved through his own experience, which means he should not be allowed to read fables until after he no longer needs the lessons they offer. The moral will become in some sense redundant. To ensure that Émile's education in reading proceeds, Rousseau suggests that the moral of the fable should be cut out or removed; if the child understands the fable only because of the explicit statement of the moral, then the child has not fully understood the fable. In withholding the fable from the child until after the child has experienced enough of life to know and understand the moral of the fable even in its absence, Rousseau guarantees that the child will read only after (and only because) he knows to read to the proper moral end. In this way, as Geoffrey Bennington writes, "the reading of fables will not simply be a pointless exercise in memorizing a text the child has not understood, but a supplement to experience which will allow the pupil to 'draw out' the maxim for himself and to profit from it."[4] The reading of fables is then one way to determine to what extent Émile knows how to read properly, whether, in other words, he reads as a child (without experience) or as an adult (with experience).

Rousseau acknowledges the dangers of reading to the wrong end. And Rousseau labors to prevent this possibility by leaving letters for Émile and dismembering the fables he reads by removing the moral and ensuring that Émile reads the fable only when he is able, in a sense, to read it without needing to read it. The chance that the child will read against authorial intention is for Rousseau a chance that must be overcome through proper instruction in reading. To learn to read fables properly is to learn that one did not, in fact, need to read them at all. In this way, reading becomes both necessary and irrelevant, and Émile's attention can thus be devoted to things.

❖ The Necessity of History

Reading, despite the potential threats it raises, plays an important role in Émile's education.[5] Rousseau asserts the importance of reading in several ways in the second half of *Émile,* and while Rousseau "hates books," learning to read properly is essential to Émile's education. In the opening of book 4, Rousseau introduces the necessity of history books to Émile's education. At this point in the narrative, Émile is an adolescent, approximately fifteen years old. With book 4, Rousseau begins to describe the importance of Émile's (re)introduction into society, but he also explains how delicate will be this introduction. Up until this moment in Émile's education, the boy has been kept from others and has learned to rely only on himself and his own experiences. He must now learn to think about others as well as himself. He must no longer think of himself alone but must come to integrate into his consciousness the experience of society.

Émile must be introduced to human society, but how is this to be accomplished without ruining the education that he has received thus far? If Émile is introduced to others too early, then he might lose track of himself and begin to think of himself only in his relations with others. Instead of judging his neighbor by himself, by his own standard, he will judge himself by his neighbors. He will become a product of the society that he has been produced to change. If he is introduced to society too late, then he might become a scandalmonger and a satirist, peremptory and quick to judge. He will look upon the world with disgust and become either accustomed to vice or resigned to solitude.[6]

To mediate these dangers and make possible Émile's reintroduction to society, Rousseau turns to history: "je voudrois lui montrer les hommes au loin, les lui montrer dans d'autres tems ou dans d'aurtres lieux, et de sorte qu'il put voir la scène sans jamais y pouvoir agir" ("I would want to show him men from afar, to show him them in other times or other places and in such a way that he can see the stage without ever being able to act on it") (*Oc,* 526; *OE,* 237). Paradoxically, perhaps, Rousseau calls on history for the same reasons that he denigrated books in the past; books were accused of causing problems for Émile's education because they made it possible to speak about things without having direct experience of them. Now, history books are necessary to his future education precisely because Émile will read about human society without directly experiencing it. In the beginning, direct experience is privileged over signs, doing and acting over reading; now reading is privileged over direct experience of society.[7] If Émile's education proceeds without the mediating presence of history, then all the effort spent keeping Émile safe from the untoward influence of society will have been wasted. Rousseau aims to introduce Émile to society indirectly via signs.

The reversal that takes place between book 3 and book 4, between the first half of *Émile,* which describes Émile's isolation from society, and the second half of *Émile,* which describes his (re)introduction to society, has the shape of a rhetorical trope, chiasmus. Rousseau's distrust of human society has been consistent from the beginning. But his newfound reliance on history books presents a potentially surprising reversal of Rousseau's opinion of books. The turn from nature to society, which corresponds to Émile's return from the isolation imposed on him by his tutor, is made possible precisely by those same things (books) which should have no place in Émile's early education. In the initial parts of *Émile,* things are privileged absolutely over signs, and direct experience is privileged absolutely over verbal lessons; now, however, signs are privileged over unmediated contact with society. While Émile is not to encounter books at all in the first years of his education, his education could never be completed and he could never pass from nature to society without them. In *Émile,* Rousseau works to systematize the relation between nature and society through a tropological model of substitution.

Given the tropological (and so linguistic) structure of *Émile,* it may be no surprise that at the center of *Émile* is the story of Émile's learning to read; at the center of *Émile* is the story of Émile's reading of *Robinson Crusoe,* the one book that will teach him to read all others. Émile's reading of *Robinson Crusoe* is of great importance, for only after he reads Defoe's book will it be possible for him to encounter history without the accompanying threat that signs had posed to his education. If he were introduced to history without *Robinson Crusoe*—without knowing how to manage the difficulty that reading poses—then the same problems that reading poses in the first half of *Émile* would remain to threaten Émile's reading of history books. Just as he might draw the wrong lessons from fables—learning to employ rather than eschew false flattery—so too might he learn to emulate the wrong historical figures or take from history books the wrong lesson. For the chiasmatic reversal to take place, Émile must learn to read properly. And more specifically, he must learn to read *Robinson Crusoe.*

❖ Reading *Robinson Crusoe*

As a result of his hatred and distrust of books, Rousseau seeks the one book that will guide Émile's future reading and prevent him from being waylaid by books. Daniel Defoe's *Robinson Crusoe,* read in translation, is the one book that will teach Émile to avoid the dangers of signs as Rousseau has defined them.[8] Rousseau turns to *Robinson Crusoe* repeatedly throughout his works, also celebrating it in his *Confessions* and *Dialogues,* for Crusoe is afforded a long-term respite from society; he is granted the opportunity to learn anew the value of nature free from the confines of human society.[9] Rousseau recognizes that *Robinson Crusoe* must mean something else to Émile. Unlike Rousseau, Émile does not need respite from the demands of society for he has had no (or at least limited) contact with it. Émile's reading of *Robinson Crusoe* is meant, instead, to prepare him for his introduction into society. Crusoe's departure, coupled with his inevitable return, serves as a model for Émile, whose journey will follow the second half of Robinson Crusoe's—from nature to society.

Robinson Crusoe is to provide Émile with a model of self-sufficiency. Deprived of the company of fellow human beings, Crusoe must successfully fend for himself, and so should Émile learn to fend for himself. More important, perhaps, Rousseau argues that this book, more than any other, upholds the true value of things over signs and emphasizes the need for the practical over the rhetorical. Crusoe's survival depends on his quickly learning the "real" value of things rather than being distracted or swayed by a thing's symbolic value or by the value another might ascribe to it. When, for example, he returns to the ship to salvage materials necessary for his survival, he must act decisively and with purpose. He must not linger, for the ship is in danger of being torn from the rock upon which it has become temporarily anchored. He must act decisively to collect the things that will give him the best advantage for survival.

To survive, Crusoe must learn that the value of a thing is not arbitrary but determined by what it will help him accomplish. Things are instruments; their value is their utility—this is the same lesson, of course, that the notes offer Émile. Learning to value the utility of a thing is crucial to both Crusoe's survival and Émile's future success as a model citizen. As a result of reading *Robinson Crusoe,* Émile will be inspired to know all that is useful, and he will base appropriate judgments on the utility of objects. He will also learn to value signs for their utility, which explains one other, and perhaps the most significant, reason for Rousseau's selection of *Robinson Crusoe.* Émile will learn from *Robinson Crusoe* to relate even to language as a tool, as if it were a thing.

Though many have noted that *Robinson Crusoe* is to be Émile's first book, the story of Émile's reading of *Robinson Crusoe* is complicated by a performance of overidentification with Crusoe that unsettles Émile's identity.[10] Rousseau puts great pressure on what *Robinson Crusoe* will do for Émile; it must effectively ensure Émile's mastery over reading and so, by extension, the world of conventions and signs. As a result, Rousseau pushes his rhetoric toward hyperbole. Émile is not simply to read *Robinson Crusoe;* he is to dress like Robinson Crusoe, putting on his skins, carrying his cutlass and umbrella, and so on. He is to perform the role of Robinson Crusoe and, in the process, come to believe that he *is* Robinson Crusoe. The literal self-forgetting that Rousseau requires of Émile—if Émile is to be prepared to read the books of history—is meant to overcome the trouble with books.[11] To direct Émile's reading to its proper end and limit the possibility that Émile will be led astray by the books that he will read, Rousseau introduces a performative aspect of reading:

> Je veux que la tête lui en tourne, qu'il s'occupe sans cesse de son château, de ses chèvres, de ses plantations, qu'il apprenne en détail non dans ses livres mais sur les choses tout ce qu'il faut savoir en pareil cas; qu'il pense être Robinson lui-même, qu'il se voye habillé de peaux, portant un grand bonnet, un grand sabre, tout le grotesque équipage de la figure, au parasol près dont il n'aura pas besoin. (*Oc,* 455)
>
> I want that his head should be full of it, he should always be busy with his castle, his goats, his plantations. Let him learn in detail, not from books but from things, all that is necessary in such a case. Let him think he is Robinson himself; let him see himself clad in skins, wearing a tall cap, a great cutlass, all the grotesque get-up of Robinson Crusoe, even to the umbrella that he will not need. (*OE,* 185)

Robinson Crusoe will have the desired effect on Émile only if he comes to think of himself as also marooned. Only then will he be able accurately to judge things for their utility. But Émile's reading is not complete until

Robinson Crusoe also becomes real for him, that is, only once he becomes Robinson Crusoe through an almost mad act of absolute identification.[12] To learn to read and for his education to progress, Émile's head is to be so full of *Robinson Crusoe* that he begins not only to imagine but also literally to see himself as Crusoe; he is to see himself clad in Crusoe's skin(s). While this phrase presumably refers to the animal skins that Crusoe wears after the clothing he was wearing before the shipwreck deteriorates, the phrase is itself a sign of the violence present in the scene. The literal desire for Émile to wear the animal skins worn by Crusoe becomes a metaphoric desire for Émile to get inside Crusoe's skin (to become him).[13] In other words, Émile is to forget, at least for a moment, that he is Émile and come to believe that he is another.

The chiasmatic reversal in *Émile,* from the privileging of things and the denial of signs to the acceptance of signs (as history books), makes possible a metaphoric union of nature and society through an Émile who knows himself as self-sufficient. Unlike a dialectic in which society would function as the determinate negation of nature, or in which nature would function as the determinate negation of society, in the tropological model that Rousseau develops and relies on in *Émile,* Émile should learn to take Robinson Crusoe as an example. However, even accepting Crusoe's exemplary status, it is not clear why he should need to *become* Crusoe. The adequate systematization of the tropological model, Rousseau's text implies despite itself, depends upon evicting the very idea of a reading subject from the model of education asserted positively in *Émile.* There is no more reading subject, only the endless repetition of Robinson Crusoes. If the point of *Émile* is to produce a self-sufficient and self-identical model citizen, why should Émile need to see himself as another to learn to read as himself?

As Christopher Kelly notes, Émile's identification with Robinson Crusoe is meant to be short lived. Kelly writes, "Immediately after saying that Émile will think he is Robinson, Rousseau indicates that the boy will constantly be made 'to examine his hero's conduct; to investigate whether he omitted anything, whether there was nothing to do better; to note Robinson's failings attentively; and to profit from them so as not to fall into them himself in such a situation' . . . In other words, the intensity of Émile's identification with his hero is considerably diluted by an actively critical spirit."[14] Rousseau, in other words, suggests Kelly, acknowledges that the goal of Émile's reading is not full identification with Robinson Crusoe. Rousseau revises and retreats from his initial position, but in a sense the damage has been done. Every act of reading becomes an almost mad identification—a too literal identification—with a literary character *and* a critical reflection on the failings of "Robinson" (i.e., Émile, himself, as reader).

To become himself, Émile must become two; he must be himself *and* Robinson Crusoe when he reads. And this splitting of the reading subject, I argue, has consequences for Émile and the version of the reading subject that emerges with *Émile.* Rousseau's pedagogical treatise is meant to guarantee that reading never derail his pupil and ensure (however impossibly) his pupil's self-sufficiency even when confronted by societal pressures; and yet for reading never to derail the reader, Rousseau must introduce the necessity of Émile's reading as another, as someone he is not (Robinson Crusoe).

Émile's encounter with *Robinson Crusoe* is a memorable scene of reading, but the language of the passage introduces some complexities that are difficult to resolve, specifically with respect to the inclusion or exclusion of the umbrella (which Crusoe uses to shade himself from the harsh sunlight): "qu'il pense être Robinson lui-même, qu'il se voye habillé de peaux, portant un grand bonnet, un grand sabre, tout le grotesque équipage de la figure, au parasol près dont il n'aura pas besoin" (*Oc,* 455). The expression "au . . . près" can be positive or negative depending on the context. Two common English translations of *Émile* offer opposing translations of this passage. Barbara Foxley translates the passage positively: "let him see himself clad in skins, wearing the tall cap, the great cutlass, all the grotesque get-up of Robinson Crusoe, even to the umbrella which he will scarcely need."[15] Allan Bloom translates the passage negatively: "I want him to think he is Robinson himself, to see himself dressed in skins, wearing a large cap, carrying a large saber and all the rest of the character's grotesque equipment, with the exception of the parasol, which he will not need" (*OE,* 185). Given that the expression "au . . . près" comes after the phrase "tout le grotesque équipage de la figure," it follows that the parasol would be included in "all of the equipage." But the context does not adequately control the two readings. If one translates the passage as "even to" or "including" the umbrella, then Rousseau is violating the very point behind Émile's reading of *Robinson Crusoe,* which is meant to teach him to relate to things for their usefulness. Why should Rousseau want Émile to include in his costume something for which he will explicitly have no use? And yet, translating the passage as Bloom does also fails to resolve the complexity. What reason is there to draw a distinction between the cap and saber that Émile does need and the parasol that he will not need? In what ways does Émile "need" a cap and saber but not a parasol? At the very moment that Rousseau introduces the importance of a divided reading subject (Émile as himself *and*

Robinson Crusoe), he also introduces textual complexities that are difficult to control. The attempt to control Émile's reading produces a text that is itself difficult (if not impossible) to read. The story of Émile's reading undoes one's reading of *Émile.*[16]

Émile must learn how to read *Robinson Crusoe* if he is to learn to read properly. And he must learn to read properly before he is introduced to history books that will help him articulate natural and civil man. And *Émile,* in a sense, is all about attempts to articulate opposing forces, as the complete title suggests. But here, in the story of Émile's learning to read, *Émile,* the text, is itself disarticulated. It cannot decide whether or not Émile needs, of all things, an umbrella. Determining what is useful is, of course, the point of Émile's reading *Robinson Crusoe,* and *Émile* does not seem to know at this all-important moment what it means to "say" about the usefulness of an object.

Reading as Robinson Crusoe is to help Émile learn to read properly, always to the right end, and so prepare him for the encounter with history books. Without *Robinson Crusoe* and without the performance of reading that Émile will learn from Robinson Crusoe, the chiasmatic reversal upon which the whole of *Émile* depends will not be realized. Émile will fail to enter society without being mastered by it because he will fail to master his relationship to signs. And yet Rousseau's attempt to control Émile's reading introduces textual difficulties that demand more and not less reading, just as Rousseau's attempt in book 2 of his *Confessions* to speak only once and no more of the ribbon-stealing incident results, almost mechanically, in his repeated returns to it (in the *Fourth Rêverie,* for instance).

While Rousseau does not seem to acknowledge the strangeness inherent in this scene, the sequel to *Émile, Émile et Sophie, ou les solitaires,* offers Rousseau a chance to return to the pedagogical reading practices he describes. After yet another scene of reading, this time Sophie's reading of François Fénelon's *Telemachus,* which she too reads literally, *Émile* concludes with the marriage of Émile and Sophie. Sophie's reading of *Telemachus* prepares her for her meeting with Émile, as she identifies him with the hero and so falls in love with him. In *Émile et Sophie, ou les solitaries,* which Rousseau never finished, Émile recounts the failures of his life to his tutor. After many adventures, including being taken prisoner by pirates and surviving a period of enslavement, Émile realizes (that is, literalizes) his reading of *Robinson Crusoe. Émile et Sophie* shows that Émile's reading of *Robinson Crusoe* may indeed have had negative consequences, for Émile does become his ideal—and literally finds himself on a desert island.[17] *Émile* is governed by Rousseau's attempt to turn two into one (Émile represents the possible articulation of natural and civil man just as *Émile* concludes with the marriage of Émile and Sophie). Both of these unions depend upon Émile's learning to read; and yet in the attempt to guarantee Émile's reading, Émile himself becomes two: Émile *and* Robinson Crusoe. And the splitting of Émile in and through the attempt to learn to read eventually results in the splitting of *Émile* into *Émile* and *Émile et Sophie, ou les solitaires.* The presence of *Émile et Sophie* acknowledges the very instability Rousseau happens upon and repeats with the attempt to control Émile's reading—and therefore, in closing, reading itself.[18]

❖ Two for One

I began by claiming that *Émile* is Rousseau's most sustained attempt to think together two competing discourses, the philosophical and the literary, and that Rousseau pursues the opposition of these two discourses via the structural opposition of nature and society. For *Émile* to be successful, Émile must manage to unite these two competing states, the natural and the social, which also correspond to two competing relationships to signs. In the early books of *Émile,* Émile is to have a very limited number of encounters with signs; in fact, the fewer encounters with signs, the better off Émile will be and the more perfect his education will become. For this reason, Émile is not to read fables until later in his life, not until after the chance that reading books will lead him astray is minimized. However, in the second half of *Émile* Rousseau asserts the importance of reading and of books to Émile's education; without books Émile will never marry Sophie and his education will never be complete. I have argued that this reversal depends upon the scene of Émile's reading *Robinson Crusoe,* which occurs midway through the text of *Émile* and subsequently midway through Émile's education and development.

The complexity of Émile's reading of *Robinson Crusoe,* however, suggests that more is at stake than Émile's development. We can understand the necessity of *Robinson Crusoe* to Rousseau's argument as expressed in *Émile* in slightly different terms. While Rousseau pretends that Émile's education is governed by—and must respond to—natural changes, *Émile* is an imagined experiment and not an empirical one; as such *Émile* offers itself as an allegory and not an empirical model of development. From the moment Rousseau begins to depend upon a substitutive system, from the moment, in other words, that he stresses through hyperbole the need for Émile to become Robinson Crusoe, it is clear that Rousseau's concerns are also linguistic and not simply psychological.

In linguistic terms, Émile's reading of *Robinson Crusoe* functions as an attempt to articulate two competing and potentially incompatible linguistic models: the natural and the differential. The natural man has no relation to anything else. In Émile's early education, which is to correspond to the condition of nature, signs have meaning because they have a unique and natural relationship to the things to which they are said to refer. This is why, for instance, Émile is to learn to decode signs through the notes left for him that refer to particular outings and events that he will miss because he is not yet fully literate. He is to relate to signs for the signifieds they represent. Rousseau continues and extends the importance of the sign's relationship to its signified with *Robinson Crusoe,* in which utility in the world of things is the ultimate signified. Émile's reading of *Robinson Crusoe* will teach him to relate to signs as the things they signify. The civil man, on the other hand, is defined by his relationships with others. In the opposing linguistic model, that is, signs have value not because they refer to things but because of the network of signs of which they are a part. Signs are granted meaning and value by the system that produces them and through their difference from other signs, not by the things to which they refer. Just as Rousseau finds both the natural and the civil man lacking, he is also dissatisfied with either linguistic model; the goal of *Émile* and the goal of Émile's reading is to unite these two models, the natural and the differential.[19]

As a reader, Émile is to unite the natural relationship to signs (as things) with the conventional relationship to things (as signs). Émile achieves this, or so Rousseau imagines, but only to the extent to which the experience of reading belongs to another, namely, Robinson Crusoe. When this moment of identification is translated back into a psychological vocabulary, and it must be possible to do so since readers of *Émile* should not forget that this is also a pedagogical treatise that aims for a degree of practical applicability, then certain difficulties arise for Rousseau's model of education. In particular, certain difficulties arise concerning the relationship (or nonrelationship) between experience and education, particularly the experience of learning to read.

It may be possible (however unlikely) to unite a natural and differential understanding of signs, but only at the expense of the one who would know that such a passage (as an event available to individual consciousness) occurs. For Émile to unite the natural and civil—for Émile to pass into human society—he must learn to "read" *Robinson Crusoe.* To read *Robinson Crusoe,* though, he must learn to read *as* Robinson Crusoe. Dressed in Crusoe's skins, Émile is not to recognize himself as Émile. As a result, Rousseau's *Émile* suggests that reading is to be taught only if the one who reads forgets he reads as himself, only, that is, if the experience of learning to read is missed. It may not be a surprise, then, that *Émile,* which inscribes within itself a story of the difficulty of knowing that one knows how to read, should also raise persistent questions about its own readability, disguised for example at first in the "or" that divides its title. Each time Rousseau attempts to control how this text is read, the text merely produces more problems for reading. How to read the "or" that divides its title is a question that returns within *Émile* at the very moment Rousseau most powerfully articulates reading's usefulness. But if readers are unsure whether Émile needs his umbrella, a small thing for sure, how do they move ahead? How does one judge the text's defense of the utility of reading if the text is unsure of the utility of an umbrella? Émile will come into being as a proper reader only to the extent to which he is split into two, the very thing Émile (and *Émile*) is meant to overcome. In splitting Émile, however unproblematic this split may seem at first, Rousseau also inadvertently splits his own text, and this split has repercussions. How does one learn to read from *Émile* if one cannot even learn to read *Émile*? *Émile* testifies to a truth about education that may be difficult to integrate into any systematic understanding of education. Though Rousseau makes fun of Locke's die-rolling game, *Émile* inadvertently repeats Locke's suggestion that learning to read is an event that is missed and suggests that education—specifically an education in reading—is not an experience that can be claimed by the one who reads as himself, which may explain why readers, including Rousseau himself, so often fail to remember learning to read at all.

In the second part of this book, I turn to particular examples of lyric address in poems by Thomas Gray, William Wordsworth, and John Keats. Locke, with his die-rolling game, introduces a necessary attention to signifiers in the absence of considerations of address and meaning. Rousseau's *Émile* highlights the importance of considerations of address and meaning to reading instruction but also discloses the consequences that accompany the attempt to secure language from the lyric, from language's potential to transmit unanticipated meaning or refer aberrantly. In situating poems that feature figures of lyric address in relationship to Locke's and Rousseau's pedagogical experiments, I show how poems inherit a pedagogical concern even as they question and depart from it. Poems repeatedly return readers to the event of learning to read as they consistently raise questions of address by foregrounding the figures that make address possible. One is returned to an event one missed to catch up to a knowledge one cannot yet claim as one's own.

Part II

Lyric—Pedagogy

3

Leaving the World to Darkness: Gray

> The way to solve the problem you see in life is to live in a way that makes the problem disappear.
>
> —Ludwig Wittgenstein

Although Thomas Gray later became suspicious of its success, "Elegy Written in a Country Churchyard" (1751) was immensely popular from its first appearance.[1] And its continued popularity led Edmund Gosse in 1882, more than a century after initial publication, to describe Gray's "Elegy" as the ideal English "poem of poems," an epithet one might not associate with a poem capable of producing controversy.[2] And yet, in the middle years of the twentieth century the poem inspired the so-called Stonecutter Controversy, the result of several competing readings of the poem's enigmatic figures of address. It may be that controversies are most likely to erupt around poems previously identified as ideal.

In their treatises on education, Locke and Rousseau offer practical advice for improving reading instruction, but how does one teach children to read when, as the text of Rousseau's *Émile* demonstrates, the attempt adequately to formalize language introduces its own textual complexities? Locke offers lessons in reading through a "chance-writing" that cannot easily be said to address the pupil, since it comes from no authoring consciousness, and Rousseau offers a lesson in reading that turns on the ability of one text (*Robinson Crusoe*) to control one's experience of others, as if *Robinson Crusoe* were not subject to the same textual drifting found within *Émile* and "Elegy Written in a Country Churchyard." If poetry is frequently celebrated for its ability to introduce the textual drifting that reading pedagogues, such as Rousseau, abhor, what do poems teach readers about the rhetorical tropes that determine discussions of reading? Famous for a problematic figure of address, what does Gray's "Elegy" show readers about language's tendency to address in the absence of meaning or mean in the absence of address? Significantly, Gray's poem not only inspires numerous and competing interpretations but also anticipates and allegorizes the effort to read it. Gray's "Elegy" foregrounds the tropological dimension of reading that

Locke and Rousseau, for example, labor to eliminate in their drive to secure the relationship between language, address, and cognition. If the term "literature" has come to include those texts capable of producing and sustaining divergent interpretations, then Gray's "Elegy" reflects on the emergence of this definition and on its pedagogical power.

❖ From the "Poem of Poems" to a "Controversy"

Gray's "Elegy" achieved immense popularity before the controversy it inspired in the twentieth century in part because it was strikingly unoriginal. In his *Lives of the English Poets,* Samuel Johnson, who for the most part is critical of Gray's poems, celebrates the "Elegy" because it "abounds with images which find a mirrour in every mind, and with sentiments to which every bosom returns an echo."[3] Readers find their thoughts and feelings echoed back to them as the poem accurately anticipates and captures what is common to "every" reader. Like Johnson centuries earlier, I. A. Richards in 1929 similarly describes the poem's universal appeal: "It would be difficult to maintain that the thought in this poem is striking or original, or that its feeling is exceptional. It embodies a sequence of reflections and attitudes that under similar conditions arise readily in any contemplative mind."[4] Richards celebrates the poem not because it is bold or original but because it is powerfully commonplace. The poet-speaker stands for a universal contemplative mind. In this way, the poem's success is linked to Gray's ability to communicate "unexceptional" thoughts and feelings and so move from the particular experience of the poet-speaker to general reflection.[5] The poem is understood to achieve epistemological certainty in uniting the particular (experience, sensation, phenomenon) and the general (reflection, cognition, understanding), and readers who find themselves in the poem find themselves as universally recognizable, unexceptional, "mirroured," and so addressed.[6] One learns to read the poem with a properly contemplative mind. And perhaps for this reason, its place in school curricula was for centuries unquestioned.

The critical reception of Gray's "Elegy" in the twentieth century, however, was complicated by attempts to account for the identity of the youth commemorated in the concluding epitaph.[7] "The problem," as Herbert W. Starr writes in *Twentieth Century Interpretations of Gray's Elegy,* "is essentially one of pronominal reference."[8] The poet, having established the universal sentiments admired by the poem's aforementioned critics, turns to address an unidentified "thee":

> For thee, who mindful of th' unhonour'd Dead
> Dost in these lines their artless tale relate;
> If chance, by lonely contemplation led,
> Some kindred Spirit shall inquire thy fate.
> ("Elegy," ll. 93–96)

Unclear is who, here, is addressed. Does the poet address himself, some lost relative or friend, another poet, or the reader?[9] If this "thee" is also the one elegized in the poem's conclusion, who is the subject of the epitaph? Limiting his reading to the text itself, Cleanth Brooks in *The Well Wrought Urn* counters those such as Odell Shepard who argued that with "thee" Gray addresses his recently deceased close companion, Richard West.[10] Instead of focusing on history and biography, Brooks argues that Gray's poet means "for me" when he writes "for thee." As a result, the epitaph that concludes the poem is in fact the poet's, and the shift in pronoun is meant to communicate the force of mortality, which cannot be faced directly but only ever indirectly. Brooks notes that in the first stanza the speaker is willing to say "me," but by this later point in the poem the poet has become so carried away by his own meditation that he addresses himself in the second person. Brooks summarizes: "Dramatically, what has happened is that the meditation has gone on so fervently that in talking to himself, the speaker has lost his identity as an ego . . . he is willing to see himself as he shall be, merely one with the others in the country churchyard."[11] Dissatisfied with Brooks's rewriting of the poem (a sign that the poem is not as "well wrought" as *The Well Wrought Urn* implies?), Frank Ellis, in "Gray's *Elegy:* The Biographical Problem in Literary Criticism," argues that in the crucial stanza of the poem the poet turns to address a stonecutter responsible for engraving the names and dates on the monuments before which the poet ruminates. "For thee" is an address to "the Stonecutter," writes Ellis, "on whom the villagers rely for a more substantial and enduring tribute."[12] As a result of the introduction of the stonecutter, "these lines" no longer refer to the poem the poet is in the process of composing but to the names and dates inscribed on the face of the grave markers. What has come to be called the "Stonecutter Controversy" erupted in response to Ellis's close examination of the poem, which attempts to account for a number of textual complications but thereby increases the number of figures within the poem.[13] All too often, the more closely one examines a text, the more complicated it becomes.

For some readers, the compositional history of the poem makes clear that by "thee" Gray meant the poet-speaker. The "Elegy" exists in two manuscript versions. The first, titled "Stanzas Wrote in a Country Churchyard," appears in the Eton manuscript. The second is the version found in later manuscripts, the Pembroke and Wharton, as well as in publication. In the earlier manuscript, "Stanzas," the address is most likely to the poet-speaker who has written the poem. H. W. Starr summarizes:

> In the first version of the *Elegy* (the "Stanzas") the final reference is clearly to a Narrator who has written the poem, but this cannot be regarded as certain proof that Gray did not change his mind in the second draft. On the whole, a knowledge of Gray's writing habits suggests that the ambiguity is accidental—and very natural. A man who carefully revises a poem over several years will devote great thought to such minute details as substituting "noiseless" for "silent" in "silent tenor"—doubtless to avoid the clash of two dentals—but will easily overlook the ambiguity of an important pronominal reference which has always been clear in his own mind but is not clear to a reader. Undoubtedly this is a flaw in workmanship, undoubtedly either interpretation is possible, and undoubtedly Gray himself would have been annoyed, amused, and embarrassed by the whole controversy.[14]

Starr does his best to acknowledge the validity of the reading that sparked the controversy while simultaneously dismissing it as politely as possible. "Undoubtedly"—writes Starr—"thee" and "thy" may be read as referring to a village poet, the stonecutter, and "these lines" to those inscribed on the grave markers, but to do so is to risk annoying, amusing, and even embarrassing Gray. As Starr makes clear, it may only be through reanimating the figure of Gray that the so-called controversy can be put to rest. In other words, the rhetoric that puts an end to the controversy—and transforms it into a historical event safely inscribed in the past, a record of past readings from which the critical discussion around the poem has moved away—repeats the central question *of* the poem. How does one know and remember the dead? To end the controversy, Starr must employ the same figures—anthropomorphism, apostrophe, prosopopoeia—that feature prominently within the poem and that have come to define poetry.[15]

Gray's "Elegy" not only poses unique challenges to literary interpretation but also reflects on the degree to which reading is determined by tropes of animation. We read, suggests Stephen Greenblatt in the opening of *Shakespearean Negotiations,* because we wish to speak with, and so animate, the dead.[16] Locke and Rousseau attempt to align writing with intention and voice, the inscription with the continuous lived presence of the author extended through space and time. To do so requires avoiding the ways "voice" results from the employment of particular rhetorical figures that preoccupy the poets. One finds oneself addressed only to the extent to which one grants life to the inscription. Can one hear the voice of an inscription without bringing the dead back to life? Can an inscription and a voice ever be aligned perfectly? These questions emerge from "within" the poem, as the poet reads the inscriptions of the grave markers in an attempt to know the dead; it is also true of the poem's reception, as critics have struggled to explain what Gray meant with the address to "thee." What is the poet of Gray's "Elegy" teaching readers about reading, about the tropes of voice and address so important to instruction in reading for Locke and Rousseau? The poem's closing lines reassure the reader that he or she knows how to read and so knows how to respond adequately to the dead—"Approach and read (for thou can'st read)" ("Elegy," l. 115)—and yet the poem stages as a question what it means to read. While the Stonecutter Controversy has largely receded from critical view, situating this poem in relation to Locke's and Rousseau's pedagogical writing brings out some potentially confusing aspects of a poem so important to school curricula for centuries. One could not follow the text's command to approach without of course already knowing how to read to some minimal extent. Why reassure the reader that he or she knows how to do what he or she is already doing? And perhaps more to the point, how does one respond to this reassurance when the poem itself inspires a controversy, when the poem itself produces disagreement over how (and whether one "can'st") read it? The poem's concluding lines reassure readers that they know how to read even as the poem's own rhetoric—its preoccupation with figures of address—throws such assurance into question.[17]

❖ The "Elegy" and Forgetting

Gray's "Elegy" investigates the power of animating tropes and explores the connection between reading and figures of facing, figures that grant a voice—and so life—to an inanimate object. Two contrasting senses of the poet emerge with the enigmatic address "for thee" in line 93 and from the so-called Stonecutter Controversy. The poet is concerned either with himself or with some nameless other. If one, following Brooks, substitutes "me" for "thee," then the concluding epitaph is the poet's own. Struck by thoughts of his own mortality, the poet-speaker is inspired to write his own epitaph with the hope that in the future someone will stand before his grave marker and remember him. But if one takes "thee" as an address to the stonecutter (an address, in other words, to some other village poet), then the poem attempts in conclusion to provide an epitaph for the poet responsible for the epitaphs the poet-speaker reads on other grave markers. Without the names and dates inscribed on the grave markers, one suspects that the poet-speaker would not have been moved so profoundly to compose the poem in the first place. The one who engraved the lines the poet-speaker reads upon the markers requires his own epitaph. The poet-speaker concludes his poem with the epitaph the stonecutter could never have cut for himself. In moving through the churchyard, the poet-speaker is provoked to contemplate his own death; or, in reading the epitaphs inscribed on the grave markers by some other hand, he is provoked to reflect on the death of the one responsible for the memorials he reads. Does the poet turn inward and compose his own epitaph, or does he turn outward and compose an epitaph for another, the mute inglorious Milton responsible for the "poems" (however unpoetic) in the country churchyard?

In presenting two contrasting senses of the poet-speaker, Gray's "Elegy Written in a Country Churchyard" also presents two competing theories of poetry. One need not think of "thee" as an address to the stonecutter for these two senses of poetry to emerge, and yet the possibility of competing addressees draws attention to the difference, a difference that concerns the poet from early in the poem. In offering competing theories of poetry, the poem reflects *on* poetry, its aims and ambitions, its limitations and enabling questions. The lyric poem offered by the poet-speaker that imagines the villagers in "their lowly bed" ("Elegy," l. 20) is countered by the artless lines inscribed on the grave markers, the names and years that supply "the place of fame and elegy" ("Elegy," l. 82). The poet-speaker acknowledges that the names and dates inscribed on the grave markers do not elegize the dead. They "supply the place" of an elegy. The poem stages an encounter between one understanding of poetry as capable of animation and another that refuses (or refuses fully to employ) this same power.

Unlike the names and dates, which supply the place of elegy but do not elegize—they mark the absence of a proper elegy—the elegy produced by the poet-speaker seeks to call to life with the help of his imagination those buried in the country churchyard the better to memorialize them. The power of the poet-speaker's imagination is present from the outset of the poem, from the moment he first turns to the graves of the villagers: "Beneath those rugged elms, that yew-tree's shade, / Where heaves the turf in many a mould'ring heap, / Each in his narrow cell for ever laid / The rude Forefathers of the hamlet sleep" ("Elegy," ll. 13–16). The poet-speaker's imagination blurs the boundary that separates the flight of his imagination from a natural description of the churchyard. By "heaving," the poet-speaker describes the lay of the land; however, one is also invited to imagine the earth heaving as the dead begin to stir. The choice of "heaves" to describe the ground suggests that the dead are not quite dead. Through the poet-speaker's imagination the dead villagers begin to stir as he proceeds to grant the dead villagers a second life. In the stanzas that follow, he imagines the dead villagers (who should be "sleeping" in their narrow cells, already a metaphor) running, climbing, and harvesting. The poet-speaker asks, "Can storied urn or animated bust / Back to its mansion call the fleeting breath?" ("Elegy," ll. 41–42). As a rhetorical question, the poet-speaker announces in these lines the inevitable failure of storied urn or animating bust to "soothe the dull cold ear of Death" ("Elegy," l. 44). But to the extent to which the poet-speaker has already begun his elegy, he has, through the power of his imagination, granted the dead new life. With special power, he is able to "see" again the villagers at work: "How jocund did they drive their team afield! / How bow'd the woods beneath their sturdy stroke!" ("Elegy," ll. 27–28). While the storied urn or animated bust cannot call the dead to life, the poet-speaker uses the muteness of the monuments he encounters, their inability to "call," as the occasion to reflect on the imaginary lives the dead villagers may possibly have lived. In imagining the past lives of the dead, the poet-speaker means to honor the previously unhonored. To honor them requires bringing the dead back to life through story. Despite Gray's chosen adjectives, the storied urn and animated bust cannot call the dead to life. Poetry, however, or so Gray's poet implies, can.

"Elegy" reflects on the recuperative reach of such a poem. If the poet's elegy attempts, like Orpheus, to bring the dead back to life, to what extent does such an elegy resist loss and at what cost? The poet-speaker has earlier suggested that the names and years "spelt by th' unletter'd Muse" ("Elegy," ll. 81–82) supply the place of fame and elegy; in producing an elegy, the poet substitutes his own for the names of the unhonored dead. In celebrating the lives of the unhonored, the poet substitutes his poem for all that is known of them. The "Elegy" takes the place of the only marks that refer to the specific lives of the dead (even if the only specifics included on the grave markers are names and years). The poet's "Elegy," which honors the unhonored and mourns their loss, offers itself in place of the dead, whose names are erased from the historical record. In this way the poem records the poet-speaker's desire to celebrate the lives of the deceased villagers, but what it "does" is offer one elegy, the poet's, for another.[18] The lives lived are erased even as they are remembered and raised to the subject of poetry.

The poet brings the dead villagers to second life but consigns the names and years to oblivion. While the "Elegy" seems to mourn the unhonored dead, it also records the poet-speaker's self-conscious celebration of his own poetic powers. As Diana Fuss writes, "The Orphic elegy may be less an homage to the dead than a self-indulgence of the living."[19] The poet-speaker finds his "voice" through the encounter with the mute call of the storied urn and the inscriptions on the grave markers. The names and years fail to provide a proper elegy, at least from the perspective of the poet-speaker who is compelled to produce another one. This failure of the names and years to provide a proper elegy offers the occasion for the poet-speaker to exercise his imagination, writing villagers into a kind of second life that erases—by refusing to record—the evidence present on the grave markers. By virtue of the "Elegy," the unhonored dead become, once again, anonymous.[20] Their anonymity makes possible the assertion of the poet-speaker as subject, as his elegy takes the place provided for it.[21]

The poet-speaker's elegy gathers its force from this metaphoric substitution of his own elegy for the simpler "elegies" already inscribed on the grave markers. It supplements the grave markers but in supplementing them also replaces them. In this way, the poem theorizes the elegy as a poetic form that labors to remember the dead only by first overcoming that death. In so doing, the elegy, like so-called successful mourning, overcomes loss. The elegy labors to overcome loss in order to move away from loss—and redeem loss as the condition of possibility for future hope. The self-invention and self-animation the elegy makes possible is, Gray's poem reveals, complicit in new forms of historical forgetting.[22]

❖ Marked Loss

In contrast, Gray's "Elegy" also offers a theory of poetry conceived around metonymy, as the crude names and years supply the place of elegy; they stand beside or next to the dead and do not, at least not in comparison to the force of the poet-speaker's metaphoric substitution of one elegy for another, raise the dead to new life and, consequently, doom them to the oblivion of historical forgetfulness.

Unlike the poet who labors to revivify the dead, the "poems" of the stonecutter—the "uncouth rhymes and shapeless sculpture" ("Elegy," l.

79)—merely mark a death. They announce the absence of speech but do not call back breath. The "artless" tales and uncouth rhymes inscribed on the grave markers stand in contrast to a model of the poem that aims through the creative act of the imagination to redeem loss. This is, in part, why the figure of the stonecutter remains relevant to the poem; of interest is not the simple fact that one can read "thee" as referring either, as Brooks suggests, to "me," or, following Ellis, to the stonecutter or village poet, but that in opening a gap between these two antecedents, Gray's "Elegy" draws attention to competing theories of poetry and poetry's relationship to loss. The lines inscribed on the grave markers, which are aligned with a different sort of poem, do not offer the promise of future life. They do little more than supply the place of elegy. The sparseness of their detail sparks the poet-speaker's response to them—his desire to replace them with another tribute. What is "spelt by th' unletter'd muse" ("Elegy," l. 81) does not bring the dead to life but resigns them, however unforgotten, to history—as the apostrophes figured prominently in Gray's line mark a space that is removed from the lines when voiced aloud.

The speed with which the poet-speaker substitutes his elegy for the names and years implies the failure of the names and years to authorize the poetic subject. But what if the speed with which the poet-speaker replaces the names and dates is also a sign of his resistance to a form of poetry—however minimally "poetic"—that marks but does not redeem loss? What, in other words, if one reads Gray's "Elegy" as staging the poet-speaker's confrontation with a second form of elegy, his confrontation with the "place of . . . elegy," an elegy that does not aim to overcome loss?[23] What supplies the place of elegy does not supply an elegy. As a result of the confusion surrounding Gray's enigmatic address to "thee," there is, perhaps, reason to be suspicious of the poet-speaker's drive to replace the "place" these elegies provide with his "Elegy," as this effort demonstrates a drama of self-consciousness that risks substituting the story of "me" for the story of "thee."[24] Whether or not it is in fact possible to resist the power of figure to revivify the dead remains an open question.

The poem stages the difference between the grave markers the poet-speaker reads and the poem he writes (and that his own reader reads). "Elegy Written in a Country Churchyard" stands as a symptom of the desire to replace the specific death with a more general elegy; simultaneously, it allegorizes such a desire and presents the effort to read, as illustrated by the poet-speaker, as a form of resistance to the encounter with the unlettered tales engraved on the monuments. The poet's desire to compose an elegy (a desire that results from the encounter with the mute, unlettered, artless monuments) can itself be read, then, as a resistance to the muteness of the monument—a desire to ascribe to the monuments a face, a life, and so a history.

❖ "You Shall Flit Among the Fading Corpses"

What one calls literature may emerge from the various and often competing ways texts subvert any authoritative reading by anticipating and inscribing within their own structures the reading strategies brought to bear on them. If reading is often figured as an attempt to reconcile form and content, grammar and rhetoric, then it may be no surprise that in the attempt to reconcile available readings of the poem, critics should have turned from the poet and the stonecutter to the reader. In the wake of the Stonecutter Controversy, critics attempted to move beyond the impasse by offering the reader as yet another antecedent for "thee." Bertrand H. Bronson and W. K. Wimsatt, for instance, each suggest that the movement in the poem from "me" to "thee" represents a broadening perspective; the poet addresses not a single subject (he addresses neither himself nor the stonecutter only) but a more universal subject position. As Bronson writes, the poet "has so long ceased to mention himself that we have been projecting into his lines our own identity, so that it is our voice which has been speaking *our* own train of thought all this while. It seems, therefore, perfectly natural to be addressing another as 'thee.' This transference is surely one of the subtlest effects in our literature. For now we join the poet in addressing himself in the second person, continuing the identification as we imagine 'some kindred spirit' inquiring about *us*."[25] Like Brooks before him, Bronson replaces "thee" with another pronoun—this time not "me" but "us." Readers take themselves as addressed by the poem and substitute themselves for "thee," thus confirming, once again, the poem's universal appeal. Readers hear their own voice in the poem they read, a result of the very tropes the poem foregrounds. W. K. Wimsatt similarly suggests in *Hateful Contraries* that "the term 'thee' . . . refers to the same person as the 'me' of stanza 1 . . . and this person is any sensitive, melancholy, unknown poet . . . and hence again, by extension, any person at all who happens to be reading the poem."[26] In response to the critical disagreement surrounding the Stonecutter Controversy, such readings of the poem employ a dialectical logic: the two possible identities for "thee" are figuratively joined together in a third, more fluid and dynamic subject position ("us," the reader, any person who happens to be reading the poem).

In taking "thee" as an address to the reader of the poem, Bronson and Wimsatt mediate between the two existing interpretations that sparked the Stonecutter Controversy, but in the process they also return readers to the controversy, for the poem raises as a question how the reader is to respond to the poem. That the reader is now included within the poem (as one addressed) only intensifies the difficulty of reading the poem because the poem already reflects on (and questions) the poet's ability to animate. Unlike Samuel Johnson and I. A. Richards, who suggest that the poem's success results in part from its ability to reflect back to the reader certain shared feelings, experiences that would be common to all people under similar conditions, Bronson and Wimsatt account for the poem's power by suggesting that the poem universalizes its subject not only through particular content but also through a particular rhetorical procedure. What was once viewed as the result of the poem's content is now viewed as a result of the poem's rhetorical structure. While such a turn closes one interpretative dilemma, it simultaneously opens others. If reading is itself an attempt to speak with the dead (in other words, if reading itself is dominated by tropes that animate the inanimate word, that throw or transfer the voice of the poet), then readers who "hear" their own voice in the poem they read are aligned with the poet of Gray's "Elegy" as he animates the inanimate dead. The transference of voice is precisely what the poem questions by staging it as a form of resistance to the muteness of the monuments the poet encounters.

More troublingly, if the reader is addressed as "thee," then the epitaph that concludes the poem is the reader's own. In this way the call to the reader in Gray's "Elegy" echoes Sappho's fragment 55: "Dead you will lie there and no memory of you / Shall there be and no desire for you in time to come; for you have no share / In the roses of Pieria, but unseen even in the house of Hades / You shall flit among the fading corpses, flown away."[27] One's future death is inscribed within the address, within the epitaph, as an event already missed. Yopie Prins describes the poem's proleptic force: "instead of bringing the dead to life, [fragment 55] finds the living dead."[28] In calling attention to its own dependence on figures of address (such as apostrophe and prosopopoeia), these poems foreground their own status as inscriptions, as representations of voice and not voices themselves. In "Repetition, Refrain, and Epitaph," Debra Fried quotes two epitaphs from a Quaker graveyard. Like Sappho's fragment 55, both address the reader. Epitaphs generate through the power of direct address the comforting fiction of speaking dead (the dead are not entirely absent if they are still granted life enough to "speak"). But in positing a voice for the inanimate text, writes Fried, "epitaphs predict the collapse of reader and poem and a consequent proliferation of more epitaphs."[29] This collapse of living reader into dead speaker is foretold with frightening directness by another stone, that marking the grave of Betsey Lewis, from the same Quaker graveyard: "What thou art reading o'er my bones / I've often read on other stones / And others soon shall read of thee / What thou are reading now of me."[30] The epitaph relies upon a disturbing chiasmus. "According to this inscription," continues Fried, "the very act of reading an epitaph is almost like a curse, an unfailing omen of the reader's own death."[31] Just as Betsey Lewis, now a corpse, was once a living reader of epitaphs, so too will the reader of her epitaph soon become a corpse. Chapter 5 of *The Poetics of Unremembered Acts* takes up this thread more explicitly.

❖ "To the Moon Complain"

Gray's "Elegy" foregrounds its investigation into the animating power of tropes (and so, as well, its investigation into the tropological dimension of reading) from its opening stanzas, which anticipate and frame the latter address to "thee." In demonstrating the similarity between the poet-speaker's animating power and the reader's, the poem calls attention to the degree to which "life-giving" tropes condition the possibility of reading. The poet-speaker's willingness to grant the villagers a second life anticipates what readers may be called to do in taking themselves as addressed by a written call, an inscription, or an epitaph.

The poem's opening stanzas announce the poet's growing solitude. With the curfew tolling the parting day, the poet is left alone with darkness:

> The curfew tolls the knell of parting day,
> The lowing herd wind slowly o'er the lea,
> The plowman homeward plods his weary way,
> And leaves the world to darkness and to me.
>
> Now fades the glimmering landscape on the sight,
> And all the air a solemn stillness holds,
> Save where the beetle wheels his droning flight,
> And drowsy tinklings lull the distant folds;
> ("Elegy," ll. 1–8)

As Vincent Newey explains, the opening stanzas suggest a "trance or half-conscious state in which the sights and sounds of the external world are interiorized as vivid slow-motion dream-impressions and sensations."[32]

The poet's solitude is first a result of nature's departure, signaled by the "parting" of day. The second line announces the departure of the animal world, as the lowing herd winds over the lea. And the third line announces the departure of other men, as the plowman plods his weary way. One senses a shift in the third line when one follows the subject-verb constructions of the first several lines. The curfew tolls, the herd winds, and the plowman plods; but the inclusion of "homeward" between noun ("plowman") and verb ("plods") alters the rhythm of the line. One senses that the poet, unlike the plowman, does not have a home toward which to plod. He stands still, without anywhere to go, reflecting on the departure of all around him. The first stanza is the only one in which appears any mention of the poet in the first person: the world is left "to darkness and to me" ("Elegy," l. 4). The poet is left alone "with," not simply "in," darkness, a sign of the poet's unwillingness to submit to solitude. The subtle anthropomorphism, which anticipates the owl's "complaint," prevents for however brief a moment the poet-speaker's total solitude.[33]

"Elegy Written in a Country Churchyard" records the thoughts of a last man as the light of the world is extinguished. The first stanzas mark the departure of other inhabitants as well as the light of the world. While there is perhaps some hope in the minimally anthropomorphized presence of darkness, the second stanza reduces the presence of this abstraction, as the speaker announces "Now fades the glimmering landscape on the sight" ("Elegy," l. 5). The speaker of the first stanza who stood for a moment "with" darkness is now "in" darkness. In this fashion, the poem completes its first turn. The poet is now isolated in darkness, and for however brief a moment that darkness is also a stillness: "the air a solemn stillness holds" ("Elegy," l. 6). Given the poem's location, a churchyard, this dark stillness feels ominous; the world has become all too much like a casket.

With line 7, however, a return to life begins as the dark stillness gives way to the wheeling beetle, a first new sign of life. The fact that line 7 begins with "save" instead of, for instance, "but," suggests the poet's relief at finding something capable of disturbing the dark stillness, even if at first what disturbs the dark stillness is as mechanical as it is living (not a beetle but a "wheeling" beetle). The opening of the poem describes a descent into the world-become-casket as well as an acknowledgment or discovery of new life. It is from the world-become-casket that the poet is saved by the beetle that wheels its droning flight. But there is something unsatisfying about the wheeling beetle, which is robbed of its life through the addition of "wheels," just as in the next line the living animals, the sheep, are replaced by the "tinkling" of the bells around their necks. Again the mechanical (and inanimate) intrudes as sheep are replaced by a metonymic figure that links them to that which is least alive about them. As a result, a second "save" is required.

With the second appearance of "save"—introduced at the beginning of the third stanza—the poet moves from metaphor and metonymy ("wheeling" and "tinkling") to tropes of address, as the owl's complaint to the moon turns the poet-speaker's attention to the churchyard. A switch in tropes makes possible the poet's move into the churchyard as he discovers the power of address to animate. Barbara Johnson suggests in "Apostrophe, Animation, Abortion" that poets employ apostrophe to animate themselves (as the lyric speaker of "Ode to the West Wind," for instance, apostrophizes—and through apostrophe animates—the wind so that it will animate him in return).[34] Here the poet does not animate himself directly through apostrophe but by imagining an owl apostrophizing an inanimate object, the moon:

> Save that from yonder ivy-mantled tow'r
> The moping owl does to the moon complain
> Of such, as wandering near her secret bow'r,
> Molest her ancient solitary reign.
> ("Elegy," ll. 9–12)

Conventionally, apostrophe positions the reader as one who "overhears" an address not intended for him. Precisely because this situation is not literal, readers, as Jonathan Culler suggests in his famous essay on apostrophe, ignore the presence of figures of address like apostrophe.[35] As Culler argues, apostrophe "is different [from other tropes] in that it makes its point by troping not on the meaning of a word but on the circuit or situation of communication itself."[36] It marks a deflection of the message and so disrupts the circuit of communication and "raises questions about who is the addressee"[37]—a question Gray's poem conspicuously raises as well, as we have already seen. Because the poet-speaker of Gray's "Elegy" addresses neither the moon nor the owl but instead describes the owl as addressing the moon, the poet figures himself as one turned away from. Instead of himself addressing the owl or moon, and instead of positioning himself as the one addressed by the owl—who might for instance warn him to trespass no further—the poet positions himself as excluded from the conversation he describes. He overhears the owl's complaint, the apostrophe to the moon, and is not the owl's direct addressee. This deflection of address launches the poem as it moves with the next stanza toward its larger subject, the reading of the epitaphs in the country churchyard and the poet-speaker's reflections on mortality. That the poet should go on to animate the dead follows from this opening scene. The owl "teaches" the poet-speaker about the force of apostrophe even as Gray's "Elegy" explores the limitations of such reanimating power.

Only a poet fully invested in the power of lyric tropes would hear an owl and believe it apostrophizes the moon. The poet-speaker positions himself as one ignored by the landscape he enters, but unlike the wheeling beetle, the sheep, or even the plowman, the owl, so the poet asserts, acknowledges him indirectly. The poet reaches after (and receives, though, again, only through the intervention of a particular rhetorical trope) some acknowledgment of his own continued life. The owl's complaint draws the poet back from the brink of dark solitude. He is saved. After the address by the owl to the moon, the poet-speaker turns in the fourth stanza to the graves of the rude forefathers "Beneath those rugged elms, that yew tree's shade" ("Elegy," l. 13). The owl's apostrophe to the moon—as imagined by the poet—leads the poet into the churchyard where he, like the owl, will exercise his poetic power to animate the inanimate and save the dead from darkness.

The figure of apostrophe is granted by the poet a prominent place in the poem, and this is especially significant given that the poem is famous for its later apostrophe to "thee." The poet-speaker—left for a moment in darkness—slowly recovers and with the address by the owl to the moon is able more fully to employ his own poetic power. The power of tropes to animate is precisely what saves the poet from the world-become-casket. The owl addresses and animates the moon. As a result, the poet is propelled to further anthropomorphisms as he moves from the fourth stanza to describe the "rude Forefathers of the hamlet" buried in the country churchyard as "sleeping." In other words, just as he grants the owl human emotion, the poet transforms the corpses into sleeping bodies.[38] The poet-speaker turns to the graves of the rude forefathers only after first anthropomorphizing the owl (as one who complains), an owl also capable of animating inanimate objects through the force of address.

The poet moves from an opening description of apostrophe to later employing the figure, when, first, in line 37, the poet addresses "you, ye Proud," who should not impute fault to the dead, and then, second and more famously, "thee." For a poem that concludes with an epitaph after an address to an unnamed "thee," this opening set of figures is conspicuous. In complaining to the moon, the owl transforms the moon into a subject. Similarly, Gray's poet-speaker grants life to the inanimate as he moves through the country churchyard. In reading the names and years inscribed on the grave markers, he grants to the dead villagers an imagined second life. He gives the villagers what the epitaph is meant to provide: a living voice.[39] The owl's apostrophe to the moon links the opening of the poem to the much longer discussion of the grave markers the poet-speaker comes to read and respond to in the bulk of the poem; but it also anticipates the confusing address to an unnamed "thee" and the position one finds oneself in as reader of the poem.[40] Critical arguments that take "thee" as an address to a human reader put themselves in the position of the owl (and later in the poem, the poet-speaker as he, like the owl, transforms the mute dead into living subjects). In taking oneself as addressed by the poem ("you, ye Proud," "for thee") the reader grants to the poem, the mute word, a voice and a face; one gives life to the dead letter, the inscription. This is the act the poet-speaker figures the owl performing in the third stanza as well as the act the poet-speaker goes on to perform as he moves into the country churchyard.[41] The "solution" to the Stonecutter Controversy offered by Bronson and Wimsatt has been anticipated by the poem from its opening lines. To read is to animate the dead, granting life to the inanimate—the same action the owl and poet perform, an action the poem also figures as a form of resistance to the very monuments (and so the poem as monument) encountered.

If the poet discovers the animating power of tropes in the opening stanzas through the owl, he also figures himself as ignored by this same power. He finds himself animated by the owl's indirect acknowledgment of his trespass, but his animation is also a sign of his being ignored. The force of address to animate always also misses its mark. The poet is ignored and animated at the same time. The position of the poet-speaker in the first stanza anticipates the position the poet-speaker secures for the reader. The poet positions himself as the reader as he imagines himself overhearing the owl's apostrophe. The reader hears the complaint of the "poet" and so encounters the power of figure to animate the inanimate. But the poet's address "for thee" cannot simply be said directly to address the reader without ignoring how the poet positions himself in relationship to the owl and the moon. To animate is always to ignore. To find oneself animated is to find oneself ignored.

When the poet goes on to animate the dead he also, so the opening stanzas suggest, ignores them. When the poet addresses "thee" later in the poem, the poet puts himself in the position of the owl, with "thee" in the position of the moon. The reader is therefore situated somewhere between the moon and the position formerly held by the poet. To find oneself addressed by the poem is to repeat the animating effort that begins it.

In reading Gray's "Elegy," one animates a poem that takes seriously the power of animating tropes.

❖ On Speaking with the Dead

The turn away from the Stonecutter Controversy by critics required a turn toward the reader, now included as a possible antecedent for "thee." But figures of direct address in poems are also apostrophes.[42] The fact that one might find yet another possible addressee for the line, this time the reader, only reinforces the awkward position an apostrophe produces for the reader from the start. In encountering an apostrophe to the reader, one finds oneself invited to take oneself as the poem's addressee, but one is allowed to take oneself as addressee only to the degree to which one ignores the ways in which apostrophes raise address as a question, as they trope the means by which a message is conveyed.

Two theories of poetry are explored in Gray's "Elegy," and following this discussion of the opening stanzas, it should be possible to articulate the stakes involved. The poet-speaker reads the epitaphs inscribed on the grave markers as lyric poems and imagines the lives of the dead; he grants the dead a second life, a life that replaces the names and years inscribed on the grave markers. This is the lyric's power. The effort mirrors the conceptualization of the lyric poem one often associates with a future, romantic project. As Paul de Man suggests in "Lyrical Voice in Contemporary Theory," "The principle of intelligibility, in lyric poetry, depends on the phenomenalization of the poetic voice. Our claim to understand a lyric text coincides with the actualization of a speaking voice, be it (monologically) that of the poet or (dialogically) that of the exchange that takes place between author and reader in the process of comprehension."[43] While it would be difficult to think of reading lyric texts without phenomenalizing the poetic voice, without, that is, ascribing to the inscription a voice, this voice is not present to the senses, which is why, for de Man, prosopopoeia is the master trope of poetic discourse. To read the lyric is to grant the lyric, as inscription, a voice (and so a face). There might be no reading of the lyric, and perhaps no reading more generally understood, without such granting of voices (and faces). What is striking, then, is the fact that the poem begins by reflecting on these same issues. In addressing the moon the owl transforms the moon into a subject. To a significant degree this is precisely the same action readers of Gray's "Elegy," like Bronson and Wimsatt, perform in response to the poem's own muteness about its proper addressee. In response to "thee," readers transform the figure of address into a direct address, thereby granting the poem a voice and the power to address one. One finds oneself addressed by an inanimate object, words inscribed on a page. In interpreting the address to "thee" as a direct address, readers transform the relationship between owl and moon into one between speaker and listener; but the poem has already warned readers that to do so is possible only because of figure, only because various figures, here apostrophe as well as anthropomorphism and prosopopoeia, condition the possibility of communication. Bronson and Wimsatt close the Stonecutter Controversy by suggesting that one might read "for thee" as a direct address. Closing the controversy, however, requires missing the ways the opening stanzas anticipate the later address to "thee." Through its sophisticated attention to the power of apostrophe and prosopopoeia, the poem offers a chance not to ignore the figures of address that condition the possibility of the lyric and of lyric reading. What Rousseau calls reading, it seems, belongs to the poets.

Instead of critical consensus, Gray's revision of "Stanzas" into "Elegy" produced a "problem poem." Gray's revisions turn the poem itself into an epitaph, into an inscription that anticipates and frustrates readers' attempts to limit the possible number of addressees for the poem. The epitaph, like poetry more generally, is always open to being read and is therefore, as Wordsworth writes of epitaphs, addressed to no one in particular.[44] The poem is addressed to all who read, which may help explain the hoary-headed swain's enigmatic aside: "Approach and read (for thou canst read) the lay, / Graved on the stone beneath yon aged thorn" ("Elegy," ll. 115–16). But the act of reading, as the opening stanzas to the poem indicate, is always already a sign of one's exclusion. This is the lesson the poem attempts to "teach." One "canst read" precisely because to read means to have been—and to continue to be—excluded from the poem one reads.[45] Gray's poet responds to the "anonymity" of the dead buried in the country churchyard; he responds to the encounter with the names and years spelled "by the unlettered Muse"; he responds, that is, to the fact that the names and years are unable to "speak" of those whose lives they mark. The epitaph, as Paul Fry suggests in *A Defense of Poetry,* "is not the pursuit of voice but the burial of voice."[46] The muteness of the buried voice, I suggest by way of conclusion, gives rise to the poem and raises as a question what it means "to read" a monument, a monument that marks a death but cannot (or does not) speak for that death. Gray's "Elegy," however, refuses to assume any simple understanding of such a wish and instead is offered by Gray as an allegory of reading displaced as commemoration. The language of the poem refuses to align reading with any simple idea of response to, of responsibility for, the dead. And yet the poem also acknowledges the power and unavoidability of address, of finding oneself "as if" addressed by the dead and so burdened by the responsibility to respond.

This model of the poem is countered by another, represented by the uncouth rhymes inscribed on the grave markers that strive merely to mark the dead and testify to the death of the dead without simultaneously bringing the dead to new life—a poem that calls for a type of reading that testifies to loss but does not strive (however heroically or unheroically) to overcome that loss. Gray's "Elegy" and the history of its reception demonstrate the difficulty of such a project. As a literary critic, one is perhaps always in danger of defining reading not as the uncomfortable (and potentially alienating) encounter with the mute inscription but as speaking with the dead, as bringing the dead back to life to speak again through the apocalyptic force of the imagination, something that might be unavoidable. The poem stages just this sort of trap and anticipates (as it simultaneously mirrors back) the resistance that readers manifest in their unwillingness to acknowledge the muteness of the monuments, the monument's own material unwillingness to "speak" what the poet most wishes to know.[47]

The "poem of poems," which forcefully announces that "one can'st read," also allegorizes the difficulty—or impossibility—of reading.[48] It does so, however, while at the same time gesturing toward what it might mean to read in such a way that one bears witness (merely, just barely) to the impossibility of recovery. That all of this is "for thee" means, in other words, that all of this—this chance for something else—is not for "us."

4

The Craving for Incidents: Wordsworth

Watch over absent meaning.
—Maurice Blanchot

If Gray's "Elegy" concludes with a pronouncement that one "can'st" read even as the poem challenges readers who struggle to make sense of it, Wordsworth's "Simon Lee" poses a similar challenge in taking on poetry's social function. How does one learn to read poetry, and what is poetry good for?

In his preface to *Lyrical Ballads* from 1800, William Wordsworth famously, if also enigmatically, defines poetry as "the spontaneous overflow of powerful feelings: it takes its origin from emotion recollected in tranquility."[1] Readers of Wordsworth's preface often concentrate on one half or other of this formulation. Readers who privilege the spontaneous overflow of powerful feelings produce an understanding of Wordsworth's poetry, and of romantic poetry more generally, that relies heavily on theories of expression and aligns poetic power with spontaneity. The fact that for Wordsworth these powerful feelings are "recollected in tranquility" remains enigmatic in part because it introduces a necessary temporal delay, a level of mediation that is difficult to reconcile with the unmediated access to powerful feelings the first half of Wordsworth's formulation promises. Readers who privilege the importance of "recollection" have linked Wordsworth's commitment to tranquillity to a civilizing process that subordinates immediate sensation to reflective judgment. Tranquillity marks a necessary temporal and psychological distance from the initial sense-experience and becomes one way for the poet to maintain control over such experiences. As Noel Jackson summarizes, "Wordsworth's claim that the poet is capable of formally abstracting from and exerting control over the immediacy of 'vulgar' sense-experience has often been read as the signature proposition of Wordsworthian aesthetics and a crucial expression of its ideological character."[2] Through reflection, in other words, the poet learns to impose continuity on discontinuous sense-data. Such readings of Wordsworth find in the movement from a spontaneous overflow of feeling to the recollection of these feelings in tranquillity a model for the development, as enculturation, of the individual, society, and the nation-state.

However, Wordsworth's introduction in the preface to *Lyrical Ballads* of a necessary temporal delay and an accompanying psychological distance from immediate sensations, made possible by what he calls "tranquility," also introduces an interpretive dilemma. At some key moments, Wordsworth invites readers to conclude that the feelings recollected are not exactly the poet's, which results in an idiosyncratic understanding of tranquillity. Famously, Wordsworth writes in *The Prelude* (1805) of his past self: "so wide appears / The vacancy between me and those days, / Which yet have such self-presence in my mind / That, sometimes, when I think of them, I seem / Two consciousnesses, conscious of myself / And of some other Being."[3] Wordsworthian tranquillity may not always denote an experience of calm but an experience of estrangement from the very things one hopes never to feel estranged from, such as oneself. With "tranquility," I suggest, Wordsworth not only describes a psychological state belonging to a "civilized" subject but also introduces a certain interpretive dilemma that poetry poses for its readers, even when the reader is also the poet himself.

The concluding lines of "Simon Lee: The Old Huntsman with an Incident in Which He was Concerned" mark the delay required for Wordsworthian tranquillity typographically with the inclusion of a dash separating the final four lines of the poem from what has preceded them. This delay, far from enabling an assertion of control over the experience recorded, produces instead two competing reflections on or responses to the incident. What Wordsworth's poem demonstrates in closing is a poet-narrator less in control of his responses to the incident with which he was concerned than has previously been noted in the body of criticism that responds to the poem. The concluding lines of Wordsworth's poem suggest that one danger of tranquillity—of the necessary temporal and psychological distance from incidents—may be a sort of estrangement, for the poet-narrator himself as well as for the reader, the interpreter, from the incident the poem describes.

Readings of Wordsworth's poetry that privilege the spontaneity of powerful feelings have missed other passages from the preface to *Lyrical Ballads* that have, in recent years, come to a renewed legibility. In his preface Wordsworth identifies a modern dilemma: "A multitude of causes, unknown to former times, are now acting with a combined force to blunt the discriminating powers of the mind, and unfitting it for all voluntary exertion to reduce it to a state of almost savage torpor. The most effective of these causes are the great national events which are daily taking place, and the increasing accumulation of men in cities, where the uniformity of their occupations produces a craving for extraordinary incident, which the rapid communication of intelligence hourly gratifies" (*LB*, p. 249). For Wordsworth, the health of the mind is threatened by the too-rapid communication of intelligence about events "daily taking place." Certain technological advances, such as newspapers, make it possible for the mind to be supplied with extraordinary incidents (and so momentarily gratified). But the cost of such a craving is alienation, solipsism, and even death, what Wordsworth describes as the absence of all "voluntary exertion." The rapid communication of intelligence gratifies a craving for extraordinary incidents, but gratification is opposed to voluntary exertion and thus also to anything like willed action.

In this way, Wordsworth's fear as it is expressed in 1800 anticipates the failure of realistic, real-time media today to bring about proper political action, even as it perfects the transmission—the rapid communication—of intelligence.[4] The numbness that consumers of realistic, real-time media experience today when confronted with massive amounts of information may be a version of the blunted modern mind Wordsworth diagnoses in the preface. As Geoffrey Hartman writes in *The Longest Shadow*, "Even while deploring and condemning the events, we experience what the poet John Keats called 'the feel of not to feel it,' as we continue with everyday life."[5] While information is consumed at a great rate, one fears that the greater the rate of transmission, the less effective the intelligence becomes. News of events daily taking place momentarily satisfies the craving for shock and surprise but at the expense of the mind's ability to respond to the events. The rapid communication of intelligence becomes one way among many of blunting the impact of events—or, more strongly put, of avoiding the impact of events—rather than a means to understand or respond to them.[6]

The idea of reading as decoding and as the reception of information has its strongest articulation in the writings of Enlightenment pedagogues who themselves struggled with the very idea of reading they espoused. Wordsworth aligns the idea of reading as decoding with the desire for rapid communication and extraordinary incidents. Poetry offers the possibility of rethinking reading not as the negation of communication but as an intervention into the rhetoric that determines and overdetermines communication. While the extraordinary incident seems to offer some escape from the uniformity of history, nothing is more uniform in modernity—Wordsworth suggests indirectly—than the craving for extraordinary incidents produced by the rapid communication of intelligence. In this light, the clamor for shock and surprise, for intense experience, is possibly the modern mind's last great defense against experience; the rapid communication of intelligence becomes a way not to experience events or the feelings they inspire. As Giorgio Agamben writes in *Infancy and History,* "the question of experience can be approached nowadays only with an acknowledgment that it is no longer accessible to us."[7]

A somewhat embarrassed Wordsworth situates poetry—specifically the poetry of *Lyrical Ballads*—in relation to this dilemma and so raises the ethical stakes of reading poetry: "When I think upon this degrading thirst after outrageous stimulation, I am almost ashamed to have spoken of the feeble effort with which I have endeavoured to counteract it" (*LB,* p. 249). What role does poetry play in counteracting this thirst after outrageous stimulation without retreating into another, aesthetic form of solipsism? How does poetry "unblunt" the mind or make possible alternative forms of response to events daily taking place? If experience is no longer accessible, can poetry make experience possible again? It is clear from Wordsworth's preface that poetry is not to guard readers against stimulation as such. It is not the role of poetry to isolate readers from the world—though this is one way in which the function of the aesthetic has been misunderstood. But neither is poetry, worries Wordsworth, to satisfy readers' thirst for "outrageous stimulation," which is satisfied by the works Wordsworth opposes: "frantic novels, sickly and stupid German Tragedies, and deluges of idle and extravagant stories in verse" (*LB,* p. 294).

While powerful feelings and their spontaneous overflow are necessary for poetic production, Wordsworth is keenly aware of the dangers presented by this thirst after "outrageous stimulation," linked as it is to the craving for immediate communication of extraordinary incidents. Wordsworth challenges the popular sentimental literature of his day, which stimulated quickened emotional responses to representations of events. If poetry is only the expression of the powerful overflow of spontaneous feeling, then it is always in danger of satisfying the craving for extraordinary incidents and so participating in the blunting of the mind that Wordsworth diagnoses in his preface.

Poetry, hopes Wordsworth, makes possible some form of response that is neither an abdication of the responsibility to respond nor a thirst for more "outrageous stimulation," for more rapid communication of intelligence. In turning away from an intensity of feeling, in mediating the experience of spontaneous feeling, Wordsworth hopes to make possible the return of—the return to—feeling. Tranquillity, however, understood as the interpretive dilemma that poetry poses, interrupts the redemptive trajectory suggested here, for if tranquillity mediates the craving for spontaneity, aligned as it is with "outrageous stimulation," it also alienates oneself from oneself. Feeling returns but only as unclaimed by consciousness.[8]

❖ O Gentle Reader!

To consider some of the issues Wordsworth raises in his preface in more specific detail, I turn now to one of Wordsworth's "Lyrical Ballads," first published anonymously in 1798, "Simon Lee: The Old Huntsman with an Incident in Which He was Concerned." The poem describes an old man, Simon Lee, struggling to survive and a young man's offer of aid when he happens to come upon Simon working to sever a root. In its complicated concluding lines, the poem raises as a question the ability of the young poet-narrator to respond appropriately to Simon Lee's struggles, both his more general struggle to survive in a modern world that has no use for him and his more specific struggle, described in the second half of the poem, to sever a root. To the extent to which the poem raises as a question the ability of the poet-narrator to respond appropriately to one in need, it also questions the ability of poetry to function as a bridge between sympathetic identification (in the form of spontaneous and powerful feeling) and political or ethical action (in the form of humanitarian aid). What is, in other words, the relationship between powerful feelings and action, especially given Wordsworth's suggestion in the preface that a craving for incidents capable of producing powerful feelings threatens to produce apathy and not action?

The poem has challenged readers for centuries. It perhaps challenged its first reader, Wordsworth himself, most of all. As Ernest de Selincourt writes, "On the text of no other short poem did W. expend so much labour as on *Simon Lee.*"[9] Wordsworth repeatedly revised the poem over the years, returning to it again and again; unlike other poems originally published in *Lyrical Ballads,* by the time "Simon Lee" appeared in *The Poetical Works of William Wordsworth* in 1832, it had changed considerably. "Simon Lee" also challenges readers more directly; the poem is likely most famous for the apostrophe to the reader that Wordsworth includes between the balladlike first part of the poem (which corresponds roughly to the first part of the poem's subtitle: "The Old Huntsman") and the lyriclike second part of the poem (which corresponds roughly to the second part of the poem's title: "with an Incident in Which He was Concerned"). Like "Hart-Leap Well," which begins the second volume of *Lyrical Ballads* published with the addition of several poems in 1800, "Simon Lee" participates in an experiment in poetic form. Generated by the tension

Wordsworth perceived between narrative and lyric poetry, "Simon Lee" moves the reader from the ballad, with its emphasis on narrative action, to the lyric, with its emphasis on emotional intensity.[10] In situating the direct address to the reader between the ballad and the lyric, the poem aligns the ballad (the narrative of suffering chronicled in the first half of the poem) with the sensationalism the poet-narrator criticizes.[11]

In the balladlike first part of the poem, the poet-narrator describes Simon Lee in his youth: "No man like him the horn could sound, / And no man was so full of glee" (*LB*, ll. 17–18). Simon's youth is celebrated, but it is celebrated for it to be more effectively contrasted with his present condition, the condition in which the poet-narrator finds him. In the past, Simon was a famed hunter, but now he has grown old: "he is lean and he is sick" (*LB*, l. 33). In this way, the poem reminds one of—and responds to—other poems published during this period that chronicle the experiences of the poor, the forgotten, the mad, and the like, such as Robert Southey's "The Widow" and "The Idiot" and Charlotte Smith's "The Dead Beggar," in other words, the humanitarian protest poem.

However, in "Simon Lee" the poet-narrator anticipates and then actively frustrates the expectations of the imagined reader in addressing the reader directly after narrating Simon Lee's decline: "My gentle reader, I perceive / How patiently you've waited, / And I'm afraid that you expect / Some tale will be related" (*LB*, ll. 69–72). After contrasting Simon's youth with his present condition, the poet-narrator abruptly announces that the poem will move now in a new direction, which calls attention to the imagined reader's investment in sensationalism. The apostrophe questions the reader's desire for narratives of suffering. With the apostrophe the poet-narrator turns, as the second half of the poem's subtitle warns readers he will, to an *incident* in which Simon Lee is concerned. The poem moves from a detached third-person narrative to a more intimate first-person perspective, in which the poet-narrator's encounter with Simon vainly attempting to sever a root is described. A reader of what Wordsworth calls "extravagant stories in verse," the apostrophe implies, is not likely to believe that such an unremarkable incident will produce an emotionally intense experience. As Stephen M. Parrish suggests, however, the goal of a poem like "Simon Lee" is to "reduce the role of story or event in narrative, in favor of passion or feeling—to internalize the action."[12] The poem focuses on an unremarkable incident to aid the reader to invest in a passion or feeling that is not reducible to sentimentalism or sensationalism. The stress is not placed on the incident but on the reader's ability (or inability) to "take it." As the poet-narrator explains, "What more I have to say is short, / I hope you'll kindly take it; / It is no tale; but should you think, / Perhaps a tale you'll make it" (*LB*, ll. 77–80). At the same time, the presence of the apostrophe suggests that the reader is in need of some instruction. The poet-narrator anticipates and intentionally thwarts the narrative expectations of his imagined reader, expectations that he has helped produce in the first half of the poem. As James Averill notes in *Wordsworth and the Poetry of Human Suffering,* "Expectation, the craving for the 'moving accident,' the desire for the stimulus of fictional suffering, becomes a symptom of deficiency."[13] The first half of the poem produces in the reader just the sort of desire for fictional suffering the poet-narrator criticizes. Precisely because the poet-narrator's imagined reader is not likely to find the incident emotionally powerful, the poet-narrator sets out to frustrate (and alter) the imagined reader's expectations. As Wordsworth explains in the preface to *Lyrical Ballads,* his goal, specific to "Simon Lee," is to produce "another and more salutary impression than we are accustomed to receive" from ordinary moral sensations (*LB,* p. 293).

As a result, though, "Simon Lee" questions the goals of the humanitarian protest poem by drawing attention to its own narrative frame. In stimulating moral sensations, fictional suffering always risks generating the craving for extraordinary incidents Wordsworth criticizes in his preface to *Lyrical Ballads.* Similarly, humanitarian protest poems may challenge readers to rethink the prevailing assumptions that govern responses to the poor, but they also risk substituting sympathetic identification with the representation of suffering for sympathetic identification with what one might call actual suffering. Does the fictionalization of suffering inspire readers to put an end to suffering, or does it relieve readers of the responsibility to act because it allows readers to view the suffering of others as fictional?[14] In a reading of *The Ruined Cottage,* Karen Swann explores Wordsworth's use of narrative frames. Wordsworth, writes Swann, uses "a mediating narrative consciousness to interpose distance between the reader and the narrative of suffering—thus encouraging a meditative rather than a stimulated response to painful events." Wordsworth often complicates the narrative frames of his poems to draw attention to the "narrative acts themselves and thus invite[s] the public to reflect on its own investments in sensationalism."[15]

Like *The Ruined Cottage,* the goal of "Simon Lee" is not merely to inspire within the reader great feelings of sympathy for Simon Lee, or even for those who exist in a similar condition. If such were the case, it is not clear that Wordsworth—or the poet-narrator—should need to interrupt the narrative the ballad constructs. One suspects that sympathy is more easily produced in a reader when it is not demanded of him or her in quite so direct a manner. In moving from the narrative quality of the first half of the poem to a specific incident that testifies to Simon's weakened condition, the poet-narrator calls for the reader to make a tale of this incident, to discover feeling in those moments others pass over in the search for "extravagant stories in verse." In turning to such an unremarkable incident, and yet one capable of producing great feeling, the poet-narrator reminds readers that the desire for extraordinary incidents may preclude and not enable feeling. The desire for sensational tales may be one way in which feeling is evaded.

❖ Alas!

In frustrating the imagined reader's expectations, the poet-narrator foregrounds the poem's didactic aims. While the apostrophe implies the presence of a knowing poet-narrator who can instruct his reader in how to read poems and so come to experience the world differently (as well as respond to those in need appropriately), the closing lines suggest an alternative reading at odds with this apparently didactic aim.

In the second part of the poem, the poet-narrator writes of his encounter with Simon toiling away at a tangled root. Simon is so weak that it seems he might toil forever at the task. But the poet-narrator kindly takes the mattock and severs the root with one stroke:

> "You're overtasked, good Simon Lee,
> Give me your tool" to him I said;
> And at the word right gladly he
> Received my proffer'd aid.
> I struck, and with a single blow
> The tangled root I sever'd,
> At which the poor old man so long
> And vainly had endeavour'd.
> (*LB*, ll. 89–96)

The helpful action produces in Simon an overwhelming response. The poem concludes:

> The tears into his eyes were brought,
> And thanks and praises seemed to run
> So fast out of his heart, I thought
> They never would have done.

—I've heard of hearts unkind, kind deeds
With coldness still returning.
Alas! the gratitude of men
Has oftner left me mourning.
(*LB*, ll. 97–104)

The poet-narrator severs the root, and this act of kindness inspires such gratitude in Simon Lee that the poet-narrator is almost unsure how to respond. In fact, instead of narrating how he responded to Simon's effusive expressions of gratitude, the poet-narrator turns to address the reader again in the concluding four lines of the poem. The poet-narrator pauses (a pause marked by the inclusion of the dash) and then begins to reflect on the incident. The poet-narrator remarks not simply on the fact of Simon's tears but the fact that tears of gratitude surprise him and transmit great emotional force. Simon's gratitude produces a strong emotional response in the poet-narrator, who, it seems, begins to mourn. The poet-narrator writes that he has heard of "hearts unkind" that have failed to express gratitude. He has, in other words, heard of ingratitude. And while ingratitude might cause one to mourn, sometimes gratitude, strangely enough, causes one to mourn more. Why precisely Simon's gratitude should cause the poet-narrator to mourn is left unexplained. The dash separating the memory of the incident from the self-conscious reflection on the incident marks a silence in the text. It may be that Simon's tears expose the poet-narrator's inability to respond in kind. For what sort of response do tears of gratitude call? Or, the poet-narrator may mourn Simon's condition. He may mourn, in other words, the fact that such a simple act, the severing of a root, should produce tears in Simon, pointing to the discrepancy between the excessive nature of Simon's expressions of gratitude and the poet-narrator's accomplishment. After all, the poet-narrator has merely severed a root. There is little to suggest that in the near future Simon will not be faced with a similar dilemma.

Or, the poet-narrator may mourn the unanticipated and potentially negative significance of the action that he has performed. The presence of "seems" in the lines preceding the dash ("And thanks and praises seemed to run / So fast out of his heart") raises as a question whether Simon is in fact grateful for the action performed by the poet-narrator. By severing the root, the poet-narrator has freed Simon from the mechanical repetition of his own actions. Simon "gladly" receives the proffered aid and the poet-narrator saves him from what seems like ceaseless toil. However, what is true in the underworld may be true on earth as well; what one endeavors forever to accomplish may be the one thing that grants one's existence meaning. While Simon's vain endeavor inspires great pathos in readers, it is also one of the few remaining signs that Simon lives. One could contend, in other words, that the root roots Simon's existence and is not simply an obstacle that must be overcome. The poet-narrator's inclusion of "seems" suggests that he recognizes this troubling possibility but only too late. The ease with which the poet-narrator severs the tangled root would confirm what Simon may already have suspected, that he is old and weak and so near death. More dramatically stated, if the root stands for Simon's life thread, then the poet-narrator plays the role of Atropos, one of the three Moirai, or Fates, who cuts the thread of life. Simon welcomes the poet-narrator's aid but then is forced to bear the poet-narrator's symbolic announcement of his death.

This is an unpleasant suggestion, but the assumption that the poet-narrator is reliably responsive to Simon's needs has led to some selective quotation by readers of the poem. Don Bialostosky, for example, in *Making Tales,* which takes "Simon Lee" as a point of departure in its discussion of Wordsworth's narrative experiments, writes, "The warm thanks are evident enough in the way Simon's 'thanks and praises' are described running 'So fast out of his heart.' "[16] Despite Bialostosky's claim that these warm thanks are "evident enough," he elides from the poem Wordsworth's poet-narrator's troubling use of the word "seems," which raises as a question the poet-narrator's confidence to relay to the reader what he thinks Simon's tears signify. In the language of apostrophe present in the first address to the reader, the poet-narrator adopts the role of a benign pedagogue but in the closing lines of the poem the poet-narrator "seems" uncomfortable with his ability to narrate the significance of the incident he describes. It may, however, be the poet-narrator's difficulty narrating the incident that grants it significance.

Wordsworth's poems often remain stubbornly silent at those moments one most wishes for them to "speak," to disclose their meaning and narrow the possible range of interpretations. While the language of Wordsworth's poetry is famously reserved and reticent, John F. Danby's reading of the poem, from *The Simple Wordsworth,* remains the accepted one: " 'Simon Lee' exists as a poem, I think, to carry these lines [the concluding four] to the reader in the precise way it does: with the weight, the depth, the soberness, the measured seriousness and overflowing tenderness that they have. It exists, that is, to ensure the 'comprehensiveness in thinking and feeling' which Wordsworth thought the great poet should possess and the good reader acquire."[17]

Though one does not know definitively why the poet-narrator mourns, one assumes that the incident, together with or perhaps as a result of

Simon's simple expressions, affects the poet-narrator powerfully; the incident has a power to which the poet-narrator wishes to testify. The poem aims to transmit this effect to the reader. The power may be the result of the emotions expressed by Simon or the moral outrage—to the point of disgust—the poet-narrator seems to feel toward a society that allows its members to exist in such a state of poverty.[18] The power may even result from the poet-narrator's belated recognition of the negative significance of the action he has performed. Each of these suggestions, however (and there are others not pursued here), assumes that the poet-narrator experiences strong feelings in response to the incident. The assumption is (and has been) that the poet-narrator, following Danby, exists as a model of "thinking and feeling" that the good reader should emulate.

Yet the conclusion to the poem complicates such a reading. As R. F. Storch notes in "Wordsworth's Experimental Ballads," the final stanza of the poem begins with a stock eighteenth-century idea, that ingratitude causes one to mourn. Wordsworth quickly overturns the conventional idea with the suggestion that it is not ingratitude that the poet-narrator mourns but gratitude. Just as the apostrophe to the reader takes readers by surprise and frustrates expectations, so too does the poet-narrator's turn from convention in the final lines of the poem. He does not simply rehearse the poetic conventions of the past. He surprises readers with his willingness to overturn poetic convention and seems only more sincere as a result. However, as Storch also notes, the use of "Alas!" introduces a bit of playacting at the most emotionally intense moment of the poem and so raises some troubling questions.[19] It may always be those expressions meant to convey sincerity that seem all too calculated and so, at least to some degree, insincere for that very reason. Such is the risk of "Oh" or "Alas!" in any lyric poem, a risk staged repeatedly by romantic poems. If the poet-narrator of "Simon Lee" is willing to play with the reader's emotions at the moment that one assumes is to carry great emotional import, how reliable is this poet-narrator? How affected has he been by his encounter with Simon Lee? Or, how affected is his response to this encounter?

If one questions the reliability of the poet-narrator, then some minor details of Wordsworth's language come into focus. Registering a turn inward by the poet-narrator, the final four lines attempt to punctuate the lesson he has learned. The dash marks some minimal degree of separation between the poet-narrator and the experience he relates, between the incident itself and the poet-narrator's reflection on the incident he records in the poem. Typographically, the dash marks the temporal delay that makes possible the psychological distance Wordsworth elsewhere in his preface to *Lyrical Ballads* links to poetic production. This emotional or psychological distance is intensified by the poet-narrator's diction. While the poet-narrator has heard of unkind hearts, his use of "oftner" in the last line of the poem implies that this is not the first time that he has encountered the gratitude of men and experienced the mourning that these encounters produce in him. The poet-narrator quickly takes Simon's tears as a type of response, one that he has encountered numerous times before. He compares Simon's specific expressions of gratitude with those of others and compares the intensity of the experience of mourning he feels with past experiences of mourning that he has felt. The force of the emotional response seems to come from the poet-narrator's surprise, but "oftner" introduces a calculating mind and an emotional or psychological distance at what one assumes is the most affectively powerful moment of the poem.

In pursuing such a reading, other complicating questions are raised. The final two lines ("Alas! the gratitude of men / Has oftner left me mourning") seem meant to counter the two preceding ones ("I've heard of hearts unkind, kind deeds / With coldness still returning"), arguing that expressions of gratitude might be more powerful than expressions of ingratitude. However, it is also possible to read these last two lines as referring back to Simon's expressions of gratitude. The final lines, then, suggest that despite their effusiveness, Simon's expressions of gratitude leave little impression on the poet-narrator. In this case, "oftner" compares the gratitude of Simon with the gratitude of other men, and the poet-narrator finds Simon's expressions of gratitude lacking. They carry little force. Recognizing in the line the pluralized "men" that the poet-narrator has, evidently, known, may help this alternative reading to emerge: alas, the gratitude of *other* men has oftner left me mourning. Such a reading presents a different poet-narrator than has been identified in the critical literature that surrounds the poem. This is a poet-narrator who is perhaps overly cynical, perhaps even unhealthily immune to others' tears. It is a reading of the poem consistent, however, with Wordsworth's all-too-theatrical inclusion of "Alas!"

In reflecting on the incident, two competing senses of the incident emerge. The incident was both powerfully felt and strangely unaffecting. In this way the poem performs the dilemma of interpretation tranquillity always possibly occasions. Readers view the poet-narrator reflecting on the incident, but in the process the poet-narrator becomes less, not more, in control of his own responses to the incident. The final lines suggest the existence of a conflict within the poet-narrator. The poem presents, in other words, a poet-narrator, like Wordsworth himself in *The Prelude*, who struggles with two "consciousnesses" within himself. It performs and bears witness to the sort of self-alienation Wordsworth describes with "tranquility" in his preface to *Lyrical Ballads,* a self-alienation that Wordsworth's poems very well may work to produce in readers to counteract the craving for the extraordinary incident whose impact is palpably felt but robbed of force for that very reason.

In this didactic poem, the poet-narrator testifies to the power of incidents as tales. He celebrates the power—the lyric potential—of the most unremarkable of events, and readers are invited to make a tale of the incident he relays. But if the final lines of the poem suggest, however obliquely, that the poet-narrator's response to Simon Lee's helplessness is itself problematic, then how are readers to respond to the poem's address, which calls for the reader to respond *to* the incident? When the poet-narrator asks the reader in the apostrophe to make a tale of the incident, is he asking readers to respond as he responded or is he asking readers to respond differently? Is "Simon Lee" meant to instruct readers of sensational ballads how to engage properly with their own emotional experiences, or is "Simon Lee" meant to warn readers not to respond as coldly, in quite so unsympathetic a manner, as the poet-narrator does when he compares Simon's gratitude to the gratitude of others?

Two seemingly incompatible readings are staged in the concluding lines of the poem. On the one hand, the poet-narrator gives voice to Simon's condition, and in testifying to the force of Simon's expressions of gratitude, he also testifies to the force of even the simplest everyday encounter. Here, the lyric triumphs over the sensational ballad. The force of the incident is transmitted to the reader, who is reminded that feeling may not be the same as sensationalism or sentimentalism. A "tale" has been related, but it is not one the reader was expecting, though it may be all the more powerful for that fact. On the other hand, if the final lines are read as referring back to Simon's expressions of gratitude, if they compare Simon's gratitude with the gratitude of other men, then the poet-narrator is testifying not to the force of Simon's simple expressions but to their powerlessness. Simon's expressions of gratitude fail to evoke in the poet-narrator an emotional response, inviting instead only a comparative assessment of Simon's ability to produce affect through the representation of his feelings. Here, the poem would seem to testify to the danger of making tales of everything.

❖ A Blunted Mind

The closing lines of the poem hinge on the reader's ability to determine whether the poet-narrator is conscious of the complexity of what he says with "Alas! the gratitude of men / Has oftner left me mourning." If the reader is to model himself or herself on the poet-narrator, then the fact that the poem's rhetoric stutters around the act it describes reveals a potential problem with the possibility of repetition on which such modeling depends. The opening line of the concluding stanza features two contrasting rhetorical schemes that foreground repetition. The lines, "I've heard of hearts unkind, kind deeds / With coldness still returning" (*LB*, ll. 101–2), are somewhat cumbersome. While many readers stumble on the awkward movement from "hearts unkind" to "kind deeds," the difficult rhythm of the poet-narrator's language may give voice to his own surprise. Like Simon, the poet-narrator has been robbed of the ability to speak fluidly and without effort. But the intrusion of rhetoric here at the end of the poem is remarkable, and Wordsworth's specific use of paronomasia and polyptoton suggests another reading. In moving from paronomasia to polyptoton, Wordsworth moves from a scheme where the similar sounds (and appearances) of words are at play ("heard" and "hearts"), to one, polyptoton, in which the same root word is repeated but in a variant form ("unkind" and "kind"). The progression from (weak) paronomasia—including a visual echo—to polyptoton suggests a focus on the root word, which is all too conspicuous given the poet-narrator's ability to sever roots with one blow. In moving from "unkind" to "kind," the poet-narrator, it seems, is looking to focus attention on the root, a root ("kind") that is also central to the apostrophe that divides the poem: "What more I have to say is short, / I hope you'll *kindly* take it" (*LB*, ll. 77–78). If the poem leaves readers unsure whether to repeat the poet-narrator's gestures and sentiments, it is hardly a coincidence that the conclusion of the poem should focus attention on the question of repetition through the employment of two rhetorical schemes, especially if the second (polyptoton) consists of circling, in this case, somewhat cumbersomely, around a root. The rhetoric of the poem returns readers to the action of the poem, the severing of the root, which is repeated linguistically by the comma that divides "unkind" from "kind." The poet-narrator's language registers, though without his seemingly becoming conscious of it, some awareness of the strangeness of his action. Here may be one clue that Wordsworth and the poet-narrator should not be collapsed too quickly into one and the same figure. The language of the poet-narrator registers a resistance to what it is he says. That this resistance is carried forward to the reader, that it becomes legible for the reader even though it remains outside of (or beyond) the consciousness of the poet-narrator testifies to the difficulty of knowing for sure whether readers should strive to emulate the poet-narrator or abstract a poet's promise behind that of the poet-narrator.

If, as Wordsworth suggests in his preface to *Lyrical Ballads,* the craving for extraordinary incidents produces a blunted mind, then what are readers to make of this incident with which Simon Lee is concerned? For Sigmund Freud, an incident must be inscribed within a narrative for psychological health to be maintained or, in the face of traumatic events, restored. And yet, at the same time, Freud acknowledges—in a text such as *Beyond the Pleasure Principle*—that to construct a narrative is always possibly a way *not* to encounter various incidents, a way to evade the incidents with which one no longer wishes to struggle.[20] "Simon Lee" is at best ambiguous about the desire to make incidents into tales, to make a tale of everything; such a desire becomes, in the light of the poem's closing lines and the questions they raise about the ability of the poet-narrator to respond to Simon's tears, a potential symptom of the blunted mind Wordsworth diagnoses in his preface. The result of making tales of everything may be the cold deafness the poet-narrator exhibits.

The poet-narrator's language undermines (or at least questions) the lesson the encounter is meant to pass on to the reader. It simplifies the poem too much to replace the sympathetic poet-narrator (one perhaps modeled on Wordsworth himself and one to whom readers of the poem have responded) with a more coldhearted poet-narrator. However, the poem's final lines point to (and index) the poet-narrator's resistance to the encounter with Simon Lee even as he relays it to the reader as one capable of producing great affect. Denial of the poet-narrator's resistance to the force of the encounter he records risks missing the way the poet-narrator opposes his own reading (or understanding) of the encounter. Language continues to act even when the consciousness of the poet-narrator holds short. The inclusion of "Alas!"—I argue—acknowledges the force of a transmission not necessarily available to consciousness but one legible nonetheless; the reperformance of the central event of the poem on the level of the signifier marks not only the intensity of the encounter but also the poet-narrator's potential self-defense from it. What is passed on to the reader is not only the force of the encounter with Simon Lee but also the degree to which he evades this force; the language of the poem passes on what the poet-narrator does not wish to describe: his own resistance to the incident in which Simon Lee is concerned. The language used to describe an experience may always tell others more than one wishes them to know.

Readers are left stranded somewhere between taking the poet-narrator as an example (to the extent that he exhibits the kind of emotional response Wordsworth is looking to produce in readers of his poems) or as a counterexample (to the extent that he suffers from an inability to hear

Simon's gratitude or witness his suffering). The poet-narrator, in addressing his imagined reader, invites readers to make a tale of the incident, but it is unclear whether making a tale of the incident results in humanitarian aid or a repetition of the poet-narrator's deafness to Simon's expression of gratitude, a deafness marked by his comparison of Simon's gratitude with the gratitude of others.

Read in this light, and given Wordsworth's description of the blunted modern mind, the poet-narrator serves as a reminder that the craving for incidents (however ordinary or extraordinary) may lead not to appropriate action but to paralysis, deafness, coldness: a failure to see, a failure to witness the suffering of another. Not to hear the warning Wordsworth subtly introduces in the final lines by opening the possibility that the poet-narrator is more interested in how Simon's gratitude compares with the gratitude of others is to miss the possibility that the making of tales risks the paralysis that Wordsworth's poetic project is itself to counteract. It is difficult to know, in other words, whether the poet-narrator (and the encounter he describes in "Simon Lee") serves as a means to counter the dilemma Wordsworth identifies in his preface or whether the poet-narrator suffers from the demands of modernity in characterizing Simon's expressions as somehow lacking in force. "Simon Lee" places readers in an uncomfortable double bind: if one does not make a tale of this incident, one is in danger of turning away from the means to counter the blunted mind Wordsworth describes; and yet, in making a tale of the incident, one risks repeating the poet-narrator's failure to respond adequately to Simon's need. One risks repeating the poet-narrator's turn from Simon. In other words, in making a tale of the incident, one is also in danger of satisfying the craving for extraordinary incidents symptomatic of what Wordsworth calls the blunted mind.

As a result, the poem complicates Enlightenment ideals of civic responsibility that are governed by the assumption that appropriate political or ethical action follows from an increase in knowledge. This may also be true of the increase in feeling. In perfecting the transmission of knowledge and in eliminating the possibility of ignorance, one seems to eliminate inappropriate political and ethical actions. In *Lyrical Ballads,* Wordsworth worries that the opposite is true: the proper political and ethical response is not guaranteed by the exponential increase in information, intelligence, or emotion. As more and more information of historical events is transmitted with greater and greater speed, the mind becomes less (not more) able to process it. "Simon Lee" suggests that such may also be true of information about the suffering of others and the most immediate emotional responses available.

In a poem like "Simon Lee," Wordsworth acknowledges that sympathy, sympathetic identification, while necessary to the project of the humanitarian protest poem and even the larger poetic project of *Lyrical Ballads,* is always possibly a form of resistance, a symptom of the blunted mind he diagnoses in the preface and no guarantee of right-minded humanitarian action. In presenting readers of the poem with a poet-narrator who seems both engaged by and disengaged from the tale of suffering he tells, Wordsworth poses a question that is difficult to acknowledge, let alone answer: what if the failure of sympathy (and humanitarian action) results not from the failure of images or texts to inspire powerful feeling but from the success of images and texts to inspire powerful feelings and so satisfy a craving for extraordinary incidents that leads to apathy and emotional detachment? As images of suffering come to dominate the news media, this may be just the sort of question most in need of an answer. But the strong need for an answer to this question may go a long way toward helping one understand why the final lines of "Simon Lee" have not occasioned the disagreement for which they call. For better or worse, one often knows enough not to acknowledge the questions one does not know enough to answer.

5

Lyric Yawns: Keats

Although he makes no large gestures nor loud cries
He willingly would make rubbish of the earth
And with a yawn swallow the world.
—Charles Baudelaire

A discouraging gulf yawns between the experience of a poem and professional explanations of the importance of this art.
—Robert von Hallberg

Early chapters of *The Poetics of Unremembered Acts* focused on Locke's and Rousseau's pedagogical treatises and specifically on their attempts to teach children how to read. While significant differences in method exist between the two, both define reading as ideally a process of decoding. The message conveyed by the text is most important. And yet the attempt to secure such a definition of reading results in texts, like Rousseau's *Émile,* that cannot easily be decoded. By foregrounding figures of address, specifically figures of address to readers, Gray's "Elegy" and Wordsworth's "Simon Lee" work to overcome the contingencies of meaning that interrupt Locke's and Rousseau's pedagogy. But by troping address, as we have seen, Gray and Wordsworth inherit and so pass along the unreadability Locke and Rousseau stumble on. The accident of reading is what (reading) poetry teaches.

Poetry tropes the communicative circuit Locke and Rousseau work to secure for proper instruction in reading. Following John Stuart Mill, William Butler Yeats offers a distinction between rhetoric and poetry: "We make out of the quarrel with others, rhetoric; but of the quarrel with ourselves poetry."[1] Unlike the reader of persuasive rhetoric, the reader of poetry is self-consciously excluded, ignored, by the poet; one takes oneself as addressed only to the extent to which one transforms poetry into rhetoric (a text, for instance, to be deciphered). Instead of articulating a determinable difference between rhetoric and poetry, the poems that I read in *The Poetics of Unremembered Acts* examine the degree to which rhetorical figures (for example, apostrophe and prosopopoeia) condition the possibility of reading. My readings of Gray and Wordsworth have emphasized the degree to which poetic texts pass along not information but the inability to guarantee in advance that signs lead to particular meanings, that phenomenal perception leads to cognition. Cognition is always possibly contingent, the result of a chance entanglement; and reading describes not only a process of understanding but also, and perhaps more importantly, a way of passing along what one does not (yet) understand. As Jacques Rancière suggests in *The Names of History: On the Poetics of Knowledge,* "to know something is not to have to think about it."[2] In other words, one says that one *understands* something when one no longer wishes to think about it.

More than most literary genres, the lyric generates its force through figures of address, which is why the trope of "voice" is so often employed in discussions of lyric. One is halted, arrested, by one's sense of the poem's unique "voice." In reading, that is, one grants the lyric poem a speaking face. And as a result the reading of lyric poems is often figured as listening to or, as John Stuart Mill famously argued by drawing a distinction between poetry and eloquence, overhearing a poet. In this closing chapter, I linger on a particular (and peculiar) image from John Keats's "Isabella or the Pot of Basil," that of a "yawning tomb." In a key stanza from the poem, the poet turns from the narrative to address his reader directly: "Why linger at the yawning tomb so long? / O for the gentleness of old Romance, / The simple plaining of a minstrel's song! / Fair reader, at the old tale take a glance."[3] Within the narrative, Isabella has perhaps lingered for too long at her dead lover's yawning tomb, but including this reference to the yawning tomb in a stanza in which the reader is encouraged to turn away from the poem, Keats offers the yawning tomb as a figure for the poem over which the reader has, in turn, been lingering. With *Isabella,* in other words, Keats offers as an alternative figure for the lyric not the speaking face but the yawning mouth. Instead of the lyric voice, that is, I trace in this chapter the lyric yawn.

Like the figures of address in Thomas Gray's "Elegy" and William Wordsworth's "Simon Lee," the yawn in Keats's poem refuses easy passage between sign and signification, word and idea, poem and meaning, and instead stages an interruption of cognition. Such an interruption, as Wordsworth's "Simon Lee" implies, may be what makes possible a response conditioned neither by the fiction of direct address nor the assurance that address is purely fictional. The image of the yawning tomb returns in the closing lines of the poem and marks poetry's ability to bear witness to suffering in the absence of full cognition or understanding. In the conclusion to "Isabella," where Keats describes most explicitly the manner in which Isabella's story of suffering is passed around the country, the story is not passed from mouth to ear (as a metonym for understanding) but from mouth to mouth. Like Locke's pupils who cannot know they have learned to read and yet read nonetheless, the transmitters of Isabella's tale, I suggest, do not (and cannot?) know what they transmit. The figure of the poem as a yawn (a contagious yawn) passed from mouth to mouth is offered by Keats as one way to describe how the romantic poem passes on an encounter unavailable to cognition.

❖ The Lure of Romance

In early poems like *Endymion,* Keats demonstrates his interest in romance, long maligned for its celebration of aesthetic illusion over complex, real-world engagement. By 1818, however, and following the painful reception of *Endymion,* Keats famously begins to question his own fascination with romance. As he writes in "On sitting down to read King Lear once Again": "O golden tongued Romance with serene Lute! . . . Shut up thine olden volume and be mute. / Adieu!" (*CP,* p. 164, ll. 1, 4). And yet, Keats does not reject romance quite so definitively as these lines suggest; many of his later poems, such as those published in his 1820 volume *Lamia, Isabella, The Eve of St. Agnes, and Other Poems,* stage a conflict between the ability of art to make "all disagreeables evaporate"[4] and the ability of art to tread "the agonies, the strife / Of human hearts" (*CP,* p. 40, ll. 124–25). This conflict leads Jack Stillinger in his readings of Keats's late romances, especially "Isabella or the Pot of Basil," to identify what he calls an antiromantic strain in Keats.[5] Responding to but also carrying forward Stillinger's reading of the poem, Tilottama Rajan suggests in particular of "Isabella" that it "represents its own discourse as alternately romantic and anti-romantic, because it is uncertain whether to value or devalue illusion."[6] In this way, the critical reception of "Isabella" circles around concepts that have become key to the reception of late Keats more generally. "Isabella," not unlike "Ode to a Nightingale," attempts to work through two competing understandings of the function of art. Does art offer respite from the world or bring one closer to it?[7]

In her reading of the poem, Susan Wolfson focuses on the ways Keats interrupts the narrative that he tells through a series of digressions that "refashion the genre of tale-telling into a more comprehensive mode of discourse."[8] If for Stillinger and Rajan, Keats is unsure of his commitment to romance, for Wolfson the poem exposes the conventions of romance to make possible some critical reflection on the genre: "the play of digressions in "Isabella" ultimately serves its purpose by becoming assimilated to an enlarged critical awareness, yielding a narrative in which the teller and the tale share the communication of a mutual 'burthen,' fully informed by the burdens of its theme."[9] The end goal of the digressions that punctuate "Isabella" is not confusion—which might be caused by an "endlessly" digressive text—but an enlarged critical awareness of the conventions and attitudes toward pleasure that the genre traditionally promotes. The poem's digressions, in other words, are principally pedagogical; they enable if not a demystified then at least a less mystified critical reading practice. Like "Simon Lee," which interrupts its balladlike first half to call for reflection on its sentimentalism, "Isabella" aims to alter the conventions of reading determined by romance and so replace a desire for romance with critical reflection.

Keats introduces a series of digressions in "Isabella," argues Wolfson, to make the art of storytelling—linked as it is to the genre of romance—all the more legible. The digressions make it more difficult to forget that one is reading a romance. If one is seduced by the story of "Isabella" and finds oneself inhabiting the imaginary world of romance, one does so only to the degree to which one ignores the poem's series of digressions foregrounding the fact that a tale is being told with persuasive gains in mind. Just at those moments when the reader might forget that he or she is reading, the poet-narrator digresses, interrupting the reader's "fall" into the story. In this way, the poem calls attention to itself, recursively points back to itself, and expresses a high degree of self-consciousness.

While Wolfson includes as examples of digression the poet-narrator's invocations to "Melancholy," "Music," and "Echo," only in the concluding pages of her own reading does she link "digression" with the rhetorical figure of apostrophe. In quoting "O Melancholy, turn thine eyes away!" Wolfson writes, "Indeed this apostrophe is a version of 'digression,' as the etymology—*apostrephein,* 'to turn away'—may remind us."[10] While an apostrophe need not always or necessarily constitute a digression—as is the case in "Ode to the West Wind," where an apostrophe constitutes the poem as a whole and so is not, at least not in any simple sense, digressive—the etymology of apostrophe aligns the apostrophe with digression. The apostrophes within "Isabella"—like the address to Melancholy—do not forward the plot but instead interrupt its momentum; the reader is invited to turn away from the story.

"Isabella" is a "digressive" text in part because Keats's poet-narrator is fascinated by figures of address.[11] Many of the poem's "digressions," as Wolfson acknowledges in closing, are in fact apostrophes, which suggests that the poem is preoccupied with questions of address. To whom is this poem addressed? How are readers to respond to it? How is it to be read?[12] In focusing on "digressions" and not apostrophes, Wolfson does not pursue directly the question of address in "Isabella." For Wolfson, one of the poem's principal aims is the production of an enlarged critical awareness. However, like Wordsworth's "Simon Lee," in raising so persistently questions of address, and even including a prominent direct address to an imagined or ideal reader, the poem reflects on and so allegorizes the very effort to achieve critical awareness. In effect, through its repeated apostrophes, the poem stages its own readability as a theme, one that is disturbingly linked to the desire of Isabella, the poem's protagonist, to bring her dead lover back to life.

❖ "Wormy Circumstance"

Keats famously opposed publishing "Isabella" and reportedly described the poem to a friend as "mawkish."[13] As he explained in a letter to Richard Woodhouse from the same period, "I will give you a few reasons why I shall persist in not publishing The Pot of Basil—it is too smokeable. . . . There is too much inexperience of [life], and simplicity of knowledge in it."[14] And indeed, though Charles Lamb, in his review of the volume, described it as "the finest thing in the volume,"[15] most readers, and many literary critics, have responded to the poem as Keats himself did, finding it sentimental, "mawkish," "smokable."[16]

Keats was inspired to write the poem after hearing a lecture by William Hazlitt in February 1818 in which Hazlitt suggested that a series of poems adapted from Boccaccio might sell well. Borrowing much from Boccaccio's *Decameron,* Keats revises the poem's plot slightly.[17] Isabella, the poem's heroine, and Lorenzo, "a young palmer" (*CP,* p. 184, l. 2) and employee of Isabella's brothers, fall in love, but Isabella's brothers, who are described by Kurt Heinzelman as "self-interested exploiters of the labor of others," would prefer "to coax her by degrees / To some high noble and his olive trees."[18] They would, that is, prefer to marry her off to a noble and thereby increase their own wealth.[19] The brothers invite Lorenzo to go hunting with them, and in the forest they murder and bury him. Upon returning home, the brothers explain to Isabella that Lorenzo took ship for foreign lands. Isabella is saddened by Lorenzo's disappearance but suspects nothing until one night Lorenzo's ghost visits her in her bedroom, tells her the story of his murder, and provides her with the location of his body. Around this point, the poem moves from the sentimental to the grotesque, as Isabella, with the help of her nurse, rides into the forest to recover the body of Lorenzo. Isabella digs up the body of her beloved only just enough to sever the head, which she takes home and plants in a basil pot and waters with her tears. When her brothers discover Lorenzo's head in the basil pot, they steal the pot from Isabella, who soon dies. The poem concludes, "And so she pined, and so she died forlorn, / Imploring for her basil to the last. / No heart was there in Florence but did mourn / In pity of her love, so overcast. / And a sad ditty of this story born / From mouth to mouth through all the country pass'd" (*CP*, p. 198, ll. 497–502).

Keats did, of course, publish the poem but includes within the poem a number of apostrophes that signal the poet-narrator's discomfort (or seeming discomfort) with the tale he is telling. Early in the poem, the poet-narrator turns from the tale to apostrophize the original author of the tale Keats reads in translation: "O eloquent and famed Boccaccio! / Of thee we now should ask forgiving boon, / . . . Grant thou a pardon here, and then the tale / Shall move on soberly, as it is meet" (*CP*, p. 188, ll. 145–46, 153–54). The poet-narrator pauses to ask forgiveness for the poem he is in the midst of composing. And he promises to move on more "soberly."[20] But with the next apostrophe, an address this time to his reader, the poet-narrator begins, "Ah! Wherefore all this wormy circumstance?" (*CP*, p. 195, l. 385), thus implying that the attempt to move on more soberly has failed. He must pause the story yet again, and this time he urges the reader to turn back to Boccaccio's original for those parts of the story that he cannot bear: "Fair reader, at the old tale take a glance, / For here, in truth, it doth not well belong / To speak" (*CP*, p. 195, ll. 389–91). But the poet-narrator, of course, continues; one senses that either the power of a nonsober poem, one filled with "wormy circumstance," is too much for the poet to resist or that he is pretending to have been overcome by the "wormy circumstance" that actually fascinates him.

Indeed, if one follows the poet-narrator's suggestion and "at the old tale take[s] a glance," one finds that Keats's poet-narrator has in fact increased the "wormy circumstance" from which he claims to recoil. In stanza 50, which follows the apostrophe to the reader and the complaint over "wormy circumstance," the poet-narrator describes Isabella severing the head of her beloved:

> With duller steel than the Persean sword
> They cut away no formless monster's head,
> But one, whose gentleness did well accord
> With death, as life. The ancient harps have said,
> Love never dies, but lives, immortal Lord:
> If Love impersonate was ever dead,

> Pale Isabella kiss'd it, and low moan'd.
> 'Twas love; cold,—dead indeed, but not dethroned.
> (*CP,* p. 195, ll. 393–400)

The poet-narrator increases the "wormy circumstance" in part by refusing to offer any motivation for Isabella's severing the head of her beloved. Boccaccio, for instance, provides a rationale. The body is too heavy for Isabella to carry home; she takes of Lorenzo only what she can carry.[21] Keats's poet-narrator provides no reason for the decapitation, giving the reader the sense that Isabella is simply drawn to possess the head, a sense that is increased by the order of events at the tomb. Isabella severs the head of her beloved and *then* kisses it. Presumably Isabella might have kissed the head of her beloved before removing it.

❖ Lyric Address

Many readings of "Isabella," like those discussed in the previous sections, focus on the poem's "wormy circumstance" as a way of teasing out Keats's response to the aestheticized world of romance; instead, I focus on Keats's many figures of address, his apostrophes (including those to Boccaccio and to Melancholy), for the stanza in which Keats's poet-narrator struggles with "wormy circumstance" also prominently features an apostrophe to the reader. Keats aligns the desire for "wormy circumstance" and the figurative power of the lyric (and so of lyric reading) to make the dead speak.

The modern conception of the lyric still owes much to John Stuart Mill. In defining poetry, Mill draws a contrast between poetry and eloquence: "Poetry and eloquence are both alike the expression or utterance of feeling. But if we may be excused the antithesis, we should say that eloquence is *heard,* poetry is *overheard.* Eloquence supposes an audience; the peculiarity of poetry appears to us to lie in the poet's utter unconsciousness of a listener."[22] For his definition, Mill draws on romantic poets, such as Keats, who often turn away from their readers to address absent subjects or inanimate objects (like Boccaccio in the lines quoted earlier or, perhaps more famously, a Grecian urn). In reading "Ode on a Grecian Urn," one catches the poet with his back turned away from his human audience. In reading, one "overhears" the conversation between poet and inanimate object. In *Anatomy of Criticism,* Northrop Frye defines the lyric (more specifically) along similar lines: "The lyric poet normally pretends to be talking to himself or to someone else: a spirit of nature, a Muse, a personal friend, a lover, a god, a personified abstraction, or a natural object. . . . The poet, so to speak, turns his back on his listeners."[23] Frye's definition helps make clear the ways apostrophe (from the Greek *apo,* away, and *strephein,* to turn) and prosopopoeia (from the Greek *prosopon,* mask, and *poiein,* to make) define the lyric. The poet turns his back on his audience and grants a speaking face to an absent subject or inanimate object. These figures, I think, help explain the emotional impact of the lyric. The poet's lack of interest in a present, human audience only increases the perceived sincerity of the poet. Who would question the sincerity of the poet-speaker's expression in "Ode on a Grecian Urn," for who would lie to an inanimate object? The expressive nature of romantic poems is often the effect of a particular set of rhetorical figures.

In his influential chapter titled "Apostrophe" from *The Pursuit of Signs,* Jonathan Culler notes how embarrassing apostrophes can seem; it is often easier to ignore them than to take them seriously, which, Culler argues, is precisely what has happened to apostrophes. They have been ignored. Culler, however, links apostrophe with the power of lyric poetry.[24] The apostrophe, as a performative gesture, constitutes encounters with the world as relationships between subjects. The world is animated though the power of poetic voice: "O wild West Wind, though breath of Autumn's being";[25] "Thou still unravish'd bride of quietness" (*CP,* p. 282, l. 1). In addressing the west wind or a Grecian urn, poets grant these entities the capability of speech. As was previously explored in the reading of Gray's "Elegy Written in a Country Churchyard," the address accomplishes that for which the poets have often been understood to strive. The object becomes a sentient subject through the power of the lyric address; and, as a result, a harmony between subjects is made possible. In addressing a Grecian urn, for instance, Keats grants the inanimate object a face through the power of address. The address to the urn turns the inanimate object into a subject (an interlocutor, one with a face, a voice, and the capability of responding to the poet). And the poem literalizes the impact of address (the transformation of an inanimate object into a subject) when in the closing lines the urn speaks: "Beauty is truth, truth Beauty" (*CP,* p. 283, l. 49).

Keats's frequent use of apostrophe in "Isabella" demonstrates his interest in the very figures of address that define the lyric, figures that are also central to the lyric structure of reading. While apostrophe can and frequently does function as a digression, in thinking of apostrophes as digressions a critic such as Wolfson disguises the degree to which apostrophe, as a trope of address, is foundational to the lyric. As J. Mark Smith, for instance, has suggested, "where there is lyric there is apostrophe."[26] The opposite may be true as well: where there is apostrophe there is lyric.[27] What is most interesting about the lyric, in other words, is not the poet's seeming lack of interest in a human audience but his willingness to transform the object into a subject. The lyric does not simply exclude its listener; in its most extreme examples, the poet turns his back on his listener and addresses an inanimate object, thereby animating it through the power of address. Through figures like apostrophe and prosopopoeia, the inanimate is granted a face and a voice. This may seem a strange thing that poets do, animating the inanimate, giving life—a face and a voice—to the dead. Following Culler, one might even be a bit embarrassed by this strange thing the poets do. But if the lyric poet animates the inanimate through various figures of address, then the critics I have quoted in this chapter rely on the same set of figures. In identifying as a listener the one who "overhears" the poem, Mill transforms the mute word into living speech; he grants to the mute text (an inanimate object) a voice. One may snicker at the poet, like Keats, who talks to Boccaccio (who is dead) or a Grecian urn (an object), but before one does, one should acknowledge that what look like extreme examples of the lyric poet animating an inanimate object turn out to describe what one does—perhaps unavoidably—when one "reads." One posits oneself as the text's addressee and thereby transforms the object of the poem into an interlocutor, an interlocutor with a face and a voice, one with whom one may have a conversation.

The figures one commonly employs when one reads are the same ones that lyric poets employ, the same figures that define the poem as poem. We read as poets; the often-mourned resistance to poetry prominent today is also, then, a resistance to the rhetorical and tropological dimension *of* reading. Keats's preoccupation with apostrophe and his inclusion of an apostrophe to the reader in "Isabella" acknowledges the ways figures of address that define the lyric condition the activity of reading. The lyric poem may be potentially alienating not simply because it excludes one (turns its "back" on one) but because it shows one something about how one reads, about the figures one employs as one reads. Like the lyric poets, we grant the inanimate, the nonliving, the dead (the mute, written word) a face, a voice, a new life. It may be that one sometimes finds lyric poems boring or uninteresting not because they are too distant but because they show one something about how one reads that one would rather forget. Reading—in the light of lyric address—can come to seem a somewhat ghoulish exercise.

Paul de Man explores the sinister quality of apostrophe and prosopopoeia. In giving voice to the inanimate, the absent, or the dead, he writes, "the symmetrical structure of the trope implies, by the same token, that the living are struck dumb, frozen in their own death."[28] That which figures the possibility of a relationship between subject and object, a relationship that is posited by granting the object a voice, also always necessarily risks the reverse—the subject becomes an object. This symmetrical structure is explored by Debra Fried with respect to the rhetoric of epitaphs: "the very act of reading an epitaph is almost like a curse, an unfailing omen of the reader's own death."[29] To be dead, suggests Fried, is to be read, just as, unfortunately, to read is (soon) to be dead. In her 2008 book *Persons and Things,* Barbara Johnson discusses the frequency with which modern advertisers employ prosopopoeia. As she explains, "We are supposed not to notice how absurd it is to be addressed by the Maalox Max bottle, or Mr. Clean, or Mrs. Butterworth, or the Quaker Oats man, or Aunt Jemima, or the Elidel man, or the Aflac duck."[30] In these advertisements, the objects sell themselves so that consumers feel uninfluenced by human manipulation. For Johnson, this is the darker side of late capitalism. Objects are given life so that consumers will not think about how they are being manipulated. In this way, late capitalism's goal is the production of consumers who behave more like objects, for objects are more easily manipulated. The object is given a voice so that consumers will not use theirs.

The plot of Keats's "Isabella" elaborates the risk of destruction that accompanies efforts to reanimate the dead. The heroine of the poem returns home from the grave of her beloved with his severed head, which she plants in a basil pot; but she is soon trapped in a terrible melancholia. After looking upon the face of her beloved, and after severing the head of her beloved with a knife duller than Perseus's sword, Isabella undergoes a figurative death long before her literal one. Like those who look upon Medusa, Isabella, figuratively, is turned to stone. The poem, in other words, tells the story of a woman robbed of her ability to speak her grief, a woman struck dumb and driven mad by her attempt to animate her dead beloved. The attempted reanimation results in Isabella's deanimation. While tropes of address make communion between living and dead possible, they also force on readers recognition of the fact that what one calls "life" may be the result of figure, especially if the "dead" can so quickly be returned to the living. One's death is inscribed within the effort to read, since in reading one grants the mute word a voice, the dead new life. Isabella's melancholia leads to her demise, and, in this way, "Isabella" anticipates and outlines the risks that may always accompany one's attempts to animate the inanimate and speak with the dead. Such risk may always accompany what Stephen Greenblatt, in other words, calls reading.

❖ Lingering with the Dead

In recent years, debates over ethical and political questions have persistently been raised through attention to mourning and melancholy. Giorgio Agamben provocatively describes melancholy as a disguised attempt at mastery. Melancholy does not respond to loss but, as a "pre-emptive strike," protects the ego *from* loss. "Melancholy," writes Agamben, "offers the paradox of an intention to mourn that precedes and anticipates the loss of the object." The melancholiac is caught up in a "desperate attempt to protect itself from the loss of the object and to adhere to it at least in its absence."[31] Unlike mourning—which might in this context be understood as an attempt to survive loss—melancholy, for Agamben, anticipates loss and thereby prevents the ego from experiencing loss. The object is mastered in advance as lost. And so, the end goal of melancholy is the mastery of loss itself, since loss is no longer loss but a means by which the ego appropriates what cannot otherwise be appropriated. What can be lost is by definition not mastered, and so "loss" names the impossibility of the ego's absolute mastery over objects (as well as itself). If loss is a means to mastery, then loss is no longer loss, at least not in any familiar sense of the term. Unresolved mourning, or melancholy, is a means by which the ego protects itself from objects. Given such an understanding of melancholy, one might argue that Isabella removes the head of Lorenzo and buries it in the basil pot to protect herself from the loss of Lorenzo. He is not lost. Her melancholy is a sign of her unwillingness to experience loss and so a sign of her unwillingness to mourn.

Freud, however, suggests that an inability to mourn successfully may communicate an unwillingness to forget the lost object.[32] Melancholy may, in other words, signal a resistance to mourning and the necessary distance from the love object successful mourning requires. Melancholy marks an ethical imperative not to substitute for or forget the love object. It signals a commitment to the other as lost and so a commitment to loss. In contrast to Agamben's sense of melancholy as a means to preempt loss, the impossibility of mourning takes on ethical importance, for the one suffering retains his or her fidelity to the love object as other and, in some way, unforgettable. Slavoj Žižek, writing in 2000, somewhat dismissively identifies this critical position as the "predominant opinion": "Mourning is a kind of betrayal, the second killing of the (lost) object, while the melancholic subject remains faithful to the lost object, refusing to renounce his or her attachment to it."[33]

An example of the kind of work Žižek may be singling out—and identifying as the predominant opinion—is R. Clifton Spargo's 2004 *The Ethics of Mourning: Grief and Responsibility in Elegiac Literature,* which draws heavily on the work of Jacques Derrida and Emmanuel Levinas. Spargo focuses on melancholy as the persistent sign of dedication to the time and realm of the other: "unresolved mourning" is "a dissenting act, a sign of an irremissible ethical meaning."[34] If for Agamben, unresolved mourning is understood as a means to appropriate a lost object in the only way that it can be appropriated, as already lost; if, in other words, unresolved mourning is a means to protect oneself from loss itself, for Spargo unresolved mourning introduces ethical questions "insofar as it supposes an imaginative protection of the other who has already been lost."[35] Spargo figures what he calls the "ethical" imagination as determined precisely by a mission of protecting the dead from history. On the one hand, unresolved mourning is the least ethical response to the other as lost because it protects the ego from the other, from the other as lost, and so from loss itself. On the other hand, unresolved mourning is the most ethical response to the other because it refuses to consign the other to the past, it protects the other—however impossible this attempt to protect the other may turn out to be—*from* the past, from a past that always threatens to sanitize the very otherness of the other and open the lost other to substitution.

As a romantic narrative poem that explores the enigma of melancholy, Keats's "Isabella" also explores some of the ethical issues that have in more recent years been linked to mourning and melancholy.[36] As an allegory of reading, "Isabella" questions whether—and to what extent—reading, as an attempt to speak with the dead, refuses and so masters loss or, again, as an attempt to speak with the dead, bears witness, as an ethical obligation, to the dead, thereby refusing to allow the dead to slip into historical oblivion. Does refusing historical oblivion require reanimating the dead? And if so, what of the risks that "Isabella," "Elegy Written in a Country Churchyard," and "Simon Lee" so carefully outline? How, in other words, does the understanding of reading as deciphering (as "listening" to the absent and dead) risk the very idea of education Locke and Rousseau promote?

❖ Yawning Tombs

"Isabella," like the basil pot, resists the reanimating forces brought to bear on it.[37] In resisting these efforts, however, the poem also posits the impossibility of resisting as a means to transmit, however accidentally, the story of loss. I would like to turn again to the forty-ninth stanza of the poem, to the poet's apostrophe to the reader, and in particular to the line, "Why linger at the yawning tomb so long?" One might always read "yawning" as a synonym for "wide" or "gaping," which is consistent with the etymology of "yawn," but given our short history of the lyric and the lyric's preoccupation with granting faces and voices to the inanimate, the nonliving, Keats's decision to describe the tomb as "yawning" also introduces the yawn as a kind of speech act. The inanimate tomb yawns. This alternate meaning is a confusion that the word's etymology does not clear up; "yawn," from Old English, is also related to the Greek *khainein,* to gape. From the start, it seems the word could refer either to a landscape or to a human face. And as a result it is impossible to know whether "yawning" was first used to refer to the human face and transposed onto the landscape, thus anthropomorphizing the landscape, or the reverse—whether the word was used to refer to the landscape and then transposed onto the human, thus naturalizing the human face. In the passage from Keats, to read "yawning" as a synonym for "wide" or "deep" posits the tomb as a chasm; the reader lingers at the edge. But the reader might also focus on "yawning" as a participial adjective. In this way, "yawning" is understood as an action performed by the tomb, which is thereby granted a yawning face. To read "yawning" as a participial adjective is to find lurking in the word itself another figure—another form—of address.

The poem's next lines make it clear that this question ("Why linger at the yawning tomb so long?") is addressed not only to the poet himself, or Isabella, but also to the reader: "O for the gentleness of old Romance, / The simple planning of a minstrel's song! / Fair reader, at the old tale take a glance" (*CP,* p. 195, ll. 387–89). As a result, the poet-narrator turns the yawning tomb—at first a literal enough description of the scene—into a figure for the poem itself. Why linger before this "yawning tomb" of a poem, fair reader, when one might instead take a glance at an "old tale"? Two speeds of reading are opposed (reading as lingering versus reading as taking a glance) as well as two textual models (the yawning tomb versus the old tale).

In the light of the discussion of figures of address that grant a face and a voice to the inanimate object, Keats's figure here begins to feel like a comment on our whole tradition of reading lyric poems. Unlike the Grecian urn, in other words, which speaks, this tomb yawns. A yawning tomb is not simply a threatening chasm but also an open mouth, half-vulnerable, caught midseizure. The tomb, often associated with the end of life, with death, is granted life; it is granted a face. It yawns.[38] But the tomb (as poem) is not granted a voice. In fact, one might say that the tomb is robbed of its voice, for it is difficult to speak midyawn. And in this way, the yawn offers a chance to rethink the familiar figures that govern one's "reading" of poems. It is one thing to want the dead to speak. It is quite another to want them to yawn. In "Isabella," Keats offers in place of lyric voice an open mouth, a yawn.

Keats demonstrates some awareness of the poem's potential to make us yawn when he includes emotive interjections at the beginnings of lines before and after "the yawning tomb":

> *Ah!* Wherefore all this wormy circumstance?
> Why linger at the yawning tomb so long?
> *O* for the gentleness of old Romance,
> The simple planning of a minstrel's song!
> Fair reader, at the old tale take a glance.
> (*CP*, p. 195, ll. 385–89, my emphasis)

To read these lines is to shape the open mouth the poem describes. One finds oneself repeating—even before the apostrophe to the reader is made explicit a few lines later—the figure that has come to stand for the poem. One finds oneself repeating the form of an address even before one understands one has been addressed—by a yawning tomb, a life beyond the end of life. A private utterance (like "Ah!," which Mill might take as evidence of the emotional sincerity of the poet) also performs a repetition, as one forms with one's own mouth the yawn of the tomb.

Keats returns however subtly to this figure of the yawn in the closing lines of the poem as the story of Isabella is passed through the country, thus linking the yawn to a mode of storytelling. The concluding stanza of the poem tells us that "a sad ditty of this story born / From mouth to mouth through all the country pass'd" (*CP*, p. 198, ll. 501–2). The story of Isabella is passed through all the country. But the story is not passed from mouth to ear (as a metonym for understanding or cognition) but directly from mouth to mouth; its transmission takes as its model more the contagious yawn (with its awkward mechanics) than the more familiar tale of human suffering that is knowingly shared. The end of the poem, in other words, returns one to the apostrophe to the reader in stanza 49 and to the description of the poem as a "yawning tomb."

Studies have shown that roughly half of human adults will yawn during or shortly after seeing a videotape of repeated yawns of other human beings.[39] The rate for contagious yawning is much smaller with children under age five, which has led scientists to link yawning to self-consciousness and empathy. As an interruption of speech, the yawn is passed from adult to adult, a sign of empathetic identification that is not entirely available to consciousness. Here, empathy is communicated not through the voice but through the interruption of the voice, the passing along of an open (a yawning) mouth.

For Keats, I argue in conclusion, the poem as yawn, as a lyric yawn, exposes one to modes of transmission that cannot simply be claimed or grasped. The poem opens a way of passing on, and so bearing witness to, what one does not comprehend, a silence within one's speech passed from open mouth to open mouth. One passes on another, a different story with the fragile call of a mute repetition. To yawn before the poem, before the lyric, to yawn in response to the yawn of the lyric, such may be the strange legacy for which "Isabella" calls. The poem offers itself as an encounter with a face, a yawning tomb, but a face without a voice. It issues a mute call to which one responds in kind, passing on the interruption of one's own voice. With these closing lines, Keats begins to articulate an alternative understanding of poetry's role in education. One reads not simply to understand. Reading is not simply a question of deciphering the message. For Keats in "Isabella," poetry offers a form of transmission whereby one passes on the story of another's suffering precisely at those moments when understanding fails, when one finds oneself repeating to another a story not yet fully available to understanding. What one passes on is what one cannot speak about.

Conclusion

> We're going to go ahead and go on, we're going on to do the reading thing anyway.
>
> —President George W. Bush (attributed)

> To know something is not to have to think about it.
>
> —Jacques Rancière

In moving from Locke's die-rolling game to Keats's yawning tomb, we have passed from one form of repetition to another. Both Locke's game and Keats's yawn allegorize the transformation of a mechanical repetition into a speech act, one divorced, however, from familiar notions of subjectivity, will, and intention. My point is not simply to identify the ways intention is undermined by linguistic structure. I am more interested in the ways texts—approached as literary—offer, without openly advocating for what they offer, an attention to figure that invites rereading the very idea of reading, as fully neither a process of decoding nor free play. With the story of learning to read that Locke tells in *Some Thoughts Concerning Education,* he discovers, however much he resists the insight, that one learns to read because the difference between a human utterance and a chance operation is beyond formalization.[1] The difference cannot be known in advance and is not manageable without the structuring intervention of figure. However displaced and unrecognizable, this confusion of human utterance and chance operation returns in Keats's yawn—and the figures of address that have come to define the lyric.[2] With Keats's yawn, the lyric voice is aligned with an utterance that does not, at least not in any simple way, speak even as its impact—excessively minimal—is registered and transmitted.

In the story of learning to read that I have pursued in *The Poetics of Unremembered Acts,* minimal acts of repetition haunt the more common and less alienating story of learning to read that fully locates reading, and so the moment of learning to read, within consciousness. The pedagogical texts of the opening chapters attend to those minimally mechanical or automated acts that remain forever beyond, because present from the start within, language's ability to activate the conscious intentions of an author. For Locke, one learns to read only because there is no way to formalize in advance the difference between "words" and "noise." The structuring openness of words to repetition makes learning to read possible even as the results of this structure must be kept from the one who learns to read. Rousseau's attempt to formalize reading through, of all things, a literary text, in fact results in his reader becoming Robinson Crusoe. As Émile becomes a reader able to glean information from the texts he reads, he does so only in taking himself as addressed as another. Rousseau introduces a split within Émile's identity that the text of *Émile* cannot manage or control, as the competing translations of the passage demonstrate.

Gray's "Elegy Written in a Country Churchyard," Wordsworth's "Simon Lee," and Keats's "Isabella" take up the questions that emerge from Locke's and Rousseau's attempts to formalize reading. The interruption of reading returns in these poems at the moment they seem most directly to address their readers and so articulate sign and meaning. In each instance, the attempt at articulation produces instead a moment of missed comprehension, which extends what Locke and Rousseau discover as if by accident; what "happens" in their texts happens even as they attempt to secure reading from such events. However, one finds in the lyric a chance to rethink reading as something other than communication even as one is confronted by the lyric's refusal to articulate a negative or counter pedagogy. The poems enact the event of a missed reading. The story of Isabella's suffering, for instance, is passed from mouth to mouth; bypassing the ear (as a metonym for understanding), the story is not fully integrated into understanding. Wordsworth hopes in "Tintern Abbey" that such "unremembered acts" open the chance to hear the "still, sad music of humanity."[3] The moment of missed comprehension is precisely what is passed on (if not communicated) through the invocation of lyric address. As Shoshana Felman writes of traumatic events, "because trauma cannot be simply remembered, it cannot simply be 'confessed': it must be testified to, in a struggle shared between a speaker and a listener to recover something the speaking subject is not—and cannot be—in possession of."[4] What one says is always possibly more than what one meant. All too often what has been passed on has also been passed over in silence.

❖ Reading Not Reading

How do the Enlightenment pedagogical texts that resist their own insight into reading inexperience, an insight that returns in the thinking of lyric figures offered by Gray, Wordsworth, and Keats, help us think (or rethink) reading itself? In recent years, we have begun to explore alternatives to critical reading, as it emerged so powerfully in the eighteenth century. In *The Poetics of Unremembered Acts*, I have worked to show that such attempts to pursue alternative reading strategies often repeat the questions posed within the texts we are trying to learn to read. In the introduction to their provocative special issue of *Representations*, Stephen Best and Sharon Marcus offer surface reading as an alternative to symptomatic (or critical) reading, as it has been developed by Marxist and psychoanalytic readers invested in the importance of reading "with suspicion." As Best and Marcus explain, "when symptomatic readers focus on elements present in the text, they construe them as symbolic of something latent or concealed."[5] The reader's pursuit of a text's buried, latent content enables a defense of reading as critically important. A critical reader is able to resist dominant ideologies. Best and Marcus argue that such a defense of "critical" reading ignores what is present to the senses. They promote attention to the literal surface: "a surface," they explain, "is what insists on being looked *at* rather than what we must train ourselves to see through."[6] Surface reading helps make legible certain recent critical preoccupations that have not been adequately acknowledged or theorized.

In aligning surface reading with the literal, however, Best and Marcus celebrate "just" reading as an acceptance of what one sees, as if the literal could be conceived without the figurative, as if seeing and perception were not themselves subject to differential structures (and so, as a result, to the intrusion of figure). As Emily Apter and Elaine Freedgood explain in the afterword to the issue, literal reading is—of course—always already figurative. The "literal," in other words, does not refer to the absence of rhetoric but to one type of rhetoric among others: "Literal reading is of course a metaphor; we cannot stick to the letters of the text, even metaphorically."[7] In another context, Rei Terada has similarly explored the ways in which seeing, or an attention to the surface, what is looked at as opposed to what is seen through, *is* reading, it being impossible to distinguish between the two or to understand one without the other. Seeing always includes reading; and reading, in turn, cannot be conceived without some empirical or phenomenal moment (even if or especially because language is a system of differences without positive terms). As Terada writes, "there is no nonmetaphorical way of talking about even what a perception is."[8] Indeed, when Best and Marcus attempt to define surface reading as literal meaning, they necessarily turn toward figurative language. When they write that "it is enough simply to register what the text itself is saying,"[9] they draw upon the very tropes of lyric address emphasized throughout this book and transform the mute text into a living subject capable of speech. This effort is made all the more plain when they describe the "emerging interest in literal readings that take texts at face value,"[10] which grants the concept of value a face. The point here is not to identify the rhetorical figures at work in their introduction. Best and Marcus would easily agree that one cannot, even if one wanted to, rid the world of rhetoric. The call for surface or literal reading is no simple return to Locke, as if Locke's own writings were so simple. Locke himself famously employs a host of rhetorical figures in the paragraphs from *An Essay Concerning Human Understanding* in which rhetoric is condemned, thus making it difficult *not* to recognize the irony implicit in Locke's condemnation. And yet in describing the ways in which one might "do" surface reading, Best and Marcus first define "attention to surface as a practice of critical description,"[11] thus aligning their enterprise with a certain tradition of empiricism or phenomenology. If symptomatic or deep reading is aligned with the nineteenth century—with Marx and Freud and so with legacies of romanticism—surface or literal reading defines not only the way we read "now" but also the way we read then, "before" romanticism.

The question is not whether one can read literally but whether one can formalize or control the difference between the literal and the figurative (uncritical and critical, surface and symptomatic reading). This difficulty controlling the difference is precisely one that lyric poems present over and over again. When Wordsworth addresses his imagined reader in "Simon Lee," one must take the address as both an apostrophe and, more literally, a direct address, even if address by now is not easily collapsed into expression.[12] To understand the address as merely an apostrophe is to ignore the degree to which the poem calls to its present reader. As William Waters writes in *Poetry's Touch,* "the poem has incessantly sought its true addressee, the one for whom it is meant, and in finding and reading it, you are discovered as (made into) that one."[13] And yet, to understand Wordsworth's figure as a direct address is to ignore the degree to which figures of direct address are still apostrophic and so ignore (or are positioned as if to ignore) the reader. Any accidental reader can position himself as the unique and intended one; to the extent to which such a written address includes anyone who happens to be reading it, though, it is also always on the way to another. It "speaks" to any and all, and so to none. One cannot (and yet of course one can) choose. In this regard, following Wordsworth, all texts are epitaphs. But to what or for whom?

❖ Reading (in) Events

I write this conclusion on the tenth anniversary of the terrorist attacks of September 11, 2001, and am having a difficult time not remembering the fact that on that morning then-President George Walker Bush visited Emma E. Booker Elementary School in Sarasota, Florida, to promote his new education initiative. As he sat in front of the classroom helping to teach children to read, he was informed by an aide of the first attack on the World Trade Center, even as its full import failed to register (at first, the attack was thought to be an accident). After a short meeting, the decision was made to continue the photo op, forever linking in U.S. history instruction in reading, the effort to teach children to read, and the failure to register the full import of an event. While one might wish that President Bush had responded differently to the news of the first attack, the texts that make up *The Poetics of Unremembered Acts* suggest that the failure to register the full import of an event is constitutive of learning to read. September 11, 2001, changed everything. This may be true. What would it mean to know this? But even as Emma E. Booker's heroic efforts to teach African American children to read—at a time when their educational opportunities were severely limited—remind us of the importance of reading to general education, the scene in Emma E. Booker Elementary School in 2001 stages the irresolvable tension between reading and consciousness, poetry and experience, a tension that has been the subject of this book.

As I have worked to show through readings of Gray's "Elegy," Wordsworth's "Simon Lee," and Keats's "Isabella," poems we commonly associate with romanticism—or, in the case of Gray, romanticism's precursors—take up and so carry forward the story of our having missed the event of learning to read, an event that returns with each attempt to begin again to read as if for the first time. One learns to read what one has missed; one misses what one has learned to read. To encounter the singularity of any text, to encounter a text as a singularity, is to expose oneself to being "taught" how to read as if for the first time; to read is to find oneself exposed to one's not-knowing how to read in advance.[14] And yet there would be no reading, one would never read, without some minimal knowledge of or familiarity with reading. One reads, but in reading, or, due to one's advance knowledge of reading, one fails inevitably to encounter the poem in its singularity, its absolute alterity or otherness. Precisely because one "can'st read," as Gray reminds us in his "Elegy," one fails to read *this* poem *here*. The legacy of one's having missed, of one's continual missing, the moment of reading instruction, as Locke and Rousseau demonstrate, preserves one's ignorance of how to read this particular or singular text, the particular and singular text before one. But one's ignorance of reading makes reading possible. Far from confirming one's sense of self, the importance of the self, or the mastery of self over experience, romantic poets find in the familiar tropes of the lyric, paradoxically even those of direct address, the repetition of this (missed) event—reading. As a result, reading remains exterior to the experience of the one who reads, even when a poem's rhetoric claims a knowledge of reading it simultaneously denies: "Approach and read (for thou can'st read)." But what is reading if in the very line that orders one to read, one must be reminded that one knows how? To read, one must already have forgotten what one learned?

In *The Poetics of Unremembered Acts,* and in the constellation of texts that constitute *The Poetics of Unremembered Acts,* learning to read comes to have the force of an event.[15] Because one is not entirely present for the moment one learned to read, learning to read has not yet happened (to "me"). As Rousseau describes in the opening of his *Confessions,* his first awareness of himself does not precede but follows from knowledge of reading that "he," a Rousseau conscious of and aware of himself as himself, has not experienced and so does not know. One learns to read, and yet to the extent to which the event of learning to read is missed, it "happens," it happens again as if for the first time, with each and every attempt to read. This is, I argue in closing, what romantic poetry has yet to teach us about our reading, in particular our reading of romanticism but as well of all that goes by the name "reading." One reads in the wake of one's inexperience, in the wake of one's having missed the moment one "learned to read." One reads in the dark not because all reading is figurative (open to a hermeneutics of suspicion) or literal (as if the sign could be known only as and for what it is) but because one cannot know in advance—one cannot learn—how to formalize absolutely the difference between the literal and figurative. As is likely clear by now, *The Poetics of Unremembered Acts* aims to take its place within a legacy of rhetorical reading by acknowledging the ways in which the opposition of critical and uncritical reading repeats the Enlightenment pedagogical texts of Locke and Rousseau and poetry's investigations into the force of lyric figures.

What we want is to know how to read, to know best how to teach reading, how to guarantee the teaching of reading, but what poems show, what texts approached as literature more generally show over and over again, is our ignorance of reading—an ignorance that emerges from the attempt at an adequate, critical reading.[16] This moment of missed comprehension may be romanticism's most important legacy and one against which many definitions of romanticism have been marshaled. The story of our having missed the moment of our having learned to read, and so the moment from which we date coming to consciousness (following Rousseau), goes unexperienced and unremembered. But the story of our not yet knowing fully how to read is one the poems pass on as they make possible future encounters with what we do not yet know (even what we do not yet know about reading)—and so what we are constantly thinking about. There are of course many ways not to think about what we are most thinking about, and I will hazard in conclusion that a fascination with speed, with the speedy transmission of information and an overcoming of the vagaries of interpretation that reading so often produces, is one sign of just how much we are thinking about not thinking about reading, about poetry, about literature. As Wordsworth suggests in his preface to *Lyrical Ballads,* this fascination with speed risks paralysis and inaction, blunts the mind's response to the suffering of others, and therefore puts responsibility to an end. And perhaps for this very reason, however impossible a project it may be, however minimal a difference it makes, this insignificance being part of the point, we go on doing the reading thing anyway. This may be the chance we have.

NOTES

Introduction

1. *The Letters of William and Dorothy Wordsworth: The Middle Years, Part I*, 2nd ed., edited by Ernest de Selincourt, revised by Mary Moorman (Oxford: Clarendon Press of Oxford University Press, 1969), 195. See also Stephen Gill, ed., *The Cambridge Companion to Wordsworth* (Cambridge: Cambridge University Press, 2003), xvi.

2. While Wordsworth opposes teaching and nothing, the relationship between them has a long history. Most famously, Socrates declares in contrast to one who "thinks he knows something when he does not": "when I do not know, neither do I think I know." Plato, *Complete Works*, edited by John M. Cooper (Indianapolis: Hackett, 1997), 21. Socrates does not claim that he knows "nothing," but he does align teaching with one's willingness to admit when (if not precisely that) one knows nothing. Elsewhere, Socrates more dramatically draws together teaching proper and "nothing" with his suggestion that he does not teach anything: "Meno," says Socrates, "you are a rascal. You now ask me if I can teach you, when I say there is no teaching" (Plato, *Complete Works*, 881). For Socrates there is no opposition between teaching and nothing. Or, in a sense, teaching is nothing (one of the three impossible professions, according to Sigmund Freud). Nothing is what one teaches. Moving from the figure of Socrates to the French psychoanalyst Jacques Lacan, Shoshana Felman persuasively explains how psychoanalysis throws into question the usual pedagogical pose of mastery. Just as Socrates's willingness to acknowledge his lack of knowledge transforms the very idea of the teacher, so too does psychoanalysis: the teacher as a "figure of infallible human authority implicitly likened to a God, both modeled on and guaranteed by divine omniscience, is based on an illusion: the illusion of a consciousness transparent to itself." Shoshana Felman, *Jacques Lacan and the Adventure of Insight: Psychoanalysis in Contemporary Culture* (Cambridge, Mass.: Harvard University Press, 1987), 86. With the insight of psychoanalysis, teaching no longer describes a process whereby knowledge is transmitted from teacher (one who knows and knows what he or she knows) to student. The teacher does not teach "something," something known in advance. Instead, one passes on what Jacques Lacan calls the "insistence . . . of ignorance." Jacques Lacan, *The Seminar of Jacques Lacan: Book II, The Ego in Freud's Theory and in the Technique of Psychoanalysis, 1954–1955*, edited by Jacques-Alain Miller, translated by Sylvana Tomaselli (New York: W. W. Norton, 1991), 207. Wordsworth, in his letter, holds firm to an opposition between teaching and nothing (an opposition between knowledge and ignorance) that Socrates and Lacan—as well as, I argue, Wordsworth's own poetry—throw into question.

3. William Wordsworth, *The Prelude: 1799, 1805, 1850* (New York: W. W. Norton, 1979): 1805 version, book 5, lines 10–13.

4. Ibid., 1805 version, book 5, lines 230–31. Geoffrey Hartman, summarizing Wordsworth's celebration of books, writes, "The books of adventure, poetry, and imagination to which Wordsworth refers gradualize our break with nature; they delay the overquick maturation of the child." Geoffrey Hartman, *Wordsworth's Poetry, 1787–1814* (New Haven, Conn.: Yale University Press, 1967), 226.

5. The fifth book of *The Prelude* is famously about accidents, as Cynthia Chase has shown. See Cynthia Chase, *Decomposing Figures: Rhetorical Readings in the Romantic Tradition* (Baltimore: Johns Hopkins University Press, 1986), 13–31. For a related but more recent investigation into the question of error and accident in philosophy and literature of the period, see Zachary Sng, *The Rhetoric of Error from Locke to Kleist* (Stanford, Calif.: Stanford University Press, 2010).

6. Paul de Man engages the opening of book 5 in "Wordsworth and the Victorians" and suggests that the opening lines, which grant a "speaking face" to earth and heaven, "are not simply an anthropomorphism, a conceit by which human consciousness is projected or transferred into the natural world. They assume the recognition of an entity or agency that bridges the distinction between mind and world by allowing them to exist in the proximity, in the dialogue of this distinction." Paul de Man, "Wordsworth and the Victorians," in *The Rhetoric of Romanticism* (New York: Columbia University Press, 1984), 89. Nature bridges mind and world and seems to offer the possibility of a union between subject and object. The reason that this figure is not "simply an anthropomorphism" is because these words are not addressed to nature but to man: "Thou also, man, hast wrought, / For commerce of thy nature with itself, / Things worthy of unconquerable life" (Wordsworth, *Prelude,* 1805 version, book 5, lines 17–20). The encounter with nature's speaking face makes possible dialogue between men. De Man argues that what Wordsworth's poem shows is that "man can address and face other men, within life or beyond the grave, because he has a face, but he has a face because he partakes of a mode of discourse that is neither entirely natural nor entirely human" ("Wordsworth and Victorians," 90). The encounter with the speaking face of earth and heaven precedes and so makes possible human discourse; but this encounter is not dialogue. Wordsworth's only response is to look. In this way, then, Wordsworth suggests that the condition of possibility of articulate language between men is the condition of impossibility of articulate language between this speaking face of nature and the subjective consciousness of man. I speak with others because I do not "speak" with nature; I merely look upon its speaking "face." De Man goes on to suggest that this incompatibility "would become even more manifest if, instead of considering such obviously figural terms as 'face' or 'hangs,' we considered the syntactic and grammatical backbones of Wordsworth's diction, words such as 'even' or 'but' or the ever-recurring 'not' and its many cognates" ("Wordsworth and Victorians," 92). One might say the same thing about "as."

7. Perhaps this reading of "as" helps one understand Wordsworth's repeated (and seemingly unnecessary) use of "as" in the 1808 letter: "as a teacher, or as nothing." Why should Wordsworth not have written that he wishes to be considered a teacher or nothing? Why "as" a teacher? Why "as" nothing?

8. See for instance Paul de Man, *Allegories of Reading: Figural Language in Rousseau, Nietzsche, Rilke, and Proust* (New Haven, Conn.: Yale University Press, 1979), 3.

9. Marjorie Levinson, "What Is New Formalism?" *PMLA* 122, no. 2 (2007): 558–69, at 560.

10. Franco Moretti, "Conjectures on World Literature," *New Left Review* 1 (January–February 2000): 54–66.

11. For "paranoid" and "reparative" reading, see Eve Kosofsky Sedgwick, "Paranoid Reading and Reparative Reading; or, You're So Paranoid, You Probably Think This Introduction Is About You," in *Novel Gazing: Queer Readings in Fiction,* ed. Eve Kosofsky Sedgwick (Durham, N.C.: Duke University Press, 1997), 1–37. For "critical" and "uncritical" reading, see Michael Warner, "Uncritical Reading," in *Polemic: Critical or Uncritical,* ed. Jane Gallop (New York: Routledge, 2004), 13–38. For "postcritical" reading, see Rita Felski, "After Suspicion," *Profession 2009*: 28–35. For "hyper" and "machine" reading, see N. Katherine Hayles, "How We Read: Close, Hyper, Machine," *ADE Bulletin* 150 (2010): 62–79. For "surface" reading, see Stephen Best and Sharon Marcus, "Surface Reading: An Introduction," *Representations* 108, no. 1 (Fall 2009): 1–21. As Lee Morrissey argues in *The Constitution of Literature: Literacy, Democracy, and Early English Literary Criticism* (Stanford, Calif.: Stanford University Press, 2008), literary criticism as a discipline emerges in an effort to keep in check just such a proliferation of reading forms, styles, and methods.

12. Jane Gallop, "The Historicization of Literary Studies and the Fate of Close Reading," *Profession 2007*: 183.

13. Marjorie Garber, "Shakespeare in Slow Motion," *Profession 2010*: 151.

14. To the extent to which Garber's call for slow reading is, itself, a return to Reuben Brower's "Reading in Slow Motion," it is difficult to divorce close and slow reading. See Reuben Brower, "Reading in Slow Motion," in *In Defense of Reading: A Reader's Approach to Literary Criticism,* ed. Reuben A. Brower and Richard Poirier (New York: E. P. Dutton, 1962), 3–21. Slow reading, like close reading, emerges from New Criticism, even if the spatial as opposed to temporal metaphor has, historically, carried greater weight and influence. "Returning" to slow reading offers the chance simultaneously to depart from New Criticism and to continue its legacy.

15. Levinson, "What Is New Formalism?" 561.

16. For more, see Rei Terada, "Seeing Is Reading," in *Legacies of Paul de Man,* ed. Marc Redfield (New York: Fordham University Press, 2007), 162–78. In response to earlier deconstructive materialists who opposed seeing, which assumes the possibility of phenomenal cognition, and reading, which, simply put, does not, Terada suggests that "seeing" stages many of the same questions as "reading": "attempts to use 'seeing' narrowly, over and against 'reading,' can

entangle themselves in aesthetics" (164)—the very entanglement "reading," in the strong sense, was supposed to resist.

17. Levinson, "What Is New Formalism?" 568.

18. Barbara Johnson suggests in "Nothing Fails Like Success" that "if the deconstructive impulse is to retain its vital, subversive power, we must therefore become ignorant of it again and again. It is only by forgetting what we know how to do, by setting aside the thoughts that have most changed us, that those thoughts and that knowledge can go on making accessible to us the surprise of an otherness we can only encounter in the moment of suddenly discovering we are ignorant of it." Barbara Johnson, "Nothing Fails Like Success," in *A World of Difference* (Baltimore: Johns Hopkins University Press, 1998), 16. Johnson's final sentence is particularly interesting for the repeated use of "it." In the final sentence, the "it" of "it is" is referred to by linguists as a dummy pronoun; and it seems hardly by coincidence that a sentence describing the necessity of ignorance should begin with a pronoun without an antecedent, just as "deconstruction," too, must always be in excess of any identified antecedent for it to retain its capacity to surprise.

Anne-Lise François has explored the ways literature makes "nothing" happen. Literary texts, she argues, repeatedly explore the importance of making as little impact as possible. The move from intrinsic (broadly formalist) to extrinsic (broadly historicist) criticism is predicated on defending literary criticism's ability to make an impact. François's *Open Secrets* provocatively challenges literary critics to think differently about the role of literature in education, as if what one most needs to learn from literature is how not to make an impact. See Anne-Lise François, *Open Secrets: The Literature of Uncounted Experience* (Stanford, Calif.: Stanford University Press, 2007).

19. In "On Incomprehensibility," Friedrich Schlegel expresses the hope that soon "humanity will finally . . . learn to read [die Menschheit werde sich endlich . . . lesen lernen]." In attempting to come to terms with his own critical age, Schlegel posits a notion of reading that is "to come," one toward which humanity must strive. But in so doing he distinguishes one form of reading from another (or others), a reading deferred into the future. While one must be literate—to some minimal degree—to read Schlegel's text, unclear is whether the hoped-for reading for which Schlegel calls organizes texts in advance and transforms reading into an act that could be "finally" learned; or, whether the reading for which Schlegel calls opens readers to reading, to what cannot be anticipated. Friedrich Schlegel, *Kritische Schriften,* ed. Wolfdietrich Rasch (Munich: Carl Hanser Verlag, 1958), 342. See also Jochen Schulte-Sasse et al., eds., *Theory as Practice: A Critical Anthology of Early German Romantic Writing,* (Minneapolis: University of Minnesota Press, 1997), 120.

20. Paul de Man, *The Resistance to Theory* (Minneapolis: University of Minnesota Press, 1986), 4. One might object to de Man's claim and argue that the choice he offers is false. One should teach what is in fact true. Only teaching what is true is true teaching. As de Man argues in *The Resistance to Theory,* literary theory began with an attempt to describe what can be known scientifically about literature. Far from an attack on truth, it emerges,

paradoxically, from the very attempt to describe what is true about the literary text. These questions raised for me at the time a more pragmatic one: how can I secure a position in a college or university literature department defending the importance of failing in teaching?

21. De Man, *Resistance to Theory,* 3.

22. Barbara Johnson, "Deconstruction, Feminism, and Pedagogy," in *World of Difference,* 43.

23. Thomas Keenan, *Fables of Responsibility: Aberrations and Predicaments in Ethics and Politics* (Stanford, Calif.: Stanford University Press, 1997), 1.

24. William Wordsworth, *Lyrical Ballads* (New York: Routledge, 2005), 157.

25. Ibid.

26. Jean-Jacques Rousseau, *Confessions,* trans. Angela Scholar (Oxford: Oxford University Press, 2000), 8.

27. One might hear echoes of Freud's theories of the traumatic event from *Beyond the Pleasure Principle* in my description of Locke's die-rolling game and in particular in my focus on the child's missing of the experience of learning to read. When Sigmund Freud encounters the dreams of soldiers returning from the war, he is forced to rethink his theory of dreams. In *Beyond the Pleasure Principle,* Freud suggests that traumatic events fail to enter fully into consciousness and so return in the form of flashbacks. "Dreams occurring in traumatic neuroses," writes Freud, "have the characteristic of repeatedly bringing the patient back into the situation of his accident, a situation from which he wakes up in another fright. This astonishes people far too little." Sigmund Freud, *Beyond the Pleasure Principle,* vol. 18 of *The Standard Edition of the Complete Psychological Works of Sigmund Freud,* ed. James Strachey (London: Hogarth, 1955), 13. I am unprepared to suggest that instruction in reading for Locke's child reader is "traumatic." Of interest, however, is the way that reading, and instruction in reading in particular, should share a similarly enigmatic temporal structure with the traumatic event, which is perceived only in its return in the form, for instance, of the flashback. As Cathy Caruth summarizes in *Trauma: Explorations in Memory* (Baltimore: Johns Hopkins University Press, 1995), "The pathology [posttraumatic stress disorder] consists, rather, solely in the structure of its *experience* or reception: the event is not assimilated or experienced fully at the time, but only belatedly, in its repeated *possession* of the one who experiences it" (4). As I will show in the first chapter, for Locke we read only because we missed the event of learning to read.

28. As Blanchot suggests in *The Writing of the Disaster,* "We constantly *need* to say (to think): that was quite something (something quite important) that happened to me. By which we mean at the same time: that couldn't possibly belong to the order of things which come to pass." Maurice Blanchot, *The Writing of the Disaster,* trans. Ann Smock (Lincoln: University of Nebraska Press, 1995), 9. Strangely, those events that might be said to make the greatest impact are also those that fail fully to enter consciousness. To defend the humanities, and in particular the reading of literary texts, it has become increasingly important for literary critics to explain how literature teaches,

how it, for instance, teaches students to think critically. At this point it may be impossible to question (if one wanted to question) the importance of critical thinking to defenses of the humanities. Surprising, however, is the degree to which texts by Locke and Rousseau, texts central to theories of education, raise questions about one's ability to align teaching and cognition.

29. Barbara Johnson, "The Pedagogical Imperative: Teaching as a Literary Genre," *Yale French Studies* 63 (1982), vi–vii.

30. Ibid., vii.

31. One distinguishing aspect of the literary text is its willingness to allegorize this tension between reading and experience. Literary texts reflect on one's attempt to decode a message and so offer themselves as allegories of language's compulsion to repeat, like the mariner, what has not yet been understood. As Shoshana Felman argues, "From a philosophical perspective, knowledge is mastery—that which is in mastery of its own meaning. Unlike Hegelian philosophy, which *believes it knows all that there is to know;* unlike Socratic (or contemporary post-Nietzschean) philosophy, which *believes it knows it does not know*—literature, for its part, *knows it knows, but does not know the meaning of its knowledge*—does not know what it knows." Felman, *Lacan and Insight,* 92.

32. As Cathy Caruth argues in *Empirical Truths and Critical Fictions: Locke, Wordsworth, Kant, Freud* (Baltimore: Johns Hopkins University Press, 1991), "the manner in which the *knowledge* of experience is achieved—the empirical argument—is the means by which one permanently loses the *certainty* of experience; every time the argument *claims* as *understanding* to know itself, via experience, it *tells* of its disruption of this self-knowledge as *text*" (40, emphasis in original). The attempt itself to articulate knowledge and experience disrupts the articulation. One finds, I argue, in the language of poems, registration of this disarticulation of knowledge from experience.

33. See also Elizabeth Rottenberg, *Inheriting the Future: Legacies of Kant, Freud, and Flaubert* (Stanford, Calif.: Stanford University Press, 2005); and Jacques Derrida, "Typewriter Ribbon: Limited Ink (2)," in *Materials Events: Paul de Man and the Afterlife of Theory,* ed. Tom Cohen et al. (Minneapolis: University of Minnesota Press, 2001).

34. Warner, "Uncritical Reading," 23.

35. Ibid., 34.

36. Poets, writes Roman Jakobson, express an interest in the message for its own sake, an interest not only in what words mean but also in how they appear and sound, which is why, in Jakobson's famous definition, "the poetic function projects the principle of equivalence from the axis of selection into the axis of combination." Roman Jakobson, "Linguistics and Poetics," in *Language and Literature* (Cambridge, Mass.: Belknap Press of Harvard University Press, 1987), 71. A particular word is chosen for a poem because it shares certain material features (sound, for instance, as is the case with rhyme) with surrounding words. The word's meaningful content at this moment may be of secondary interest. Edward Lear, for instance, explores the sorts of utterance possible if interest in language's semantic content is dramatically reduced in favor of its

mechanical properties, a poetics also explored by twentieth-century American L=A=N=G=U=A=G=E poets such as Bruce Andrews and Charles Bernstein. See for instance, Edward Lear, *The Complete Verse and Other Nonsense* (New York: Penguin, 2002); and Bruce Andrews and Charles Bernstein, eds., *The L=A=N=G=U=A=G=E Book* (Carbondale: Southern Illinois University Press, 1984). Poets, however, less invested in minimizing language's referential function, stage an encounter between language's competing functions, the poetic, for instance, and the referential.

37. Grammar defines the systems of relationships that generate texts independently of referential meaning. As Paul de Man writes in *Allegories of Reading,* "We call *text* any entity that can be considered from such a double perspective: as a generative, open-ended, non-referential grammatical system and as a figural system closed off by a transcendental signification that subverts the grammatical code to which the text owes its existence. The 'definition' of the text also states the impossibility of its existence and prefigures the allegorical narratives of this impossibility" (De Man, *Allegories of Reading,* 270).

38. As Sara Guyer writes, this is "a deflating acknowledgment that our understanding . . . is conditioned by acts of facing, which is to say that we are deprived of sense, a privation that figures sometimes help us to forget." Sara Guyer, "Buccal Reading," *CR: The New Centennial* 7, no. 2 (2007): 71–87, at 80. I owe much to Guyer's rethinking of trope and testimony in *Romanticism After Auschwitz* (Stanford, Calif.: Stanford University Press, 2007). Guyer argues that "when lyric figures give voice to the voiceless, make the inanimate live, and render the nonhuman human, they expose voice, life, and human beings not as givens but rather as figural effects" (218). See also Barbara Johnson, "Apostrophe, Animation, and Abortion," in *World of Difference,* 184–199, and Barbara Johnson, *Persons and Things* (Cambridge, Mass.: Harvard University Press, 2008). Johnson powerfully explores the animating power of figure (apostrophe, prosopopoeia, anthropomorphism, and personification) but also its ability to disturb any secure sense of the difference between life and death, the animate and inanimate. "A text 'speaks.' This is how texts in general are assumed to work; they 'say' something" (*Persons and Things,* 14). "Prosopopeia," writes Johnson, "is thus *the* figure for reading" (*Persons and Things,* 14). Reading, then, as an act, similarly disturbs the frontier between life and death, which may explain the dominance of the image as opposed to the text. The image does not need to be read; it does not call to be read but simply seen—or so goes the fantasy.

39. William Waters, *Poetry's Touch: On Lyric Address* (Ithaca, N.Y.: Cornell University Press, 2003). In this important book, Waters takes seriously the ways poems seek an interlocutor and call to be read: "The *you* that (perhaps) calls to the reader is a wild spot in poetics, a dynamically moving gap in whatever secure knowledge about poetry we may think we have; and 'live' as it is, this *you* makes palpable poetry's claim on being read, which is to say, its claim to make an accidental reader into the destined and unique recipient of everything the poem contains or is" (15). Waters carefully moves between formal and phenomenological vocabularies, which he describes as two sides of the same

coin. As the last footnote to his introduction discloses, though, the coin, once flipped, lands on one side: "my interest here is [in] what I call phenomenology: namely, *what it is like to be someone reading* (here, now)" (15). In *The Poetics of Unremembered Acts,* I take seriously the rhetorical structure of such "addressability" or "addressivity." If Waters is interested in the ways the accidental reader becomes the destined one, I am interested in the reverse. I take seriously, in other words, the ways a poem figures (and in figuring also anticipates) an always already future reader, someone else, someone who is not the present reader (reading not here, not now).

40. De Man famously discusses this passage from language modeled on cognition to one modeled on something else in *Aesthetic Ideology:* "The transition, the passage from the conception of language as a system, perhaps a closed system of tropes, that totalizes itself as a series of transformations which can be reduced to tropological systems, and then the fact that you pass that conception of language to another conception of language in which language is no longer cognitive but in which language is performative." Paul de Man, *Aesthetic Ideology* (Minneapolis: University of Minnesota Press, 1996), 132.

41. For a related discussion, see the conclusion to Paul Fry's *A Defense of Poetry,* in which he articulates what he calls "the ethics of suspending knowledge." Paul Fry, *A Defense of Poetry: Reflections on the Occasion of Writing* (Stanford, Calif.: Stanford University Press, 1995), 201.

42. My title is not meant but cannot help but allude to Toni Morrison's magisterial *Playing in the Dark: Whiteness and the Literary Imagination* (New York: Vintage, 1992).

43. See, for instance, Dana Gioia, *Can Poetry Matter? Essays on Poetry and American Culture* (St. Paul: Graywolf Press, 1992); and Jay Parini, *Why Poetry Matters* (New Haven, Conn.: Yale University Press, 2008).

44. See, for instance, Virginia Jackson, *Dickinson's Misery: A Theory of Lyric Reading* (Princeton, N.J.: Princeton University Press, 2005), esp. 1–15; and Ted Underwood, "Romantic Historicism and the Afterlife," *PMLA* 117, no. 2 (2002): 237–51. In placing three "romantic" poems (though Gray's poem is often described as "preromantic") in relationship to Locke's and Rousseau's concern with questions of address in reading instruction, I hope to disturb the still-dominant understanding of romanticism's commitment to an expressive model of poetry that is often viewed as originating *with* romanticism. In "Types and Orientations of Critical Theories," M. H. Abrams, revisiting his own *The Mirror and the Lamp,* describes the expressive orientation of the poet who "moves into the center of the scheme and himself becomes the prime generator of the subject matter, attributes, and values of a poem." M. H. Abrams, "Types and Orientations of Critical Theories," in *Doing Things with Texts: Essay in Criticism and Critical Theory,* ed. Michael Fischer (New York: W. W. Norton, 1989), 11. See also M. H. Abrams, *The Mirror and the Lamp* (New York: Oxford University Press, 1953). As Abrams writes in "Types and Orientations of Critical Theories," "Wordsworth's 'Preface' to *Lyrical Ballads* is the heir to a century of developments in this mode of thinking, and became the single most important pronouncement of the

emotive theory of poetry. His key formulation, twice uttered, is that poetry 'is the spontaneous overflow of powerful feelings.' The metaphor 'overflow,' like the equivalent terms in the definitions of Wordsworth's contemporaries—'expression,' 'uttering forth,' 'projection'—faces in an opposite direction from 'imitation,' and indicates that the source of the poem is no longer the external world, but the poet himself" (13).

45. The question remains whether or not the actual poems support the notion of the romantic expressive lyric—with an accompanying ideology of self-present immediacy—that emerges with and after their appearance. As Marc Redfield suggests in *The Politics of Aesthetics: Nationalism, Gender, Romanticism* (Stanford, Calif.: Stanford University Press, 2003), "because it is a trope for aesthetics, romanticism must turn on itself. It splits into error and critique, with the critique turning out to be another version of what was denounced as error" (31). This union of internal feeling and external appearance has been one way romantic poets have explored and exposed the aim of the aesthetic as a philosophical category: the attempt to bring together phenomenal appearance and cognition without mediation or interference. See Marc Redfield, *Phantom Formations: Aesthetic Ideology and the Bildungsroman* (Ithaca, N.Y.: Cornell University Press, 1996), esp. 1–37. The "success" of the romantic expressive lyric in substituting itself for all poetry becomes in this light a sign of the success of what Paul de Man calls "aesthetic ideology" (see de Man, *Aesthetic Ideology*). However, not simply the aesthetic ideology espoused by the poems but by those who read and define romanticism. One judges texts guilty of asserting an "ideology" they may in fact both espouse and criticize.

46. Romanticism has come to name the attempt to bring together and so make available the union of mind and nature, internal, powerful feelings, and their external representation, sign and signification. As a term, "romanticism," in other words, names the attempt to align what is read, the poem, and its significance. In this way, romanticism, following Kant, is an aesthetic project, where the aesthetic aims to articulate sensory experience with supersensory harmony, form, or meaning. This project, however, is not safely in the past. As Cynthia Chase writes in her introduction to *Romanticism*, "Romanticism resists being defined as a period or a set of qualities that can be comfortably ascribed to others and assigned to the historical past." Cynthia Chase, ed., *Romanticism* (London: Longman, 1993), 1. Romanticism is *our* past: "we carry it within ourselves as the experience of an *act* in which, up to a certain point, we ourselves have participated" (de Man, *Rhetoric of Romanticism*, 50). Romanticism names the attempt to bring together an act and its interpretation, which is precisely what one attempts in one's reading *of* romanticism. As an attempt at self-understanding, the reflexive structure of romantic poems can never be entirely self-reflexive. The reflexive turn always enacts a difference even as it offers the illusion of overcoming difference. As Deborah Elise White argues, "[the reflexive turn] always contains the surplus of difference that enables it to re-fer (or bear back) toward itself. The formalism associated with the claims of autonomy must, therefore, always allow for an other, heteronomous, and nonformalizable point of reference. The text that (re)turns

on 'itself' (re)turns as the imposition of the difference it enacts." Deborah Elise White, *Romantic Returns: Superstition, Imagination, History* (Stanford, Calif.: Stanford University Press, 2000), 8.

47. E. D. Hirsch Jr. has suggested in *The Knowledge Deficit: Closing the Shocking Education Gap for America's Children* (New York: Houghton Mifflin, 2007), in a section titled "The Curse of Romantic Ideas," that all that has gone wrong with education today in the United States can be traced back to romanticism and to the belief that there is "no boundary between the natural and the divine" (5). But are the texts Hirsch calls romantic so simple? Repeated references to feeling in romantic texts, for instance, are often taken as signs of feeling's importance and not a sign of worry, a sign that feeling might not be what one—what the poets even—hope it is. This estrangement of feeling from knowledge is what Adela Pinch explores so powerfully in *Strange Fits of Passion*. Adela Pinch, *Strange Fits of Passion: Epistemologies of Emotion, Hume to Austen* (Stanford, Calif.: Stanford University Press, 1996). For more on questions of romanticism and tropes of interiority, see Joshua Wilner, *Feeding on Infinity: Readings in the Romantic Rhetoric of Internalization* (Baltimore: Johns Hopkins University Press, 2000). Do the poems achieve a union between internal feeling and external appearance, perception and cognition, or in asserting the hope for such a union, do they stage their irreconcilability? This is, for instance, the question that Stanley Cavell finds raised by the marriage ceremony. The marriage ceremony unites two as one, but it also always performs a separation, as one becomes two. The ceremony repeats the story of our separation from others with each repetition, for were one not separated from others there would be no pursuit of union. Stanley Cavell, *In Quest of the Ordinary: Lines of Skepticism and Romanticism* (Chicago: University of Chicago Press, 1994), 100.

This is not, however, to substitute the irreconcilability of sign and signification for the perception of reconcilability, as negative knowledge of irreconcilability may be just another—and perhaps today the most prevalent—form of aesthetic ideology. In *The Poetics of Unremembered Acts,* I read the ubiquity of the still-conventional definition of "romanticism" as a cult of feeling as a sign of our resistance to romanticism. Or, to borrow from Bruno Latour, the triumph of romanticism (which may be measured by our resistance to it) is a sign that we have never been romantic enough. Bruno Latour, *We Have Never Been Modern,* trans. Catherine Porter (Cambridge, Mass.: Harvard University Press, 1993).

Chapter 1

1. Jacques Derrida, *The Margins of Philosophy,* trans. Alan Bass (Chicago: University of Chicago Press, 1982), 315.

2. As Jakobson writes in "Linguistics and Poetics," "focus on the message for its own sake . . . is the POETIC function of language." Roman Jakobson, "Linguistics and Poetics," in *Language and Literature,* 62–94, at 69. After warning that one should not limit consideration of the poetic function to poetry,

Jakobson explains that the poetic function, "by promoting the palpability of signs, deepens the fundamental dichotomy of signs and objects" (ibid., 70).

3. Locke's implicit recognition repeats throughout the poems considered in later chapters of *The Poetics of Unremembered Acts* as the poets transition from unclaimed utterances to larger questions about ethics, an ethics that emerges from the impossibility of knowing in advance how to respond adequately to such an utterance. The poems on which I focus are not simply "lyrics." They do not ignore the reader in the same way, for instance, that Keats's "Ode on a Grecian Urn" ignores its reader; these poems frequently call to the reader directly. If the point of the lyric is to deny addressing a reader (in turning away from the reader through apostrophe), then Wordsworth's "Simon Lee," for instance, which figures a direct address to the reader, stages a conflict that the lyric often labors to overcome.

4. John Locke, *An Essay Concerning Human Understanding* (Oxford: Oxford University Press, 1975), 405 (hereafter cited in text as *Essay*).

5. Ferdinand de Saussure, *Course in General Linguistics,* trans. Wade Baskin (New York: McGraw-Hill, 1959), 118.

6. See, for instance, Jacques Derrida, "Structure, Sign, and Play in the Discourse of the Human Sciences" in *Writing and Difference,* trans. Alan Bass (Chicago: University of Chicago Press, 1978), 278–94.

7. Locke grants words a central place even though as he writes in a letter to William Molyneux a few years after initial publication, "some parts of that third book . . . cost me more pains to express, than all the rest of my essay." Quoted in Hans Aarsleff, *From Locke to Saussure: Essays on the Study of Language and Intellectual History* (Minneapolis: University of Minnesota Press, 1982), 45.

8. For a more philosophical and less literary approach to this question, see E. J. Ashworth, "Do Words Signify Ideas or Things? The Scholastic Sources of Locke's Theory of Language," *Journal of the History of Philosophy* 19 (1981): 299–326. See also Paul Guyer, "Locke's Philosophy of Language," in *Cambridge Companion to Locke,* ed. Vere Chappell (Cambridge: Cambridge University Press, 1994).

9. Locke works to correct what he describes as misuses and abuses of language to guarantee that language function as a more perfect instrument for the transmission of one's ideas. He famously dismisses rhetoric because rhetoric confuses the relation between what is said and how it is said: "If we would speak of Things as they are, we must allow, that all the Art of Rhetorick, besides Order and Clearness, all the artificial and figurative application of Words Eloquence hath invented, are for nothing else but to insinuate wrong Ideas, move the Passions, and thereby mislead the Judgment" (*Essay,* 580). Much as Plato rejects the poets from his Republic to guarantee an earnest search for philosophical truth, Locke argues that for language adequately to communicate truth and for it to become serviceable in the continued progress of human civilization, rhetoric must be contained and dispatched from language use. For more on Locke's stance against rhetorical language, see Paul de Man, "The Epistemology of Metaphor," in *Aesthetic Ideology;* and

Geoffrey Bennington, "The Perfect Cheat: Locke and Empiricism's Rhetoric," in *The Figural and the Literal: Problems of Language in the History of Science and Philosophy, 1630–1800,* ed. Andrew Benjamin (Manchester: University of Manchester Press, 1987).

10. For more discussion of the role of the parrot in eighteenth-century literature, see Laura Brown, *Fables of Modernity: Literature and Culture in the English Eighteenth Century* (Ithaca, N.Y.: Cornell University Press, 2001), 245–54. See also Felicity A. Nussbaum, "Speechless: Haywood's Deaf and Dumb Projector," in *The Passionate Fictions of Eliza Haywood: Essays on Her Life and Work,* ed. Kirsten T. Saxton and Rebecca P. Bocchicchio (Lexington: University of Kentucky Press, 2000). To help him distinguish words from noise, language employed properly from "language," or what resembles language, employed improperly, Locke turns to what he names "simple ideas," ideas that are available to the mind only via the proper sensory inlet. Simple ideas are unlike other ideas because they cannot be defined for another; they are not open to tropological (or metaphoric) substitution. One example is "scarlet." To simplify Locke's more complicated point: one knows scarlet only because one sees it, receives particular sense-data through the proper sensory inlet. Another's words cannot help one achieve proper understanding of a simple idea. The larger point here is that Locke requires the idea of the simple idea—along with the accompanying idea that names of simple ideas cannot be defined for another—to mark the limit of definition; and it is only after marking the limit of definition that Locke may begin to build a philosophical model for the human understanding of language.

11. See Douglas Greenlee, "Locke's Idea of 'Idea,'" in *Locke on Human Understanding,* ed. I. C. Tipton (Oxford: Oxford University Press, 1977), 41–47. A blind man cannot understand "scarlet," argues Locke, because he cannot receive into his mind by the proper inlet the simple idea of the color scarlet. In other words, because a blind man has never seen the color scarlet he can never know what "scarlet" means, for he does not have access to the idea of scarlet. Locke writes, "A studious blind Man, who had mightily beat his Head about visible Objects, and made use of the explication of his Books and Friends, to understand those names of Light, and Colours, which often came in his way; bragg'd one day, That he now understood what Scarlet signified. Upon which his Friend demanding, what Scarlet was? the Blind Man answered, It was like the Sound of a Trumpet. Just such an Understanding of the name of any other simple Idea will he have, who hopes to get it only from a Definition, or other words made us of to explain it" (*Essay,* 425). The blind man's definition of "scarlet," which relies on his use of a simile (it is like the sound of a trumpet), is further evidence for Locke that a person without the "proper Inlet" for the reception of sense-data pertinent to the simple idea cannot know the true meaning of the name of a simple idea. "Scarlet" is a word when it corresponds to the idea of scarlet, which is available only to those people capable of perceiving the color scarlet. "Scarlet" is noise when it is spoken by a blind man. The blind man's knowledge of scarlet is not knowledge—suggests Locke—because "scarlet" has no literal referent when employed by a blind man. "Scarlet" has meaning for

the blind man only to the extent to which it is like something else, the sound of a trumpet. The blind man's knowledge of the color scarlet is poetic, which, for Locke, is hardly knowledge. To provide a ground for understanding the world, Locke asserts that names of simple ideas cannot be defined but only experienced. See Jules David Law, *The Rhetoric of Empiricism: Language and Perception from Locke to I. A. Richards* (Ithaca, N.Y.: Cornell University Press, 1993), esp. 19–50.

12. Language's aim is to point either to the speaker's ideas or to things in the world from which words receive their meaning; such an aim assumes a knowable and determinable difference between words and the ideas or things they signify, a difference that when exploited should prioritize the idea referred to over the word. In his investigation of language, Locke is forced to contend with the possibility that it may be difficult to distinguish between words and ideas. The difference may not be easily stabilized. Words, he discovers, are sometimes "scarce separable from our general knowledge": "At least they interpose themselves so much between our understanding and the truth which it would contemplate and apprehend that, like the medium through which visible objects pass, their obscurity and disorder does not seldom cast a mist before our eyes and impose upon our understandings" (*Essay,* 488). That words and ideas might be "scarce separable" is potentially troubling because, for Locke, the redemption of language—in other words, the perfection of language as an instrument capable of communicating truth and making one's ideas known to another without interfering in their transmission—is possible only if words are subject to the ideas they express, which assumes an identifiable difference between what is expressed (the idea) and how it is expressed (the word). Since the end goal of language is the communication of one's ideas, one assumes that the language adequate to the communication of an idea is found only after one identifies the existence (in the mind of the speaker) of the idea to be communicated. If words and ideas are "scarce separable," then this simple chronology of events becomes quite muddled. If words and ideas are "scarce separable," it is impossible to know that one's ideas precede one's words; words may precede and influence one's ideas, which opens the possibility that one might not be in absolute control of one's own ideas, not to mention the language used to express them. His fear that words and ideas might be "scarce separable" generates much of the energy Locke puts toward repairing the abuses and imperfections of language.

13. This is a problem that Locke, in "Of Study," identifies more generally with the reading of books. In reading books, "we furnish ourselves with arguments without a progress in the real knowledge of things." Since books are constructed of signs and not things, reading does not provide real knowledge of things. As a result, writes Locke, "we only fill our heads with empty sounds, which, however thought to belong to learning and knowledge, will no more improve our understandings or strengthen our reason than the noise of a jack will fill our bellies or strengthen our bodies. And the art to fence with them which is called subtlety is of no more use than it would be to be dextrous in tying and untying knots in cobwebs. Words are of no value or use but as they

are the signs of things; when they stand for nothing they are less than ciphers, for instead of augmenting the value of those they are joined with, they lessen it and make it nothing; and where they have not a clear distinct signification they are like unusual or ill-made figures that confound our reckoning." John Locke, "Of Study," in *The Education Writings of John Locke: A Critical Edition with Introduction and Notes*, ed. James L. Axtell (Cambridge: Cambridge University Press, 1968), 407. See also Richard Yeo, "John Locke's 'Of Study' (1677): Interpreting an Unpublished Essay," *Locke Studies* 3 (2003): 147–165.

14. In pursuit of a properly philosophical understanding of language, and to guard human society from the risks attributable to miscommunication, Locke distinguishes between articulate sounds and language, between sounds that resemble words and words themselves. This distinction has a long history that extends well beyond the scope of the current project and into, for example, the debates surrounding literary theory in the 1980s. As one salient example, Steven Knapp and Walter Benn Michaels famously attempt to align meaning and intention in "Against Theory." The essay, which was originally published in *Critical Inquiry* in 1982, has been republished with various responses in W. J. T. Mitchell, ed., *Against Theory: Literary Studies and the New Pragmatism* (Chicago: University of Chicago Press, 1985). Subsequent page references to the Knapp and Michaels essay in this note are to the book edition. For Knapp and Michaels, the debates surrounding literary theory revolve around the mistaken assumption that authorial intention and the meaning of a text are distinguishable. They write: "The mistake made by theorists has been to imagine the possibility or desirability of moving from one term (the author's intended meaning) to a second term (the text's meaning), when actually the two terms are the same" (12). This assumption is shared by those theorists who wish to recover authorial intention as well as those who "celebrate the impossibility" of recovering authorial intention (11). For Knapp and Michaels, there are no intentionless meanings. In support of their claim that there are no intentionless meanings, they offer a fable. In walking along a beach, one comes upon "a curious sequence of squiggles in the sand" (15). Upon stepping back a few paces, one notices that these squiggles spell out the opening stanza of a Wordsworth lyric, "A slumber did my spirit seal." And as one gazes at the pattern in the sand, a wave washes up and recedes, leaving the second stanza of the poem. How does one explain the event? Is this a poem or an accident of wave mechanics? For Knapp and Michaels, the explanations fall into two categories: "You will either be ascribing these marks to some agent capable of intentions, such as the living sea or the haunting Wordsworth, or you will count them as nonintentional effects of mechanical processes such as erosion and percolation. But in the second case—where the marks now seem to be accidents—will they still seem to be words?" (16). For Knapp and Michaels, and one suspects as well, John Locke, the answer is no. "They will merely seem to *resemble* words," write Knapp and Michaels (16). Like Locke, who posits a significant difference between language (sounds uttered with intention) and "articulate sounds" (sounds uttered without intention that might be mistaken for words), Knapp and Michaels's intervention rests on the difference between

actual words and sounds or marks that merely resemble words. As soon as words become intentionless—or are considered independent of intention—"they become meaningless as well" (16). Jonathan Culler notes the ways that "Knapp and Michaels themselves do not take meaning and intention to be identical, for one of the moves they characteristically make is to accuse their opponents (who include just about everybody) of failing to understand their own arguments—that is, failing to understand the meaning of their own texts. E. D. Hirsch, they write, has 'failed to understand the force of his own formulation.' He thinks his formulation means one thing, but he has failed to understand implications inherent to it—a perfectly plausible situation but one that is hard to explain if one accepts the impossibility of a text meaning something other than what the author intended." Jonathan Culler, "Resisting Theory," in *The Literary in Theory* (Stanford, Calif.: Stanford University Press, 2007), 76. Culler also shows how this claim becomes central to Walter Benn Michaels's later book, *The Shape of the Signifier* (Princeton, N.J.: Princeton University Press, 2004). See also Orrin Wang, "Against Theory / Beside Romanticism: The Sensation of the Signifier," *Diacritics* 35, no. 2 (Summer 2005): 1–29.

15. John Locke, *Some Thoughts Concerning Education,* in *Education Writings of John Locke,* 257–58 (hereafter cited in text as *Education*).

16. While Locke endorses these die-rolling games, he does not invent them. Such games were commonly used to aid instruction in reading. In *The Teaching of English from the Sixteenth Century to 1870,* Ian Michael describes numerous games employed by tutors to entice children to learn to read. Beginning as early as the sixteenth century, tutors would sometimes use picture alphabets in reading instruction, where the association between the picture and the letter was thought to help children to learn the letter more quickly. In such alphabets, objects would take the shape of individual letters. A monkey, for example, would form the shape of the letter *M* and so make *M* more memorable for the child. The invention of such picture alphabets led to further pedagogical experiments, though the success of such experiments was frequently questioned. Michael writes, "In addition to picture alphabets, the letters were also carved on dice or on blocks made from ivory, bone or wood; separate letters were made from the same materials or even from sugar, and were also printed on cards." Ian Michael, *The Teaching of English from the Sixteenth Century to 1870* (Cambridge: Cambridge University Press, 1987), 70. Conventional wisdom of the day assumed that children should begin reading letters, proceed to syllable combinations, and then finally learn to read whole words. As Joseph Aickin writes in 1693, "Letters composc Syllables: Syllables, words: words, Sentences: and Sentences make Orations or Books. Wherefore you must first learn the Letters" (quoted in Michael, *Teaching of English,* 72). Because syllable learning was dull work, and because ABC books, or reading primers, could contain only a limited number of letter combinations, numerous contrivances (so-called reading machines) were invented for the production of letter combinations. Inscribing letters on dice was one familiar contrivance. As Mitford M. Mathews writes, "The invention of such gadgets will probably continue forever." Mitford M. Mathews, *Teaching to Read, Historically Considered* (Chicago: University

of Chicago Press, 1966), 34. In *Some Thoughts Concerning Education,* Locke describes several toys or "reading machines." Each corresponds to a particular stage of reading instruction. To aid the pupil in recognizing individual letters, Locke imagines an ivory ball "made like that of the Royal-Oak Lottery" with many sides (as many as thirty-two). On several of the sides are pasted an *A,* on several others *B,* and so on. Stakes will be laid on who shall first throw an *A* or *B,* "as who upon Dice shall throw, Six or Seven" (*Education,* 257). As the pupil becomes better able to recognize *A* and *B,* then additional letters will added to the die. Once the pupil has learned the alphabet, then he or she will be ready to proceed to the game involving multiple dice and the reading of words spelled by chance.

17. On the relationship between Locke's die-rolling game and property rights, see Frances Ferguson, "Reading Morals: Locke and Rousseau on Education and Inequality," *Representations* 6 (Spring 1984): 66–84.

18. While Locke was a reader of poetry and even composed verse on occasion throughout his life, in *Some Thoughts Concerning Education* he emphatically rejects poetry. Of the child's "Poetick Vein," Locke writes, "Methinks the Parents should labour to have it stifled, and suppressed, as much as may be" (*Education,* 284). In privileging the ideas to which words refer over words as words, Locke limits the role of poetry in education; in versifying, for instance, one selects a word not simply because it fits the idea to be communicated but because it fits the required (or desired) metrical arrangement. By "poetry," Locke does not mean writing composed by throwing dice; however, like versification, writing produced by throwing dice suppresses language's referential function. See Roger Woolhouse, *Locke: A Biography* (Cambridge: Cambridge University Press, 2007), 19–20 and 222.

19. Though published anonymously in 1693, *Some Thoughts Concerning Education* began in 1684 as a series of letters composed over the course of several years in response to direct requests from Edward and Mary Clarke for advice on the upbringing of their eldest son, Edward. When it was published in July 1693, Clarke, to whom Locke dedicated it, responded via letter: "The printing of the book is certainly a great service to the public and a particular obligation on all . . . parents of children" (Woolhouse, *Locke,* 326). The impact of the book on the philosophy of education in the eighteenth century was immediate, and translation into various languages occurred soon after initial publication. Over the course of the eighteenth century, *Some Thoughts Concerning Education* appeared at least twenty-one times in English as well as in Dutch, French, Swedish, German, and Italian (see Axtell's introduction to *Education,* 17). While few educators today turn to Locke as a reliable authority on matters of child development, the volume has had a lasting effect on the philosophy of education. Perhaps most important, Locke's *Some Thoughts Concerning Education* plays a pivotal role in transforming the idea of the child from a simple animal or miniature adult to a human being with particular needs, talents, and patterns of development (see Axtell's introduction to *Education,* 64). My interest here is not in the influence of *Some Thoughts Concerning Education* on more contemporary philosophies of education, however great

it may be, but on the complications *Some Thoughts* introduces into Locke's philosophy of language as it is developed in *An Essay.*

20. This chance that letter combinations produced by rolling dice might be mistaken for words and so function (improperly) as words for the one who reads them is one reason why writing has been denigrated in philosophies of language, as Derrida discusses in *Of Grammatology.* Jacques Derrida, *Of Grammatology,* trans. Gayatri Spivak (Baltimore: Johns Hopkins University Press, 1976), 2–26.

21. Locke finds in children a certain resistance to didacticism that will be more forcefully articulated by later English romantic poets such as Keats, who writes in a letter to John Hamilton Reynolds, "We hate poetry that has a palpable design upon us." John Keats, *The Letters of John Keats,* 2 vols., ed. Hyder E. Rollins (Cambridge, Mass.: Harvard University Press, 1958), 1:224. One need only substitute "games" for "poetry" for Keats's echo of Locke to emerge.

22. Guy Wagner and Max Hosier, *Reading Games: Strengthening Reading Skills with Instructional Games* (New York: Macmillan, 1960), 6.

23. Jean-Jacques Rousseau, *Émile, or On Education,* trans. Allan Bloom (New York: Basic Books, 1979), 117. See also Jean-Jacques Rousseau, *Œuvres complètes,* eds. Bernard Gagnebin and Marcel Raymond, 4 vols. (Paris: Gallimard, 1959), 4:358.

Rousseau is not alone is disagreeing with the ideas behind Locke's die-rolling game, though he singles out Locke's die-rolling game for ridicule. Rousseau's pedagogy is part of a general shift in thinking about reading instruction. In Germany in 1793, Friedrich Gedike announces that whole words should be taught before individual letters and syllable combinations: "People for a long time have been aware of the unnaturalness and torture of the ABC method, and tried various games proposed to make learning the individual letters easier for the child" (quoted in Mathews, *Teaching to Read,* 40). Gedike, following Rousseau, is more interested in beginning with the meaning of the word and the idea it is meant to communicate: "It is neither necessary nor useful to begin learning to read with a knowledge of the individual letters, but it is not only far more pleasant but also far more useful for the child if it learns to read entire words at once, because in this way it will be occupied immediately with whole ideas" (quoted in Mathews, *Teaching to Read,* 39). Gedike, unlike Locke, reinforces the necessary connection between the word and the idea it is meant to communicate.

24. Rousseau, *Émile, or On Education,* 116; Rousseau, *Œuvres complètes,* 4:357.

25. Rousseau, *Émile, or On Education,* 117; Rousseau, *Œuvres complètes,* 4:358.

26. Ibid.

27. Quoted in de Man, *Allegories of Reading,* 300.

28. Mutlu Konuk Blasing, *Lyric Poetry: The Pain and the Pleasure of Words* (Princeton, N.J.: Princeton University Press, 2007), 2.

29. For Mallarmé's complicated commitment to symbolist poetics, see Kevin

Newmark, *Beyond Symbolism: Textual History and the Future of Reading* (Ithaca, N.Y.: Cornell University Press, 1991). As Newmark writes, we cannot dismiss (or celebrate) a poem "for embracing an aesthetic and subjective program that it takes . . . pains to interrogate and interrupt" (105).

30. De Man, *Rhetoric of Romanticism,* 261.

31. The connection between the die-rolling game and reading must remain unexamined, else the child might come to recognize that learning to read depends on the insight that *An Essay* works to expel. Figures of voice, especially those foregrounded by lyric poetry, can seem another way to mask the act of reading.

32. Rousseau, *Confessions,* 84. For the complete episode, see Rousseau, *Œuvres complètes,* 1:85–87.

33. De Man, *Allegories of Reading,* 84.

34. Rousseau, *Œuvres complètes,* 1:86.

35. De Man, *Allegories of Reading,* 294.

36. See Paul Hamilton, "Romanticism and Poetic Autonomy," in *The Cambridge History of English Romantic Literature,* ed. James Chandler (Cambridge: Cambridge University Press, 2009), 427–50. For an interesting history of how this understanding of literature has informed current pedagogy, see Hayden White, "The Suppression of Rhetoric in the Nineteenth Century," in *The Fiction of Narrative: Essays on History, Literature, and Theory 1957–2007,* ed. Robert Doran (Baltimore: Johns Hopkins University Press, 2010), 293–303.

37. Novalis, *Philosophical Writings,* trans. Margaret Mahony Stoljar (Albany: SUNY Press, 1997), 83. See also Novalis, *Novalis Schriften: Die Werke Friedrich von Hardenbergs,* 4 vols., ed. Paul Kluckhohn and Richard Samuel (Stuttgart, Germany: Kohlhammer, 1960–1981), 2:672.

38. "Vielleicht gleicht das *höchste Buch* einem Abcbuch" (Novalis, *Novalis Schriften,* 2:610).

39. Similarly, Mallarmé, a century later, writes that "the pure work implies the disappearance of the poet speaking, who yields the initiative to words." Stéphane Mallarmé, *Divagations,* trans. Barbara Johnson (Cambridge, Mass.: Harvard University Press, 2007), 208. See also Stéphane Mallarmé, *Œuvres complètes,* ed. Henri Mondor and G. Jean-Aubry (Paris: Gallimard, 1945), 366.

Chapter 2

1. It may not be a coincidence that Rousseau published *Émile* in October 1761, between *Julie,* published in January 1761, and *The Social Contract,* published in April 1762. On the question of genre, see Laurence Mall, "*Émile*" *ou les figures de la fiction* (Oxford: Voltaire Foundation, 2002), 9–44, especially 11–12. Paul de Man describes the difficulty of reading Rousseau's *Discourse on the Origins and the Foundations of Inequality Among Men* in similar terms in *Allegories of Reading,* 135.

2. Rousseau, *Œuvres complètes* (hereafter cited in text as *Oc*); *Émile* is volume 4. The English edition that I have consulted is Allan Bloom's translation

in *Émile, or On Education* (hereafter cited in text as *OE*). I have at moments silently modified the translation.

3. For more on Rousseau's desire to reconcile an education for autonomy with an education for community, see Geraint Parry, "*Émile:* Learning to be Men, Women, and Citizens," in *The Cambridge Companion to Rousseau,* ed. Patrick Riley (Cambridge: Cambridge University Press, 2001). It is perhaps important to mention that the publication of *Émile* resulted in the author's exile from France. See the third volume of Maurice Cranston's biography of Rousseau aptly titled *The Solitary Self: Jean-Jacques Rousseau in Exile and Adversity* (Chicago: University of Chicago Press, 1997).

4. Geoffrey Bennington, *Sententiousness and the Novel: Laying down the Law in Eighteenth-Century French Fiction* (Cambridge: Cambridge University Press 1985), 87.

5. See also Janie Vanpée, "Reading Lessons in Rousseau's *Émile ou de l'éducation,*" *Modern Language Studies* 20, no. 3 (1990): 40–49.

6. "Il s'accoutumera du moins au spectacle du vice, et à voir les méchans sans horreur comme on s'accoutume à voir les malheureux sans pitié" ("He will, at the least, get accustomed to the spectacle of vice and to seeing wicked men without disgust, as one gets accustomed to seeing unhappy men without pity") (*Oc,* 526; *OE,* 237).

7. Rousseau goes on to describe some of the dangers of reading history: historians are generally better at painting a negative picture of the historical figures they describe; to be read, history must be interesting, but in making history interesting, historians may be tempted to distort the facts. Rousseau recognizes the potential difficulties history poses, but he believes the potential benefits of such reading far outweigh their threat.

8. The legacy of Émile's reading is carried by the house steward, Gabriel Betteridge, in Wilkie Collins's *The Moonstone.* Betteridge explains, "You are not to take it, if you please, as the saying of an ignorant man, when I express my opinion that such a book as *Robinson Crusoe* never was written, and never will be written again. I have tried that book for years—generally in combination with a pipe of tobacco—and have found it my friend in need in all the necessities of this mortal life. When my spirits are bad—*Robinson Crusoe.* When I want advice—*Robinson Crusoe.*" Wilkie Collins, *The Moonstone* (London: Pan Books, 1967), 28–29. I thank David Sigler for the reference.

9. It is difficult to know for certain how attuned Rousseau was to the audible presence of his own name within "Crusoe." See also Geoffrey Bennington, *Dudding: des noms de Rousseau* (Paris: Galilée, 1991).

10. See also Diane Fourny, "L'*Émile* et la question du livre," *Studies on Voltaire and the Eighteenth-Century* 278 (1990): 309–20; Tetsuya Kumamoto, "Le 'Topos' de l'ile chez Rousseau et le roman *Robinson Crusoe,*" *Etudes de langue et literature françaises* 70 (1997): 42–54; Patrick Hochart, "La Bible d'Émile ou l'emule de Robinson," *Le travail des Lumières* (Paris: Champion, 2002). While this chapter has much in common with these articles, I place more emphasis on the question of reading in Rousseau and the way that Rousseau's suggestion of *Robinson Crusoe* as the one book that will help Émile read all

others is symptomatic of Rousseau's desire to put reading behind him. Laurence Mall addresses this question of reading directly but does not focus on the specifics of Émile's reading of *Robinson Crusoe.* See Laurence Mall, "Scénarios de lecture dans Émile," *Etudes Jean-Jacques Rousseau* 9 (1997): 21–40, and Mall, *"Émile" ou les figures de la fiction* (Oxford: Voltaire Foundation, 2002), esp. 69–74.

11. D. P. Leinster-Mackay, in *The Education World of Daniel Defoe* (Victoria: English Literary Studies, 1981), explores the historical reception of *Robinson Crusoe* and its central role in school curricula. Since Rousseau recognized the value of *Robinson Crusoe,* it has continued to hold a central place in children's instruction. Walter Wilson in 1830, for example, writes, "As a work of amusement, it is one of the first books put into the hands of youth; and there can be none more proper to insinuate instruction, whilst it administers delight" (quoted in Leinster-Mackay, *Education World,* 10). Even John Stuart Mill, the famed prodigy who had read everything serious before he turned twelve years old, remembers *Robinson Crusoe* as of great importance to him (quoted in Leinster-Mackay, *Education World,* 10). See also Martin Green, *The Robinson Crusoe Story* (University Park: Pennsylvania State University, 1990); and Hubert Damisch, "Robinsonnades I: The Allegory," trans. Rosalind Krauss, *October* 85 (Summer 1998): 20.

12. For a discussion of the problematic role of imitation in pedagogy, see Derrida, *Of Grammatology,* 204–5. As Derrida writes, "Pedagogy cannot help but encounter the problem of imitation. What is example? Should one educate by example or explanation? Should the teacher make an example of himself and not interfere any further, or pile lesson upon exhortation? And is there virtue in being virtuous by imitation? All these questions are asked in the second book of *Émile*" (204). Derrida goes on to show the ways that the possibility of imitation interrupts natural simplicity, for even "good" imitation carries within itself the promise of corruption.

13. On Émile's identification with Robinson Crusoe, see also Josué V. Harari, *Scenarios of the Imaginary: Theorizing the French Enlightenment* (Ithaca, N.Y.: Cornell University Press, 1987), 118–24. Harari notes that "Émile is thus commanded to identify himself with a utopic ideal of man free from *all* relationships, those of society necessarily included" (122). Harari, however, does not pursue the potentially grotesque nature of Émile's identification.

14. Christopher Kelly, *Rousseau as Author: Consecrating One's Life to the Truth* (Chicago: University of Chicago Press, 2003), 94.

15. Jean-Jacques Rousseau, *Émile,* trans. Barbara Foxley (London: Everyman Library, 1993), 177.

16. When Rousseau returns to this question later in *Émile* in the *Profession de foi,* he discloses again the unreadability of *Émile,* an unreadability that emerges in the attempt to control Émile's reading. See Paul de Man's reading of the *Profession de foi* in *Allegories of Reading,* 221–45.

17. For more discussion of *Émile et Sophie,* see Charles Wirz, "Notes sur 'Émile et Sophie ou les solitaires,'" *Annales Jean-Jacques Rousseau* 36 (1963–

65): 291–303; and Guy Turbet-Delof, "A propos d' 'Émile et Sophie,'" *Revue d'histoire littéraire de la France* 64 (1964): 44–59.

18. See also Janie Vanpée, "Rousseau's *Émile ou de l'éducation:* A Resistance to Reading," *Yale French Studies* 77 (1990): 156–76. Whereas Vanpée argues that in the sequel Rousseau critiques his previous interpretations of pedagogical models, I argue that the presence of the sequel discloses a truth about his own pedagogy (and in particular his pedagogy of reading) that only later became legible for Rousseau.

19. One might also identify the natural model as aesthetic because such an approach to language assumes that the meaning of a particular signifier is somehow related to its appearance and that one can move from appearance to signification without interruption.

Chapter 3

1. As Gray wrote of the poem in a letter to Thomas Wharton, "[it has] been so applauded, it is quite a Shame to repeat it. I mean not to be modest; but I mean, it is a Shame for those, who have said such superlative Things about them, that I can't repeat them. I should have been glad, that you & two or three more People had liked them." Thomas Gray, *Correspondence of Thomas Gray,* 3 vols., ed. Paget Toynbee and Leonard Whibley. (Oxford: Clarendon Press, 1935), 335. See also Robert L. Mack, *Thomas Gray: A Life* (New Haven, Conn.: Yale University Press, 2000), 412–13.

2. As quoted in Henry Weinfield, *The Poet Without a Name: Gray's Elegy and the Problem of History* (Carbondale: Southern Illinois University Press, 1991), 1. More recently, however, Alan Bower alludes to Gray's continuing "slide into disregard." Alan Bower, "The Eighteenth Century," *The Year's Work in English Studies,* 70 (1989): 370.

3. Samuel Johnson, *Lives of the English Poets,* 3 vols., ed. George Hill (Oxford: Clarendon Press, 1905), 2:441.

4. I. A. Richards, *Practical Criticism: A Study of Literary Judgment* (New York: Harcourt, Brace and World, 1929), 197.

5. Richards's interpretation is particularly fitting given the poem's concern with those who did not have access to the social structures (educational institutions, for example) that would have made possible boldness and originality: "Perhaps in this neglected spot is laid / Some heart once pregnant with celestial fire . . . But Knowledge to their eyes her ample page / Rich with the spoils of time did ne'er enroll." Thomas Gray, "Elegy Written in a Country Churchyard," in *The Poetical Works of Gray and Collins,* ed. Austin Lane Poole (Oxford: Oxford University Press, 1926), 91–97, lines 45–46 and 49–50 (hereafter cited in text as "Elegy" with line numbers). The speaker of the poem imagines that buried in the country churchyard are those who might have become bold and original world-historical figures had their material conditions been otherwise. Just as Gray celebrates the "noiseless tenor" of the lives of those buried in the churchyard, Richards responds to the quiet tenor of the poem, which he suggests distinguishes the poem and makes it remarkable even

though it is neither bold nor original. Like the poem itself, those buried in the country churchyard never made manifest their boldness and originality.

In this way the poem's lack of originality is intimately linked to what William Empson calls its ideology. As he suggests in *Some Versions of Pastoral* (New York: New Directions, 1950), the poem "trick[s] us into feeling it is lucky for the poor man that society keeps him unspotted from the World" (4). The poem reinforces the status quo and calls for inaction (as opposed to action): "the truism of the reflections in the churchyard, the universality and impersonality this gives to the style, claim as if by comparison that we ought to accept the injustice of society as we do the inevitability of death" (4). For Johnson and Richards, the poem is to be and has been celebrated for its commonness. In making the lives of the villagers worthy of a poem, Gray's "Elegy" lifts the villagers to become the proper subject of poetry. In the process, following Empson's reading of the poem, it simultaneously releases readers from recognizing, let alone working to change, the material conditions of the poor. The poor are worthy of a poem because they have not been corrupted by the world. The poem privileges a secluded life but is complicit in certain ideologies of the aesthetic in which a retreat from the world is also a thinly disguised acceptance of it. The poem's "commonness" is then a means by which the status quo is reinforced and perpetuated. One should be happy, in other words, to die in obscurity.

6. Critics have celebrated the poem for being unexceptional, and the poem itself offers an extended argument for honoring the unexceptional precisely for being unexceptional. After imagining the lives the villagers might have lived had their lot been different, the poet-speaker celebrates the simplicity of the lives they did live. Because the villagers were far "from the madding crowd's ignoble strife, / Their sober wishes never learn'd to stray" ("Elegy," ll. 73–74). Because their ambitions were constrained, so too were their crimes: "Along the cool sequester'd vale of life / They kept the noiseless tenor of their way" ("Elegy," ll. 75–76). In an earlier version of the poem, Gray had written "the silent Tenour of their Way." The revision accomplishes on the level of sound—as the "o" and "e" from "noiseless" are reversed in the "e" and then "o" of "tenor"—what the poem hopes to accomplish conceptually. The villagers' sacrificed potential is not to be mourned for it, instead, returned increased virtue. For Gray, the fact that these villagers led unexceptional lives is precisely the reason they should now be elegized. The poet-speaker justifies elegizing those who formerly would not have been considered worthy of a poem: regardless of achievement, all deserve "one longing lingering look behind" ("Elegy," l. 88), some pious drops from the eye of the one who reads an epitaph. This is true especially when the one mourned lived a life of sober wishes, when the epitaph consists only of a name and years "spelt by the unletter'd Muse" ("Elegy," l. 81). The legacy of Gray's "Elegy" returns in the conclusion to George Eliot's *Middlemarch* (New York: W. W. Norton, 2000): "the growing good of the world is partly dependent on unhistoric acts; and that things are not so ill with you and me as they might have been, is half owing to the number who lived faithfully a hidden life, and rest in unvisited tombs" (515).

7. Critics have frequently commented on the inclusion of the poem's epitaph, which Walter Savage Landor found unappealing and described as "a tin kettle tied to the tail of a noble dog," as quoted in Anne Williams, *Prophetic Strain: The Greater Lyric in the Eighteenth Century* (Chicago: University of Chicago Press, 1984), 94. In terms of the poem's reception, the "flaws" of the epitaph are not responsible for any confusion. For whom the epitaph is written is, however, still unclear. There exists a gap between elegy and epitaph, a gap that is bridged only with the enigmatic address to "thee."

8. Herbert W. Starr, ed., *Twentieth Century Interpretations of Gray's Elegy,* (Englewood Cliffs, N.J.: Prentice-Hall, 1968), 14.

9. "If we can answer that question," writes Williams in *Prophetic Strain,* "then we know whose epitaph concludes the poem and can presumably judge its suitability, and its relation to what came before" (94).

10. See, for instance, the discussion of Shepard's argument in Herbert W. Starr, "A Youth to Fortune and to Fame Unknown," in *Twentieth Century Interpretations,* 41–50.

11. Cleanth Brooks, *The Well Wrought Urn* (New York: Harcourt Brace, 1947), 117.

12. Frank Ellis, "Gray's *Elegy:* The Biographical Problem in Literary Criticism," in Starr, *Twentieth Century Interpretations,* 60. Ellis describes the poem as a dramatic situation including four distinct characters: the poet (the "me" of line 4); a kindred spirit; a hoary-headed swain; and, most significantly, a stonecutter (addressed by the poet in line 93). Ellis unites the figure of the poem's mute, inglorious Milton, whom Starr identifies with an unknown village poet, and the stonecutter, the one responsible for engraving the names and dates on the grave markers. "'Thee,'" he writes, "refers to the Stonecutter, not to Gray, 'these Lines' to the 'uncouth Rhimes' composed by the Stonecutter, and 'Some kindred Spirit' to the chance Enquirer. By a shift in the antecedent of a pronoun, Gray wrote himself out of the poem" (55).

13. On the history of the reception of Ellis's article and its place in "teaching through controversy," see William H. Epstein, "Counter-Intelligence: Cold-War Criticism and Eighteenth-Century Studies," *ELH* 57, no. 1 (1990): 63–99. For an example of another participant in the controversy, see John H. Sutherland, who in "The Stonecutter in Gray's 'Elegy'" takes issue with Ellis's interpretation. He returns to the Eton manuscript, where the equivalents of lines 93–94 read, "And thou, who mindful of th' unhonour'd Dead / Dost in these Notes their artless Tale relate." There is no doubt, asserts Sutherland, that in the early version of Gray's "Elegy" the speaker is referring to the "Elegy" itself, as suggested by "these Notes." There is "no real evidence," Sutherland asserts, "that Gray wished to change the reference of either 'thee' or 'these lines'" (in Starr, *Twentieth-Century Interpretations,* 80). In turning to the Eton manuscript to counter Ellis's suggestion, Sutherland, however, raises additional questions. For instance, in revising "And thou" to "For thee," Gray moves from a vocative construction to an accusative one, which produces a grammatical ambiguity not present before. Sutherland, in turning to the Eton manuscript, invokes the figure of Gray's "intentions," but he does not address the effect

of Gray's introducing into the poem a grammatical ambiguity, since "thee" now in the published version of the poem has no grammatical antecedent. In revising the poem, Gray produces a less, not a more, "commonplace" poem, if we, perhaps mistakenly, posit the "commonplace" and ambiguous grammatical construction as opposed. New Critical procedures inaugurated a controversy even as New Critics such as Cleanth Brooks labored to draw attention away from the line (by substituting "for me" for the more enigmatic and troubling "for thee"). "Mere reading, it turns out, prior to any theory," writes Paul de Man in "The Return to Philology," "is able to transform critical discourse in a manner that would appear deeply subversive to those who think of the teaching of literature as a substitute for the teaching of theology, ethics, psychology, or intellectual history" (in de Man, *Resistance to Theory,* 24). Attention to words throws into question the compatibility of aesthetic value and linguistic structure. "Close reading," continues de Man, "accomplishes this often in spite of itself because it cannot fail to respond to structures of language which it is the more or less secret aim of literary teaching to keep hidden" (24). The introduction of the figure of the stonecutter sparked a controversy in the middle of the twentieth century precisely because it complicated the critic's ability to judge the suitability of the epitaph. How does one judge the poem if one cannot know for sure whose epitaph concludes the poem?

14. Starr, *Twentieth-Century Interpretations,* 14–15.

15. See, for instance, Paul de Man, "Anthropomorphism and Trope in the Lyric," in *Rhetoric of Romanticism.* For a discussion of lyric tropes and related theories of testimony and witness, see Sara Guyer, *Romanticism After Auschwitz*, esp. 25–45.

16. Stephen Greenblatt, *Shakespearean Negotiations: The Circulation of Social Energy in Renaissance England* (Berkeley: University of California Press, 1988), 1.

17. As Thomas Keenan writes of the opening "Who's there?" of *Hamlet,* "The address is not a cognitive or constative utterance, not a demand for something in particular, not a relay between two constituted subjects or consciousness who encounter each other across a language that they share." Keenan, *Fables of Responsibility,* 28.

18. The point here is not to suggest that the poem was inspired by an actual graveyard. One does not need to assume that the poet actually walked through a country churchyard before composing the poem. But the poem stages what happens to the names (even if the scene is imagined) as a question precisely because it offers an "elegy" in place of the rude inscriptions that merely supply the "place" of elegy, as if awaiting Gray's poem.

19. Diana Fuss, "Corpse Poem," *Critical Inquiry* 30 (Autumn 2003): 25.

20. On romanticism and anonymity, see Jacques Khalip, *Anonymous Life: Romanticism and Dispossession* (Stanford, Calif.: Stanford University Press, 2008). Khalip "approaches romantic subjectivity through its fascination with anonymity as an ethics of engaged withdrawal or strategic reticence" (3).

21. That all of this happens around an apostrophe might not surprise many observers, given that, as Jonathan Culler suggests, apostrophe announces the

subject who is constituted around the muteness of the absent or inanimate object addressed. See Jonathan Culler, *Pursuit of Signs: Semiotics, Literature, Deconstruction* (Ithaca, N.Y.: Cornell University Press, 1981), 135–154. More on Culler and apostrophe below.

22. On mourning as a refusal of loss, and so for more on the "impossibility of mourning," see Jacques Derrida, *Mémoires for Paul de Man,* trans. Cecile Lindsay et al. (New York: Columbia University Press, 1986); Jacques Derrida, *The Gift of Death,* trans. David Wills (Chicago: University of Chicago Press, 1995); and R. Clifton Spargo, *The Ethics of Mourning: Grief and Responsibility in Elegiac Literature* (Baltimore: Johns Hopkins University Press, 2004). I return to these questions in chapter 5.

23. These questions are related to recent ones about mourning and melancholia. Is mourning, which aims through consolation to achieve some distance from the dead, a means to forget the dead? Does melancholia, which is the failure to mourn successfully and so the failure to move away from loss, offer a more ethical relationship to the dead?

24. In this way, Gray's "Elegy" anticipates one story of romanticism, which moves the poet front and center. As S. T. Coleridge writes, "Elegy is a form of poetry natural to the reflective mind. It may treat of any subject, but it must treat of no subject for itself; but always and exclusively with reference to the poet." Samuel T. Coleridge, *The Collected Works of Samuel Taylor Coleridge, vol. 14: Table Talk I,* ed. Carl Woodring (Princeton, N.J.: Princeton University Press, 1990), 444–45.

25. Bertrand H. Bronson, "On a Special Decorum in Gray's *Elegy,*" in *From Sensibility to Romanticism: Essays Presented to Frederick A. Pottle,* ed. Frederick W. Hillis and Harold Bloom (Oxford: Oxford University Press, 1970), 176.

26. W. K. Wimsatt, *Hateful Contraries: Studies in Literature and Criticism* (Lexington: University of Kentucky Press, 1965), 43.

27. Quoted in Yopie Prins, *Victorian Sappho* (Princeton, N.J.: Princeton University Press, 1999), 247.

28. Ibid.

29. Debra Fried, "Repetition, Refrain, and Epitaph," *ELH* 53, no. 3 (Autumn 1986): 615–32, at 616.

30. Ibid., 617.

31. Ibid.

32. Vincent Newey, "The Selving of Thomas Gray" in *Thomas Gray: Contemporary Essays,* ed. W. B. Hutchings and William Ruddick (Liverpool: Liverpool University Press, 1993), 14.

33. See also Frances Ferguson, *Solitude and the Sublime: The Romantic Aesthetics of Individuation* (New York: Routledge, 1992) for an investigation into the relationship between sublime experience and ideologies of solitude and romantic individualism.

34. Barbara Johnson, "Apostrophe, Animation, Abortion," in *World of Difference,* 184–200.

35. But what is the effect of the poet's turning away from his reader to address

an absent or inanimate object? In divulging his feelings to an inanimate object through apostrophe, the poet seems all the more sincere; he is burdened by a sincerity that he cannot express otherwise or to another sentient subject. Who attempts to deceive an inanimate object? The poet, in consciously employing apostrophe, foregrounds the persuasive effects of rhetorical figures. If sincerity results from the employment of a particular figure, how does one ensure that the sincerity perceived is not simply an effect of apostrophe? How does one tell the difference between feeling and its performance, especially when performance makes apparent the poet's supposed sincerity? Either sincere feeling leads the poet to employ apostrophe or apostrophe is employed to convince another of the poet's sincerity, which leaves one exposed to the very insincerity apostrophe denies. Is the ultimate addressee, then, the moon or the reader, who is led to mistake the appearance of sincerity for authentic sincerity?

36. Jonathan Culler, *Pursuit of Signs,* 135.

37. Ibid.

38. It is a complicated moment in the poem, for the poet-speaker does not himself employ apostrophe (he neither apostrophizes the owl nor the moon): "O Moon!" or "O Owl!" Instead, he figures the owl apostrophizing the moon. The poet moves from metaphor (the beetle's "wheeling") to metonymy (the "drowsy tinklings," which substitute for the sheep near their fold) to anthropomorphism (the owl complains) to apostrophe (to the moon). For a related but more extended discussion of anthropomorphism and survival, see Guyer, *Romanticism After Auschwitz*: "If anthropomorphism is a restorative figure, this is only because it restores man's weak power (the capacity to be destroyed, to live on) and introduces a possibility of speaking within weakness that does not recover a self or power" (129).

39. As Debra Fried suggests, epitaphs "beckon the passerby to halt and urge him to continue on his way laden with the inscription's knowledge and heeding its warning" ("Repetition, Refrain, and Epitaph," 616), and this is part of the epitaph's consoling fiction: that the dead are not quite dead. They beckon us to halt.

40. William Waters turns to Osip Mandelstam's "On the Interlocutor" ("O sobesednike") at a key moment and describes a metaphor employed by Mandelstam as a point d'appui for his argument, "which aims to bring out [the] sense in which certain poems seek an interlocutor" (*Poetry's Touch,* 151). While Waters argues that the one who reads a poem is its addressee by virtue of "finding it"—by virtue, in other words, of the fact that one reads it—along with Mandelstam, he also presents a powerful case for the necessary forgetting, the setting aside, of the idea that the poem was, if not addressed to no one, always possibly addressed to another. Only in taking myself as the poem's "secret addressee" do I even begin to read it, but in taking myself as the poem's "secret addressee," what is lost? What is missed, forgotten, set aside?

41. In opening the poem with the owl's address to the moon, Gray's "Elegy" anticipates the turn to the reader in surprising ways. The poet-speaker moves into the churchyard only after overhearing the owl's address to the moon—only after, that is, he finds himself excluded from the communicative circuit. As

a result, the poet-speaker is offered as a figure for the reader, one who witnesses the transformation of object into subject. This is precisely the power the poet-speaker goes on to wield in the churchyard. That this power is "borrowed" from the owl suggests that apostrophe, the power to apostrophize, already covers over—disguises—the work of another figure (anthropomorphism). One must take oneself as human—and so as alive—to adopt the role of poet, but this humanity is the result of particular tropes.

42. See, for instance, Garrett Stewart, *Dear Reader: The Conscripted Audience in Nineteenth-Century British Fiction* (Baltimore: Johns Hopkins University Press, 1996).

43. Paul de Man, "Lyrical Voice in Contemporary Theory: Riffaterre and Jauss," in *Lyric Poetry: Beyond New Criticism,* ed. Chaviva Hošek and Patricia Parker (Ithaca, N.Y.: Cornell University Press, 1985), 55.

44. "An epitaph is not a proud Writing shut up for the studious; it is exposed to all, to the wise and the most ignorant, it is condescending, perspicuous, and lovingly solicits regard; . . . it is concerning all, and for all." William Wordsworth, *The Prose Works of William Wordsworth,* 3 vols., ed. W. J. B. Oven and Jane Worthington Smyser (Oxford: Oxford University Press, 1974), 2:59. But to be readable by all is to be readable—in the sense that Rousseau develops in *Émile*—by none. It is, in other words, precisely such readability that Rousseau aims to eliminate in *Émile* through Émile's reading of the notes and *Robinson Crusoe:* a readability that emerges from absence, a readability free to drift independently from the willed intention to communicate.

45. For an alternative reading of this line, one attuned to the poem's debt to archaeology, see Lee Morrissey, *From the Temple to the Castle: An Architectural History of British Literature, 1660–1760* (Charlottesville: University of Virginia Press, 1999), esp. 81–107.

46. Fry, *Defense of Poetry,* 180.

47. In *Essays upon Epitaphs,* Wordsworth writes that every inscription evokes "the slow and laborious hand" with which it "must have been engraven." Wordsworth, *Prose Works,* 2:60. See also Cynthia Chase, "Monument and Inscription: Wordsworth's 'Lines,'" *Diacritics* 17, no. 4 (Winter 1987): 65–77.

48. In "Inscriptions and Romantic Nature Poetry," Geoffrey Hartman remarks on the prevalence in romantic writing of inscription poetry, noting that Wordsworth's earliest "genuine lyrical poem" is "Lines left upon a Seat in a Yew-Tree, which stands near the Lake of Esthwaite, on a desolate part of the shore, yet commanding a beautiful prospect," an inscription poem (as the title suggests). Geoffrey Hartman, "Inscriptions and Romantic Nature Poetry," in *The Unremarkable Wordsworth* (Minneapolis: University of Minnesota Press, 1987), 31–46. Hartman helps focus attention on Wordsworth's preoccupation, from the start of his poetic career, not with himself (as is all too often assumed) but with the anonymous inscription, which Hartman links to the epitaph. Hartman's focus on Wordsworth's inscription poetry produces a startling reunderstanding of Wordsworth. According to Hartman, nature comes to seem, for Wordsworth, "a larger graveyard" (34). With Wordsworth's interest in inscription poetry, "the poet," writes Hartman,

"reads the landscape as if it were a monument or grave" (40). In this light, all Wordsworth's poems are, less than metaphorically but more than literally, "written in a country churchyard."

Chapter 4

1. William Wordsworth, *Lyrical Ballads* (New York: Routledge, 2005), 307 (hereafter cited in text as *LB*). Subsequent line number references to "Simon Lee: The Old Huntsman with an Incident in Which He Was Concerned" are from this edition. "Simon Lee" appears on pages 105–8.

2. Noel Jackson, "Rethinking the Cultural Divide: Walter Pater, Wilkie Collins, and the Legacies of Wordsworthian Aesthetics," *Modern Philology* 102, no. 2 (2004): 216. Jackson specifically footnotes David Lloyd and Paul Thomas from *Culture and the State* (New York: Routledge, 1998): "The narrative by which poetry transforms the disintegrative effect of the multiplying shocks of modern experience into a principled phenomenology of perception in turn replicates the universal history of man's progression from 'savage torpor' to true culture" (78).

3. Wordsworth, *Prelude,* 66.

4. See also Thomas Keenan, "Publicity and Indifference," *PMLA* 117, no. 1 (2002): 104–16; and Luc Boltanski, *Distant Suffering: Morality, Media and Politics,* trans. Graham Burchell (Cambridge: Cambridge University Press, 1999).

5. Geoffrey Hartman, *The Longest Shadow: In the Aftermath of the Holocaust* (Bloomington: Indiana University Press, 1996), 100. In *Regarding the Pain of Others* (New York: Farrar, Straus and Giroux, 2003), Susan Sontag returns to this idea after first pursuing it in *On Photography* (1977). As she summarizes in *Regarding the Pain of Others,* "in a world saturated, no hyper-saturated with images, those that should matter have a diminishing effect: we become callous. In the end, such images just make us a little less able to feel, to have our conscience pricked" (105). In *Regarding the Pain of Others* Sontag wonders if this is true: "I thought it was when I wrote [*On Photography*]. I'm not so sure now" (105). She warns that "it is absurd to identify the world with those zones in the well-off countries where people have the dubious privilege of being spectators, or of declining to be spectators, of other people's pain, just as it is absurd to generalize about the ability to respond to the sufferings of others on the basis of the mind-set of those consumers of news who know nothing at first hand about war and massive injustice and terror" (110–11). For her short discussion of Wordsworth, see *Regarding the Pain of Others,* 106–7. Charles Rzepka also borrows the line from Keats to describe changes in the field of romantic studies. Charles Rzepka, "The Feel of Not to Feel It," *PMLA* 116, no. 5 (October 2001): 1422–31.

6. As Deborah Esch writes, "The unproblematic articulation of live TV with the real (and with real time) has its impulse in a broader realist ideology that finds its opportunity in the failure to reflect on the medium" (65). Considering the image as "live" becomes one way of substituting the voice for the complexities

of writing (and of the poem as written) outlined by Wordsworth in a poem such as "Simon Lee." Deborah Esch, *In the Event: Reading Journalism, Reading Theory* (Stanford, Calif.: Stanford University Press, 1999).

7. Giorgio Agamben, *Infancy and History: On the Destruction of Experience*, trans. Liz Heron (New York: Verso, 1993), 13.

8. Or, put another way, feeling comes to mark the self-differentiation of the subject. As Rei Terada writes in *Feeling in Theory,* "only self-differential entities—'texts'—feel." Rei Terada, *Feeling in Theory: Emotion After the "Death of the Subject"* (Cambridge, Mass.: Harvard University Press, 2001), 156.

9. Quoted in William Wordsworth, *The Poetical Works of William Wordsworth*, 5 vols., ed. Ernest de Selincourt and Helen Darbishire (Oxford: Clarendon, 1940–49), 4:413. Andrew L. Griffin makes a similar point in "Wordsworth and the Problem of the Imaginative Story: The Case of 'Simon Lee'" *PMLA* 92, no. 3 (1977): 392–409.

10. As Griffin writes, the "apology, or charge, to the reader can thus be welcomed as the death rattle of a story-monger and the birth of a poet. In the end, 'Simon Lee' finds itself . . . as a Wordsworthian lyric: three stanzas of deeply felt recollection finding unusual meaning, scarcely to be articulated, in an ordinary event" (Griffin, "Wordsworth and Imaginative Story," 401).

11. See also Garrett Stewart's discussion of "Simon Lee" in the opening pages of the second chapter of *Dear Reader:* the "passive . . . consumption of narrative is acknowledged by Wordsworth only to be rebuked and cured" (26).

12. Stephen M. Parrish, *The Art of the "Lyrical Ballads"* (Cambridge, Mass.: Harvard University Press, 1973), x.

13. James H. Averill, *Wordsworth and the Poetry of Human Suffering* (Ithaca, N.Y.: Cornell University Press, 1980), 164–65.

14. These are questions often raised by critics of sentimentalism. For general discussions of sentimentalism, see Janet Todd, *Sentimentalism: An Introduction* (London: Methuen, 1986); and Chris Jones, *Radical Sensibility: Literature and Ideas in the 1790s* (London: Routledge, 1993). For more specific readings of the relationship between Wordsworth and sentimentalism, see Averill, *Wordsworth and Suffering.* For more on questions of Wordsworth and philanthropy, see James O'Rourke, "'Goody Blake and Harry Gill,' 'The Thorn,' and the Failure of Philanthropy," *European Romantic Review* 9 (1998): 103–23; and J. Andrew Hubbell, "Wordsworth's *Excursion* in Romantic Philanthropy," *European Romantic Review* 18 (2007): 43–68.

15. Karen Swann, "Suffering and Sensation in *The Ruined Cottage,*" *PMLA* 106, no. 1 (1991): 84.

16. Don Bialostosky, *Making Tales: The Poetics of Wordsworth's Narrative Experiments* (Chicago: University of Chicago Press, 1984), 76.

17. John F. Danby, *The Simple Wordsworth* (London: Routledge and Kegan Paul, 1960), 38.

18. See also Arnd Bohm, "Nimrod and Wordsworth's 'Simon Lee': Habits of Tyranny," *Romanticism* 8, no. 2 (2002): 131–60.

19. R. F. Storch, "Wordsworth's Experimental Ballads: The Radical Uses of

Intelligence and Comedy," *Studies in English Literature 1500–1900* 11, no. 4 (1971): 621–39.

20. I am thinking in particular of Freud's definition of the origin of consciousness: "*Protection against* stimuli is an almost more important function for the living organism than *reception of* stimuli." Freud, *Beyond the Pleasure Principle,* 30.

Chapter 5

1. William Butler Yeats, *Mythologies* (New York: Collier, 1959), 331.

2. Jacques Rancière, *The Names of History: On the Poetics of Knowledge,* trans. Hassan Melehy (Minneapolis: University of Minnesota Press, 1994), 2.

3. All references to Keats's poems are from John Keats, *Complete Poems,* ed. Jack Stillinger (Cambridge, Mass.: Belknap Press of Harvard University Press, 1978) (hereafter cited in text as *CP*). "Isabella" appears on pages 184–98. The quoted lines are 386–89.

4. Letter to George and Tom Keats, December 1817, in John Keats, *The Letters of John Keats,* ed. Robert Gittings (Oxford: Oxford University Press, 1970), 42.

5. Jack Stillinger, "Keats and Romance," *Studies in English Literature 1500–1900* 8, no. 4 (Autumn 1968): 593–605.

6. Tilottama Rajan, *The Dark Interpreter: The Discourse of Romanticism* (Ithaca, N.Y.: Cornell University Press, 1980), 104.

7. For more on Keats's self-critique of an underlying therapeutic conception of art, see Emily Sun, "Facing Keats with Winnicott: On the New Therapeutics of Poetry," *Studies in Romanticism* 46 (Spring 2007): 57–75. See also Alain Badiou, *Handbook of Inaesthetics,* trans. Alberto Toscano (Stanford, Calif.: Stanford University Press, 2005).

8. Susan Wolfson, "Keats's *Isabella* and the 'Digressions' of 'Romance,' " *Criticism* 27, no. 3 (Summer 1985): 247–61.

9. Ibid., 258–59.

10. Ibid., 258.

11. In *Keats, Narrative, and Audience: The Posthumous Life of Writing* (Cambridge: Cambridge University Press, 1994), Andrew Bennett suggests that "Isabella" demonstrates Keats's anxiety of audience, which results in elaborations "of secrecy and publication": "The publication of the tragedy is itself implicated as a cause of the tragedy" (83). For Bennett's complete reading of the poem, see chap. 4, pp. 82–95.

12. Kelvin Everest defends the poem against those, like Keats, who are critical of the poem. He does, however, suggest that "the passages directly addressed from the narrator to the reader . . . lack self-assurance" and produce "an almost apologetic tone." Kelvin Everest, "Isabella in the Market-place," in *Keats and History,* ed. Nicholas Roe (Cambridge: Cambridge University Press, 1995), 108.

13. For a discussion of Keats's conflicted relationship to sensation, in particular through a reading of *Lamia,* see Orrin N. C. Wang, "Coming

Attractions: *Lamia* and Cinematic Sensation," *Studies in Romanticism* 42 (Winter 2003): 461–500.

14. Quoted in *CP,* 442.

15. Ibid.

16. James Chandler suggests that "smokabilty" "implies a conception of intelligibility or understanding that is itself understood, in its circumstance, as a vulnerability to being grasped—captured—by a higher-order intelligence. It implies a hierarchy of minds, souls, or sensibilities arranged according to the capacity to 'see through' another." James Chandler, *England in 1819: The Politics of Literary Culture and the Case of Romantic Historicism* (Chicago: University of Chicago Press, 1998), 400.

17. See Giovanni Boccaccio, *Decameron,* 3 vols., trans. John Payne, rev. and annot. Charles S. Singleton (Berkeley: University of California Press, 1982), 1:327–31.

18. Kurt Heinzelman, "Self-Interest and the Politics of Composition in Keats's Isabella," *ELH* 55, no. 1 (Spring 1988): 165, 167–68.

19. Unlike Keats's poetry more generally, which has often been viewed as celebrating aesthetic distance, "Isabella" has often been read approvingly by critics interested in the poem's criticisms of capitalism. George Bernard Shaw, for instance, finds in "Isabella" foreknowledge of Marx. See George Bernard Shaw, "Keats," in *The John Keats Memorial Volume,* ed. George C. Williamson (London: John Lane, 1921), 173–76. See also Everest, "Isabella in the Market-place," 107–26; and Jeffrey N. Cox, "*Lamia, Isabella,* and *The Eve of St. Agnes:* Eros and 'Romance,' " in *The Cambridge Companion to Keats,* ed. Susan J. Wolfson (Cambridge: Cambridge University Press, 2001), 53–68.

20. For more on romanticism's complicated relationship to notions of sobriety and its various negations, see Orrin N. C. Wang, "Romantic Sobriety," *Modern Language Quarterly* 60, no. 4 (December 1999): 469–93.

21. "Knowing that this was no place for lament, she [Lisabetta] would fain, if she but might, have borne away the whole body, to give it a fitter burial; but, seeing that this might not be, she with a knife did off the head from the body, as best she could." Boccaccio, *Decameron,* 1:330.

22. John Stuart Mill, "Thoughts on Poetry and Its Varieties," in *Dissertations and Discussions: Political, Philosophical, and Historical,* 2 vols. (New York: Haskell, 1973), 1:71.

23. Northrop Frye, *Anatomy of Criticism: Four Essays* (Princeton, N.J.: Princeton University Press, 1957), 249–50.

24. Culler, *Pursuit of Signs,* 141–43.

25. I quote the opening lines to "Ode to the West Wind." Percy Bysshe Shelley, *Poetical Works,* ed. Thomas Hutchinson (Oxford: Oxford University Press, 1988), 201.

26. J. Mark Smith, "Apostrophe, or the Lyric Art of Turning Away," *Texas Studies in Literature and Language* 49, no. 4 (Winter 2007): 411.

27. As Paul de Man asserts, "the figure of address is recurrent in lyric poetry, to the point of constituting the generic definition of, at the very least, the ode

(which can, in its turn, be seen as paradigmatic for poetry in general).” Paul de Man, “Lyrical Voice in Contemporary Theory,” in *Lyric Poetry: Beyond New Criticism,* ed. Chaviva Hošek and Patricia Parker (Ithaca, N.Y.: Cornell University Press, 1985), 61. Learning to read, following the conclusion to “Isabella,” may be one of those nameless, unremembered acts Wordsworth describes in “Tintern Abbey” and that Keats figures through the yawn, a way of passing on that which is not entirely conscious even as it, like the contagious yawn, occurs in a surprising act of repetition.

28. De Man, *Rhetoric of Romanticism,* 78. See also, among others, Prins, *Victorian Sappho,* 246–51.

29. Debra Fried, “Repetition, Refrain, and Epitaph,” *ELH* 53, no. 3 (Fall 1986): 615–32, at 617.

30. Barbara Johnson, *Persons and Things,* 19.

31. Giorgio Agamben, *Stanzas: Word and Phantasm in Western Culture,* trans. Ronald L. Martinez (Stanford, Calif.: Stanford University Press), 20. Agamben continues, “From this point of view, melancholy would be not so much the regressive reaction to the loss of the love object as the imaginative capacity to make an unobtainable object appear *as if* lost. If the libido behaves as if a loss had occurred although *nothing* has in fact been lost this is because the libido stages a simulation where what cannot be lost because it has never been possessed appears as lost, and what could never be possessed because it had never perhaps existed may be appropriated insofar as it is lost” (20).

32. See Sigmund Freud, “Mourning and Melancholia,” trans. James Strachey, in *The Standard Edition of the Complete Psychological Works of Sigmund Freud,* vol. 14 (London: Hogarth Press, 1957), 237–58.

33. Slavoj Žižek, “Melancholy and the Act,” *Critical Inquiry* 26, no. 4 (Summer 2000): 658. “With regard to mourning and melancholy, the predominant opinion is the following: Freud opposed normal mourning (the successful acceptance of a loss) to pathological melancholy (the subject persists in his or her narcissistic identification with the lost object). Against Freud, one should assert the conceptual and ethical primacy of melancholy. In the process of the loss, there is always a remainder that cannot be integrated through the work of mourning, and the ultimate fidelity is the fidelity to this remainder” (658).

34. Spargo, *Ethics of Mourning,* 6.

35. Ibid., 13.

36. In her reading of *Isabella,* Diane Long Hoeveler argues that Isabella looks to extend her inability to mourn to include attempts at reanimation of the dead. Hoeveler writes, “Lorenzo the lover may be dead, but the poem promises that something, some form of life and growth, can be salvaged, saved from the world of death. The poem refuses to mourn; it promises instead that activity generated by living bodies can redeem and renew the cycle of generation. As we read this image we know ourselves to be participating in a nostalgic recuperative gesture, the attempt of a child through magical thinking to reconstitute the life cycle as benign.” Diane Long Hoeveler,

"Decapitating Romance: Class, Fetish, and Ideology in Keats's Isabella," *Nineteenth-Century Literature* 49, no. 3 (Winter 1994): 332. Hoeveler suggests, in other words, that Isabella not only is unable to mourn but also redeems what has been lost, giving new life to a dead beloved. "Isabella" is the story of a young woman who cannot (or is unwilling to) mourn the loss of her beloved and instead nurses, like a child, the basil pot that contains his head. Following Hoeveler, Isabella gives "birth" to a second Lorenzo, a substitute Lorenzo, their child.

37. As Forest Pyle writes, "Keats's poetry compels 'thought' to encounter the resistance of 'things.' This tense confrontation throws both the humanist ethics to which Keats himself subscribed and the 'aestheticism' that would serve as a refuge or compensation into a crisis of such magnitude that the imagination is 'Lost in a sort of purgatory blind,' a crisis that warrants the name 'materialist.'" Forest Pyle, *The Ideology of Imagination: Subject and Society in the Discourse of Romanticism* (Stanford, Calif.: Stanford University Press, 1995), 130. See also Pyle's more recent article, "Kindling and Ash: Radical Aestheticism in Keats and Shelley," *Studies in Romanticism* 42 (Winter 2003): 427–59.

38. In this way I take the "yawning tomb" as a figure of life-in-death or death-in-life. For more on Keats and the ethical considerations such figures raise, see Brendan Corcoran, "Keats's Death: Toward a Posthumous Poetics," *Studies in Romanticism* 48, no. 2 (Summer 2009): 321–48; and Katey Castellano, "'Why Linger at the Yawning Tomb so Long?': The Ethics of Negative Capability in Keats's *Isabella* and *Hyperion*," *Partial Answers: Journal of Literature and the History of Ideas* 8, no. 1 (January 2010): 23–38. Castellano suggests that "lingering in uncertainty, beyond its aesthetic potential, embraces negativity and obstinately refuses established social and political constructs. In the characters of Isabella and Saturn, moreover, this being-towards-death becomes a deep-seated fidelity to the negative that, in its opposition to the values of rational calculation and accumulation, clears the ground for radical ethical transformation" (37). While I find Castellano's reading compelling, with its ties to R. Clifton Spargo's argument in *The Ethics of Mourning*, I am wary of the dialectical reversal that discovers in "being-toward-death" a more ethical way to live, an impossibility that "clears the ground" for possibility. For me, the "yawning tomb"—and so the theory of lyric poetry Keats advances in *Isabella*—bears witness to the undecidability of address without working to overcome that undecidability.

39. Robert R. Provine, "Yawning," *American Scientist* 93 (November–December 2005): 532–39.

Conclusion

1. For more on the question of linguistic formalization, see Paul de Man's reading of Kleist and Schiller in "Aesthetic Formalization: Kleist's *Über das Marrionttentheater*," in de Man, *Rhetoric of Romanticism*, 263–90; and Cathy Caruth's reading of de Man's essay in "The Falling Body and

the Impact of Reference (de Man, Kant, Kleist)," in *Unclaimed Experience: Trauma, Narrative and History* (Baltimore: Johns Hopkins University Press, 1996), 73–90.

2. As Mladen Dolar asserts in *A Voice and Nothing More,* "Obviously all the non-voices, from coughing and hiccups to babbling, screaming, laughing, and singing, are not linguistic voices; they are not phonemes, yet they are not simply outside the linguistic structure: it is as if, by their very absence of articulation . . . they were particularly apt to embody the structure as such, the structure at its minimal." Mladen Dolar, *A Voice and Nothing More* (Cambridge, Mass.: MIT Press, 2006), 32. I would add the yawn to Dolar's list. See also Thomas Keenan's "Afterward: The Demystifica-*hic*-tion of In-*hic*-formation," in *New Media, Old Media: A History and Theory Reader,* ed. Wendy Hui Kyong Chun and Thomas Keenan (New York: Routledge, 2006): 399–408.

3. William Wordsworth, *Lyrical Ballads* (New York: Routledge, 2005), 157.

4. Shoshana Felman, *What Does a Woman Want? Reading and Sexual Difference* (Baltimore: Johns Hopkins University Press, 1993), 16.

5. Stephen Best and Sharon Marcus, "Surface Reading: An Introduction," *Representations* 108, no. 1 (Fall 2009): 3.

6. Ibid., 9.

7. Emily Apter and Elaine Freedgood, "Afterword," *Representations* 108, no. 1 (Fall 2009): 139.

8. Terada, "Seeing Is Reading," 178.

9. Best and Marcus, "Surface Reading," 8.

10. Ibid., 12.

11. Ibid.

12. See, for instance, Philippe Lacoue-Labarthe's discussion of Paul Celan's poetry in *Poetry as Experience,* trans. Andrea Tarnowski (Stanford, Calif.: Stanford University Press, 1999). Focusing on the etymology of "experience" as *ex-periri,* "a crossing through danger" (18), Lacoue-Labarthe works against associating experience with what is lived: "I say 'experience' because what the poem 'springs forth' from here—the memory of bedazzlement, which is also the pure dizziness of memory—is precisely that which did not take place, did not happen or occur during the singular event that the poem relates to without relating" (18).

13. Waters, *Poetry's Touch,* 151.

14. For more on literature and exposure, see Emily Sun, *Succeeding King Lear: Literature, Exposure, and the Possibility of Politics* (New York: Fordham University Press, 2010). Literature, for Sun, exposes the impossibility of mastery and therefore the very possibility of politics as "free, plural, and non-sovereign action" (4). To subject what is read to models of reading prepared in advance is to refuse to encounter, however impossible it may be to encounter, the singularity of what is being read, the literariness of literature. See Derek Attridge, *The Singularity of Literature* (New York: Routledge, 2004).

15. As Jacques Derrida writes in "Typewriter Ribbon," "By reason of this unforeseeability, this irreducible and inappropriable exteriority for the subject

of experience, every event as such is *traumatic.* Even an event experienced as a 'happy' one" (258). Derrida, "Typewriter Ribbon," 277–360.

16. As E. S. Burt argues in *Poetry's Appeal: Nineteenth-Century French Lyric and the Political Space* (Stanford, Calif.: Stanford University Press, 1999), one cannot simply ask literature to weigh in on politics (or even, one might suspect, on its own historical moment) "if it is asking itself—as lyric poetry does—what constitutes a voice and what is left unrepresented in it" (8). The lyric's tendency to ask itself what constitutes a voice opens the possibility of rethinking politics (this being poetry's appeal to the political) precisely because the voice (as vote) is central to the origin of modern democracy.

BIBLIOGRAPHY

Aarsleff, Hans. *From Locke to Saussure: Essays on the Study of Language and Intellectual History.* Minneapolis: University of Minnesota Press, 1982.

Abrams, M. H. *The Mirror and the Lamp.* New York: Oxford University Press, 1953.

———. "Types and Orientations of Critical Theories." In *Doing Things with Texts: Essay in Criticism and Critical Theory.* Edited by Michael Fischer, 3–30. New York: W. W. Norton, 1989.

Agamben, Giorgio. *Infancy and History: On the Destruction of Experience.* Translated by Liz Heron. New York: Verso, 1993.

———. *Stanzas: Word and Phantasm in Western Culture.* Translated by Ronald L. Martinez. Stanford, Calif.: Stanford University Press, 1992.

Andrews, Bruce, and Charles Bernstein, eds. *The L=A=N=G=U=A=G=E Book.* Carbondale: Southern Illinois University Press, 1984.

Apter, Emily, and Elaine Freedgood. "Afterword." *Representations* 108, no. 1 (Fall 2009): 139–46.

Ashworth, E. J. "Do Words Signify Ideas or Things?: The Scholastic Sources of Locke's Theory of Language." *Journal of the History of Philosophy* 19 (1981): 299–326.

Attridge, Derek. *The Singularity of Literature.* New York: Routledge, 2004.

Averill, James H. *Wordsworth and the Poetry of Human Suffering.* Ithaca, N.Y.: Cornell University Press, 1980.

Badiou, Alain. *Handbook of Inaesthetics.* Translated by Alberto Toscano. Stanford, Calif.: Stanford University Press, 2005.

Bennett, Andrew. *Keats, Narrative, and Audience: The Posthumous Life of Writing.* Cambridge: Cambridge University Press, 1994.

Bennington, Geoffrey. *Dudding: des noms de Rousseau.* Paris: Galilée, 1991.

———. "The Perfect Cheat: Locke and Empiricism's Rhetoric." In *The Figural and the Literal: Problems of Language in the History of Science and Philosophy, 1630–1800.* Edited by Andrew Benjamin, 103–23. Manchester, U.K.: University of Manchester Press, 1987.

———. *Sententiousness and the Novel: Laying down the Law in Eighteenth-Century French Fiction.* Cambridge: Cambridge University Press, 1985.

Best, Stephen, and Sharon Marcus. "Surface Reading: An Introduction." *Representations* 108, no. 1 (Fall 2009): 1–21.

Bialostosky, Don. *Making Tales: The Poetics of Wordsworth's Narrative Experiments.* Chicago: University of Chicago Press, 1984.

Blanchot, Maurice. *The Writing of the Disaster.* Translated by Ann Smock. Lincoln: University of Nebraska Press, 1995.

Blasing, Mutlu Konuk. *Lyric Poetry: The Pain and the Pleasure of Words.* Princeton, N.J.: Princeton University Press, 2007.

Boccaccio, Giovanni. *Decameron.* 3 vols. Translated by John Payne. Revised and annotated by Charles S. Singleton. Berkeley: University of California Press, 1982.

Bohm, Arnd. "Nimrod and Wordsworth's 'Simon Lee': Habits of Tyranny." *Romanticism* 8, no. 2 (2002): 131–60.

Boltanski, Luc. *Distant Suffering: Morality, Media and Politics.* Translated by Graham Burchell. Cambridge: Cambridge University Press, 1999.

Bower, Alan. "The Eighteenth Century." *The Year's Work in English Studies* 67 (1989): 351–400.

Bronson, Bertrand H. "On a Special Decorum in Gray's *Elegy.*" In *From Sensibility to Romanticism: Essays Presented to Frederick A. Pottle.* Edited by Frederick W. Hillis and Harold Bloom, 171–76. Oxford: Oxford University Press, 1970.

Brooks, Cleanth. *The Well Wrought Urn.* New York: Harcourt Brace, 1947.

Brower, Reuben A., and Richard Poirier, eds. *In Defense of Reading: A Reader's Approach to Literary Criticism.* New York: E. P. Dutton, 1962.

Brown, Laura. *Fables of Modernity: Literature and Culture in the English Eighteenth Century.* Ithaca, N.Y.: Cornell University Press, 2001.

Burt, E. S. *Poetry's Appeal: Nineteenth-Century French Lyric and the Political Space.* Stanford, Calif.: Stanford University Press, 1999.

Caruth, Cathy. *Empirical Truths and Critical Fictions: Locke, Wordsworth, Kant, Freud.* Baltimore: Johns Hopkins University Press, 1991.

———, ed. *Trauma: Explorations in Memory.* Baltimore: Johns Hopkins University Press, 1995.

———. *Unclaimed Experience: Trauma, Narrative and History.* Baltimore: Johns Hopkins University Press, 1996.

Castellano, Katey. "'Why Linger at the Yawning Tomb So Long?': The Ethics of Negative Capability in Keats's *Isabella* and *Hyperion.*" *Partial Answers: Journal of Literature and the History of Ideas* 8, no. 1 (January 2010): 23–38.

Cavell, Stanley. *In Quest of the Ordinary: Lines of Skepticism and Romanticism.* Chicago: University of Chicago Press, 1994.

Chandler, James. *England in 1819: The Politics of Literary Culture and the Case of Romantic Historicism.* Chicago: University of Chicago Press, 1998.

Chase, Cynthia. *Decomposing Figures: Rhetorical Readings in the Romantic Tradition.* Baltimore: Johns Hopkins University Press, 1986.

———. "Monument and Inscription: Wordsworth's 'Lines,'" *Diacritics* 17, no. 4 (Winter 1987): 65–77.

———, ed. *Romanticism.* London: Longman, 1993.

Clement, Tanya E. "'A Thing Not Beginning and Not Ending': Using Digital Tools to Distant-read Gertrude Stein's *The Making of Americans.*" *Literary and Linguistic Computing* 23, no. 3 (2008): 361–81.

Coleridge, Samuel T. *The Collected Works of Samuel Taylor Coleridge, vol. 14:*

Table Talk I. Edited by Carl Woodring. Princeton, N.J.: Princeton University Press, 1990.

Collins, Wilkie. *The Moonstone*. London: Pan Books, 1967.

Corcoran, Brendan. "Keats's Death: Toward a Posthumous Poetics." *Studies in Romanticism* 48, no. 2 (Summer 2009): 321–48.

Cox, Jeffrey N. "*Lamia, Isabella,* and *The Eve of St. Agnes:* Eros and 'Romance.' " In *The Cambridge Companion to Keats*. Edited by Susan J. Wolfson, 53–68. Cambridge: Cambridge University Press, 2001.

Cranston, Maurice. *The Solitary Self: Jean-Jacques Rousseau in Exile and Adversity*. Chicago: University of Chicago Press, 1997.

Culler, Jonathan. *The Literary in Theory*. Stanford, Calif.: Stanford University Press, 2007.

———. *Pursuit of Signs: Semiotics, Literature, Deconstruction*. Ithaca, N.Y.: Cornell University Press, 1981.

Damisch, Hubert. "Robinsonnades I: The Allegory." Translated by Rosalind Krauss. *October* 85 (Summer 1998): 19–28.

Danby, John F. *The Simple Wordsworth*. London: Routledge and Kegan Paul, 1960.

De Man, Paul. *Aesthetic Ideology*. Minneapolis: University of Minnesota Press, 1996.

———. *Allegories of Reading: Figural Language in Rousseau, Nietzsche, Rilke, and Proust*. New Haven, Conn.: Yale University Press, 1979.

———. "Lyrical Voice in Contemporary Theory: Riffaterre and Jauss." In *Lyric Poetry: Beyond New Criticism*. Edited by Chaviva Hošek and Patricia Parker, 38–54. Ithaca, N.Y.: Cornell University Press, 1985.

———. *The Resistance to Theory*. Minneapolis: University of Minnesota Press, 1986.

———. *The Rhetoric of Romanticism*. New York: Columbia University Press, 1984.

Derrida, Jacques. *The Gift of Death*. Translated by David Wills. Chicago: University of Chicago Press, 1995.

———. *The Margins of Philosophy*. Translated by Alan Bass. Chicago: University of Chicago Press, 1982.

———. *Mémoires for Paul de Man*. Translated by Cecile Lindsay et al. New York: Columbia University Press, 1986.

———. *Of Grammatology*. Translated by Gayatri Spivak. Baltimore: Johns Hopkins University Press, 1976.

———. "Structure, Sign, and Play in the Discourse of the Human Sciences." In *Writing and Difference*. Translated by Alan Bass, 278–94. Chicago: University of Chicago Press, 1978.

———. "Typewriter Ribbon: Limited Ink (2)." In *Materials Events: Paul de Man and the Afterlife of Theory*. Edited by Tom Cohen et al. Minneapolis: University of Minnesota Press, 2001.

Dolar, Mladen. *A Voice and Nothing More*. Cambridge, Mass.: MIT Press, 2006.

Eliot, George. *Middlemarch*. New York: W. W. Norton, 2000.

Ellis, Frank H. "Gray's *Elegy:* The Biographical Problem in Literary Criticism." *PMLA* 66 (December 1951): 971–1008.

Empson, William. *Some Versions of Pastoral.* New York: New Directions, 1950.

Epstein, William H. "Counter-Intelligence: Cold-War Criticism and Eighteenth-Century Studies." *ELH* 57, no. 1 (1990): 63–99.

Esch, Deborah. *In the Event: Reading Journalism, Reading Theory.* Stanford, Calif.: Stanford University Press, 1999.

Everest, Kelvin. "Isabella in the Market-place." In *Keats and History.* Edited by Nicholas Roe. Cambridge: Cambridge University Press, 1995.

Felman, Shoshana. *Jacques Lacan and the Adventure of Insight: Psychoanalysis in Contemporary Culture.* Cambridge, Mass.: Harvard University Press, 1987.

———. *What Does a Woman Want? Reading and Sexual Difference.* Baltimore: Johns Hopkins University Press, 1993.

Felski, Rita. "After Suspicion." *Profession 2009*: 28–35.

Ferguson, Frances. "Reading Morals: Locke and Rousseau on Education and Inequality." *Representations* 6 (Spring 1984): 66–84.

———. *Solitude and the Sublime: The Romantic Aesthetics of Individuation.* New York: Routledge, 1992.

Fourny, Diane. "L'*Émile* et la question du livre." *Studies on Voltaire and the Eighteenth-Century* 278 (1990): 309–20.

François, Anne-Lise. *Open Secrets: The Literature of Uncounted Experience.* Stanford, Calif.: Stanford University Press, 2007.

Freud, Sigmund. *Beyond the Pleasure Principle.* Translated by James Strachey. Vol. 18 of *The Standard Edition of the Complete Psychological Works of Sigmund Freud.* London: Hogarth, 1955.

———. "Mourning and Melancholia." Translated by James Strachey. In *The Standard Edition of the Complete Psychological Works of Sigmund Freud,* vol. 14, 237–58. London: Hogarth Press, 1957.

Fried, Debra. "Repetition, Refrain, and Epitaph." *ELH* 53, no. 3 (Autumn 1986): 615–32.

Fry, Paul. *A Defense of Poetry: Reflections on the Occasion of Writing.* Stanford, Calif.: Stanford University Press, 1995.

Frye, Northrop. *Anatomy of Criticism: Four Essays.* Princeton, N.J.: Princeton University Press, 1957.

Fuss, Diana. "Corpse Poem." *Critical Inquiry* (Autumn 2003): 1–30.

Gallop, Jane. "The Historicization of Literary Studies and the Fate of Close Reading." *Profession 2007*: 181–86.

Garber, Marjorie. "Shakespeare in Slow Motion." *Profession 2010*: 151–64.

Gill, Stephen, ed. *The Cambridge Companion to Wordsworth.* Cambridge: Cambridge University Press, 2003.

Gioia, Dana. *Can Poetry Matter? Essays on Poetry and American Culture.* St. Paul: Graywolf Press, 1992.

Gray, Thomas. *Correspondence of Thomas Gray.* 3 vols. Edited by Paget Toynbee and Leonard Whibley. Oxford: Clarendon Press, 1935.

———. *The Poetical Works of Gray and Collins.* Edited by Austin Lane Poole. London: Oxford University Press, 1926.

Green, Martin. *The Robinson Crusoe Story.* University Park: Pennsylvania State University Press, 1990.

Greenblatt, Stephen. *Shakespearean Negotiations: The Circulation of Social Energy in Renaissance England.* Berkeley: University of California Press, 1988.

Greenlee, Douglas. "Locke's Idea of 'Idea.'" In *Locke on Human Understanding.* Edited by I. C. Tipton, 41–47. Oxford: Oxford University Press, 1977.

Griffin, Andrew L. "Wordsworth and the Problem of the Imaginative Story: The Case of 'Simon Lee.'" *PMLA* 92, no. 3 (1977): 392–409.

Guyer, Paul. "Locke's Philosophy of Language." In *Cambridge Companion to Locke.* Edited by Vere Chappell, 115–45. Cambridge: Cambridge University Press, 1994.

Guyer, Sara. "Buccal Reading." *CR: The New Centennial* 7, no. 2 (2007): 71–87.

———. *Romanticism After Auschwitz.* Stanford, Calif.: Stanford University Press, 2007.

Hamilton, Paul. "Romanticism and Poetic Autonomy." In *The Cambridge History of English Romantic Literature.* Edited by James Chandler, 427–50. (Cambridge: Cambridge University Press, 2009).

Harari, Josué V. *Scenarios of the Imaginary: Theorizing the French Enlightenment.* Ithaca, N.Y.: Cornell University Press, 1987.

Hartman, Geoffrey. *The Longest Shadow: In the Aftermath of the Holocaust.* Bloomington: Indiana University Press, 1996.

———. *The Unremarkable Wordsworth.* Minneapolis: University of Minnesota Press, 1987.

———. *Wordsworth's Poetry, 1787–1814.* New Haven, Conn.: Yale University Press, 1967.

Hayles, N. Katherine. "How We Read: Close, Hyper, Machine." *ADE Bulletin* 150 (2010): 62–79.

Heinzelman, Kurt. "Self-Interest and the Politics of Composition in Keats's Isabella." *ELH* 55, no. 1 (Spring 1988): 159–93.

Hillis, Frederick W., and Harold Bloom, eds. *From Sensibility to Romanticism: Essays Presented to Frederick A. Pottle.* Oxford: Oxford University Press, 1970.

Hirsch, E. D. *The Knowledge Deficit: Closing the Shocking Education Gap for America's Children.* New York: Houghton Mifflin, 2007.

Hochart, Patrick. "La Bible d'Émile ou l'emule de Robinson." In *Le travail des Lumières,* 339–60. Paris: Champion, 2002.

Hoeveler, Diane Long. "Decapitating Romance: Class, Fetish, and Ideology in Keats's Isabella." *Nineteenth-Century Literature* 49, no. 3 (Winter 1994): 321–38.

Hubbell, J. Andrew. "Wordsworth's *Excursion* in Romantic Philanthropy." *European Romantic Review* 18 (2007): 43–68.

Hutchings, W. B., and William Ruddick, eds. *Thomas Gray: Contemporary Essays.* Liverpool: Liverpool University Press, 1993.

Jackson, Noel. "Rethinking the Cultural Divide: Walter Pater, Wilkie Collins, and the Legacies of Wordsworthian Aesthetics." *Modern Philology* 102, no. 2 (2004): 209–34.

Jackson, Virginia. *Dickinson's Misery: A Theory of Lyric Reading*. Princeton, N.J.: Princeton University Press, 2005.

Jakobson, Roman. *Language and Literature*. Cambridge, Mass.: Belknap Press of Harvard University Press, 1987.

Johnson, Barbara. *A World of Difference*. Baltimore: Johns Hopkins University Press, 1998.

———. "The Pedagogical Imperative: Teaching as a Literary Genre." *Yale French Studies* 63 (1982): iii–vii.

———. *Persons and Things*. Cambridge, Mass.: Harvard University Press, 2008.

Johnson, Samuel. *Lives of the English Poets*. 3 vols. Edited by George Hill. Oxford: Clarendon Press, 1905.

Jones, Chris. *Radical Sensibility: Literature and Ideas in the 1790s*. London: Routledge, 1993.

Keats, John. *Complete Poems*. Edited by Jack Stillinger. Cambridge, Mass.: Belknap Press of Harvard University Press, 1978.

———. *The Letters of John Keats*. 2 vols. Edited by Hyder E. Rollins. Cambridge, Mass.: Harvard University Press, 1958.

Keenan, Thomas. "Afterward: The Demystifica-*hic*-tion of In-*hic*-formation." In *New Media, Old Media: A History and Theory Reader*. Edited by Wendy Hui Kyong Chun and Thomas Keenan, 399–408. New York: Routledge, 2006.

———. *Fables of Responsibility: Aberrations and Predicaments in Ethics and Politics*. Stanford, Calif.: Stanford University Press, 1997.

———. "Publicity and Indifference." *PMLA* 117, no. 1 (2002): 104–16.

Kelly, Christopher. *Rousseau as Author: Consecrating One's Life to the Truth*. Chicago: University of Chicago Press, 2003.

Khalip, Jacques. *Anonymous Life: Romanticism and Dispossession*. Stanford, Calif.: Stanford University Press, 2008.

Kumamoto, Tetsuya. "Le 'Topos' de l'ile chez Rousseau et le roman *Robinson Crusoe*." *Etudes de langue et littérature françaises* 70 (1997): 42–54.

Lacan, Jacques. *The Seminar of Jacques Lacan: Book II, The Ego in Freud's Theory and in the Technique of Psychoanalysis, 1954–1955*. Edited by Jacques-Alain Miller. Translated by Sylvana Tomaselli. New York: W. W. Norton, 1991.

Lacoue-Labarthe, Philippe. *Poetry as Experience*. Translated by Andrea Tarnowski. Stanford, Calif.: Stanford University Press, 1999.

Latour, Bruno. *We Have Never Been Modern*. Translated by Catherine Porter. Cambridge, Mass.: Harvard University Press, 1993.

Law, Jules David. *The Rhetoric of Empiricism: Language and Perception from Locke to I. A. Richards*. Ithaca, N.Y.: Cornell University Press, 1993.

Lear, Edward. *The Complete Verse and Other Nonsense*. New York: Penguin, 2002.

Leinster-Mackay, D. P. *The Education World of Daniel Defoe*. Victoria: English Literary Studies, 1981.

Levinson, Marjorie. "What Is New Formalism?" *PMLA* 122, no. 2 (2007): 558–69.

Lloyd, David, and Paul Thomas. *Culture and the State.* New York, Routledge, 1998.

Locke, John. *An Essay Concerning Human Understanding.* Oxford: Oxford University Press, 1975.

———. *The Education Writings of John Locke: A Critical Edition with Introduction and Notes.* Edited by James L. Axtell. Cambridge: Cambridge University Press, 1968.

Mack, Robert L. *Thomas Gray: A Life.* New Haven: Yale University Press, 2000.

Mall, Laurence. *"Émile" ou les figures de la fiction.* Oxford: Voltaire Foundation, 2002.

———. "Scénarios de lecture dans Émile." *Etudes Jean-Jacques Rousseau* 9 (1997): 21–40.

Mallarmé, Stéphane. *Divagations.* Translated by Barbara Johnson. Cambridge, Mass.: Harvard University Press, 2007.

———. *Œuvres complètes.* Edited by Henri Mondor and G. Jean-Aubry. Paris: Gallimard, 1945.

Mathews, Mitford M. *Teaching to Read, Historically Considered.* Chicago: University of Chicago Press, 1966.

Michael, Ian. *The Teaching of English from the Sixteenth Century to 1870.* Cambridge: Cambridge University Press, 1987.

Michaels, Walter Benn. *The Shape of the Signifier.* Princeton, N.J.: Princeton University Press, 2004.

Mill, John Stuart. "Thoughts on Poetry and Its Varieties." In *Dissertations and Discussions: Political, Philosophical, and Historical,* 2 vols., 1:63–94. New York: Haskell, 1973.

Mitchell, W. J. T., ed. *Against Theory: Literary Studies and the New Pragmatism.* Chicago: University of Chicago Press, 1985.

Morrison, Toni. *Playing in the Dark: Whiteness and the Literary Imagination.* New York: Vintage, 1992.

Morrissey, Lee. *The Constitution of Literature: Literature, Democracy, and Early English Literary Criticism.* Stanford, Calif.: Stanford University Press, 2007.

———. *From the Temple to the Castle: An Architectural History of British Literature, 1660–1760.* Charlottesville: University of Virginia Press, 1999.

Muller, John P., and William J. Richardson, eds. *The Purloined Poe: Lacan, Derrida, and Psychoanalytic Reading.* Baltimore: Johns Hopkins University Press, 1988.

Newmark, Kevin. *Beyond Symbolism: Textual History and the Future of Reading.* Ithaca, N.Y.: Cornell University Press, 1991.

Novalis. *Novalis Schriften: Die Werke Friedrich von Hardenbergs.* 4 vols. Edited by Paul Kluckhohn and Richard Samuel. Stuttgart, Germany: Kohlhammer, 1960–81.

———. *Philosophical Writings*. Translated by Margaret Mahony Stoljar. Albany: SUNY Press, 1997.

Nussbaum, Felicity A. "Speechless: Haywood's Deaf and Dumb Projector." In *The Passionate Fictions of Eliza Haywood: Essays on Her Life and Work*. Edited by Kirsten T. Saxton and Rebecca P. Bocchicchio, 194–216. Lexington: University of Kentucky Press, 2000.

O'Rourke, James. "'Goody Blake and Harry Gill,' 'The Thorn,' and the Failure of Philanthropy." *European Romantic Review* 9 (1998): 103–23.

Parini, Jay. *Why Poetry Matters*. New Haven, Conn.: Yale University Press, 2008.

Parrish, Stephen M. *The Art of the "Lyrical Ballads."* Cambridge, Mass.: Harvard University Press, 1973.

Parry, Geraint. "*Émile:* Learning to Be Men, Women, and Citizens." In *The Cambridge Companion to Rousseau*. Edited by Patrick Riley, 247–71. Cambridge: Cambridge University Press, 2001.

Pinch, Adela. *Strange Fits of Passion: Epistemologies of Emotion, Hume to Austen*. Stanford, Calif.: Stanford University Press, 1996.

Plato. *Complete Works*. Edited by John M. Cooper. Indianapolis: Hackett, 1997.

Prins, Yopie. *Victorian Sappho*. Princeton, N.J.: Princeton University Press, 1999.

Provine, Robert R. "Yawning." *American Scientist* 93 (November–December 2005): 532–39.

Pyle, Forest. *The Ideology of Imagination: Subject and Society in the Discourse of Romanticism*. Stanford, Calif.: Stanford University Press, 1995.

———. "Kindling and Ash: Radical Aestheticism in Keats and Shelley." *Studies in Romanticism* 42 (Winter 2003): 427–59.

Rajan, Tilottama. *The Dark Interpreter: The Discourse of Romanticism*. Ithaca, N.Y.: Cornell University Press, 1980.

Rancière, Jacques. *The Names of History: On the Poetics of Knowledge*. Translated by Hassan Melehy. Minneapolis: University of Minnesota Press, 1994.

Redfield, Marc. *Phantom Formations: Aesthetic Ideology and the Bildungsroman*. Ithaca, N.Y.: Cornell University Press, 1996.

———. *The Politics of Aesthetics: Nationalism, Gender, Romanticism*. Stanford, Calif.: Stanford University Press, 2003.

Richards, I. A. *Practical Criticism: A Study of Literary Judgment*. New York: Harcourt, Brace and World, 1929.

Rottenberg, Elizabeth. *Inheriting The Future: Legacies of Kant, Freud, and Flaubert*. Stanford, Calif.: Stanford University Press, 2005.

Rousseau, Jean-Jacques. *Confessions*. Translated by Angela Scholar. Oxford: Oxford University Press, 2000.

———. *Émile*. Translated by Barbara Foxley. London: Everyman Library, 1993.

———. *Émile, or On Education*. Translated by Allan Bloom. New York: Basic Books, 1979.

———. *Œuvres complètes*. 4 vols. Edited by Bernard Gagnebin and Marcel Raymond. Paris: Gallimard, 1959–69.

Rzepka, Charles. "The Feel of Not to Feel It." *PMLA* 116, no. 5 (October 2001): 1422–31.

Saussure, Ferdinand de. *Course in General Linguistics*. Translated by Wade Baskin. New York: McGraw Hill, 1959.

Shelley, Percy Bysshe. *Poetical Works*. Edited by Thomas Hutchinson. Oxford: Oxford University Press, 1988.

Schlegel, Friedrich. *Kritische Schriften*. Edited by Wolfdietrich Rasch. Munich: Carl Hanser Verlag, 1958.

Schulte-Sasse, Jochen, et al., eds. *Theory as Practice: A Critical Anthology of Early German Romantic Writings*. Minneapolis: University of Minnesota Press, 1997.

Sedgwick, Eve Kosofsky. "Paranoid Reading and Reparative Reading; or, You're So Paranoid, You Probably Think This Introduction Is About You." In *Novel Gazing: Queer Readings in Fiction*. Edited by Eve Kosofsky Sedgwick, 1–37. Durham, N.C.: Duke University Press, 1997.

Shaw, George Bernard. "Keats." In *The John Keats Memorial Volume*. Edited by George C. Williamson, 173–76. London: John Lane, 1921.

Smith, J. Mark. "Apostrophe, or the Lyric Art of Turning Away." *Texas Studies in Literature and Language* 49, no. 4 (Winter 2007): 411–37.

Sng, Zachary. *The Rhetoric of Error from Locke to Kleist*. Stanford, Calif.: Stanford University Press, 2010.

Sontag, Susan. *Regarding the Pain of Others*. New York: Farrar, Straus and Giroux, 2003.

Spargo, R. Clifton. *The Ethics of Mourning: Grief and Responsibility in Elegiac Literature*. Baltimore: Johns Hopkins University Press, 2004.

Starr, Herbert W., ed. *Twentieth Century Interpretations of Gray's Elegy*. Englewood Cliffs, N.J.: Prentice-Hall, 1968.

Stewart, Garrett. *Dear Reader: The Conscripted Audience in Nineteenth-Century British Fiction*. Baltimore: Johns Hopkins University Press, 1996.

Stillinger, Jack. "Keats and Romance." *Studies in English Literature 1500–1900* 8, no. 4 (Autumn 1968): 593–605.

Storch, R. F. "Wordsworth's Experimental Ballads: The Radical Uses of Intelligence and Comedy." *Studies in English Literature 1500–1900* 11, no. 4 (1971): 621–39.

Sun, Emily. "Facing Keats with Winnicott: On the New Therapeutics of Poetry." *Studies in Romanticism* 46 (Spring 2007): 57–75.

———. *Succeeding King Lear: Literature, Exposure, and the Possibility of Politics*. New York: Fordham University Press, 2010.

Swann, Karen. "Suffering and Sensation in *The Ruined Cottage*." *PMLA* 106, no. 1 (1991): 83–95.

Terada, Rei. *Feeling in Theory: Emotion After the "Death of the Subject."* Cambridge, Mass.: Harvard University Press, 2001.

———. "Seeing Is Reading." In *Legacies of Paul de Man*. Edited by Marc Redfield, 162–78. New York: Fordham University Press, 2007.

Todd, Janet. *Sentimentalism: An Introduction.* London: Methuen, 1986.

Turbet-Delof, Guy. "A propos d'Émile et Sophie." *Revue d'histoire littéraire de la France* 64 (1964): 44–59.

Underwood, Ted. "Romantic Historicism and the Afterlife." *PMLA* 117, no. 2 (2002): 237–51.

Vanpée, Janie. "Reading Lessons in Rousseau's *Émile ou de l'éducation,*" *Modern Language Studies* 20, no. 3 (1990): 40–49.

———. "Rousseau's *Émile ou de l'éducation:* A Resistance to Reading." *Yale French Studies* 77 (1990): 156–76.

Von Hallberg, Robert. *Lyric Powers.* Chicago: University of Chicago Press, 2008.

Wagner, Guy, and Max Hosier. *Reading Games: Strengthening Reading Skills with Instructional Games.* New York: Macmillan, 1960.

Wang, Orrin N. C. "Against Theory / Beside Romanticism: The Sensation of the Signifier." *Diacritics* 35, no. 2 (Summer 2005): 1–29.

———. "Coming Attractions: *Lamia* and Cinematic Sensation." *Studies in Romanticism* 42 (Winter 2003): 461–500.

———. "Romantic Sobriety." *Modern Language Quarterly* 60, no. 4 (December 1999): 469–93.

Warner, Michael. "Uncritical Reading." In *Polemic: Critical or Uncritical.* Edited by Jane Gallop, 13–38. New York: Routledge, 2004.

Waters, William. *Poetry's Touch: On Lyric Address.* Ithaca, N.Y.: Cornell University Press, 2003.

Weinfield, Henry. *The Poet Without a Name: Gray's Elegy and the Problem of History.* Carbondale: Southern Illinois University Press, 1991.

White, Deborah Elise. *Romantic Returns: Superstition, Imagination, History.* Stanford, Calif.: Stanford University Press, 2000.

White, Hayden. "The Suppression of Rhetoric in the Nineteenth Century." In *The Fiction of Narrative: Essays on History, Literature, and Theory 1957–2007.* Edited by Robert Doran, 293–303. Baltimore: Johns Hopkins University Press, 2010.

Williams, Anne. *Prophetic Strain: The Greater Lyric in the Eighteenth Century.* Chicago: University of Chicago Press, 1984.

Wilner, Joshua. *Feeding on Infinity: Readings in the Romantic Rhetoric of Internalization.* Baltimore: Johns Hopkins University Press, 2000.

Wimsatt, W. K. *Hateful Contraries: Studies in Literature and Criticism.* Lexington: University of Kentucky Press, 1965.

Wirz, Charles. "Notes sur 'Émile et Sophie ou les solitaires.'" *Annales Jean-Jacques Rousseau* 36 (1963–65): 291–303.

Wolfson, Susan. "Keats's *Isabella* and the 'Digressions' of 'Romance.'" *Criticism* 27, no. 3 (Summer 1985): 247–61.

Woolhouse, Roger. *Locke: A Biography.* Cambridge: Cambridge University Press, 2007.

Wordsworth, William. *Lyrical Ballads.* New York: Routledge, 2005.

———. *The Prelude: 1799, 1805, 1850.* Norton Critical Editions. New York: W. W. Norton, 1979.

———. *The Poetical Works of William Wordsworth.* 5 vols. Edited by Ernest de Selincourt and Helen Darbishire. Oxford: Clarendon, 1940–49.

———. *The Prose Works of William Wordsworth.* 3 vols. Edited by W. J. B. Owen and Jane Worthington Smyser. Oxford: Oxford University Press, 1974.

Yeats, William Butler. *Mythologies.* New York: Collier, 1959.

Yeo, Richard. "John Locke's 'Of study' (1677): Interpreting an Unpublished Essay." *Locke Studies* 3 (2003): 147–65.

Žižek, Slavoj. "Melancholy and the Act." *Critical Inquiry* 26, no. 4 (Summer 2000): 658–81.

INDEX